LIVES OF THE MASTERS

Atiśa Dīpaṃkara

ILLUMINATOR OF THE AWAKENED MIND

James B. Apple

Shambhala
BOULDER · 2019

Shambhala Publications, Inc.
4720 Walnut Street
Boulder, Colorado 80301
www,shambhala.com

Frontispiece of *Atisha with Twenty-Eight Great Adepts*
(Tibet, eighteenth century)
provided by the Rubin Museum of Art.
Used with permission.

9 8 7 6 5 4 3 2 1

FIRST EDITION
Printed in Canada

♾ This edition is printed on acid-free paper that meets the
American National Standards Institute z39.48 Standard.
♻ This book is printed on 100% postconsumer recycled paper.
For more information please visit www.shambhala.com.

Shambhala Publications is distributed worldwide by
Penguin Random House, Inc., and its subsidiaries.

LIBRARY OF CONGRESS CATALOGING-IN-PUBLICATION DATA
Names: Apple, James B., author. | Atiśa, 982–1054.
Title: Atiśa Dipamkara: illuminator of the awakened mind / James Apple.
Description: First edition. | Boulder: Shambhala, 2019. | Series: Lives of the masters |
Includes bibliographical references and index.
Identifiers: LCCN 2018043449 | ISBN 9781611806472 (pbk.: alk. paper)
Subjects: LCSH: Atiśa, 982–1054. |Bka'-gdams-pa lamas—Biography. |
Bka'-gdams-pa (Sect)—Doctrines.
Classification: LCC BQ7950.A877 A84 2019 | DDC 294.3/923092 [B]—dc23
LC record available at https://lccn.loc.gov/2018043449

Contents

Series Introduction

BUDDHIST TRADITIONS are heir to some of the most creative thinkers in world history. The Lives of the Masters series offers lively and reliable introductions to the lives, works, and legacies of key Buddhist teachers, philosophers, contemplatives, and writers. Each volume in the Lives series tells the story of an innovator who embodied the ideals of Buddhism, crafted a dynamic living tradition during his or her lifetime, and bequeathed a vibrant legacy of knowledge and practice to future generations.

Lives books rely on primary sources in the original languages to describe the extraordinary achievements of Buddhist thinkers and illuminate these achievements by vividly setting them within their historical contexts. Each volume offers a concise yet comprehensive summary of the master's life and an account of how they came to hold a central place in Buddhist traditions. Each contribution also contains a broad selection of the master's writings.

This series makes it possible for all readers to imagine Buddhist masters as deeply creative and inspired people whose work was animated by the rich complexity of their time and place and how these inspiring figures continue to engage our quest for knowledge and understanding today.

KURTIS SCHAEFFER, *series editor*

Preface

GESHÉ LHUNDUP SOPA (1923–2014) jovially introduced me to the life and teachings of Atiśa in the early summer of 1992 while I was on retreat at Deer Park Buddhist Center outside of Oregon, Wisconsin. Around the same time, I acquired a used copy of Phabongkhapa's *Liberation in the Palm of Your Hand* from an old bookstore on State Street in Madison, Wisconsin, and read Atiśa's life story in English as well.

When I returned to Indiana after the summer to finish my undergraduate degree at Indiana University, I worked during the 1992/3 academic year as a book shelver on the ninth floor of what was then Memorial Library. The ninth floor of the Memorial Library (now Herman B. Wells Library) at Indiana University has one of the largest collections of Tibetan books in North America. I would often look at the Tibetan books in between shifts of shelving regular bound books. One time while perusing Tibetan books, I spotted a Tibetan volume that was entitled *Writings of Lord Atiśa on the Theory and Practice of the Graduated Path.*[1] After my summer retreat at Deer Park, I was excited to see a work by Atiśa, so I unpacked the bound volume and began to flip through the Tibetan folios. My initial excitement became disappointment as the text was in a difficult to read handwritten script, which I was not yet able to read. I carefully put the volume away and explored other Tibetan works. Now, over two decades later, I have translated the works in that volume of

Atiśa's writings, and a selection is found in chapter 12 for the first time in modern publication.

I returned to Wisconsin as a graduate student at the University of Wisconsin–Madison in the fall of 1994, and in the spring of 1996, Geshé Sopa led my graduate school classmates and I through Atiśa's biography in a second-year classical Tibetan class. The following academic year we read Atiśa's *Open Basket of Jewels* (excerpt in chapter 4).

I did not intend to research Atiśa, as I was interested in Tsongkhapa Losangdrakpa (1357–1419). When I landed a tenure-track position at the University of Calgary in 2008, and having published a book related to Tsongkhapa (*Stairway to Nirvāṇa*), the works of Izumi Miyazaki on Atiśa came to my attention.[2] I immediately found my class notes from Geshé Sopa's class, revised the English translation and annotation of Miyazaki's paper, and published this in 2010 as "Atiśa's Open Basket of Jewels: A Middle Way Vision in Late Phase Indian Vajrayāna." At the same time that I arrived at the University of Calgary, the availability of the Collected Works of the Kadampas, unknown to Tibetan scholars after the seventeenth century and published in fascimiles only recently, had been announced. Over the last ten years, I have focused on these manuscripts that contain the works and teachings of Atiśa and his early Kadampa followers.

Rather than a minor figure as some modern scholars might portray him, Atiśa emerges as a fully trained and well-educated Buddhist master who was subtle in thought and cagey in action. The Tibetans at the time were seeking an authoritative Indian teacher to revitalize the dharma in West Tibet. In coming to Tibet, Atiśa was a great Indian Buddhist master who fulfilled, and in a number of ways even exceeded, the expectations of the Tibetans.

In the study of Indian and Tibetan Buddhism, it is often said that the study of Sanskrit and classical Tibetan is like the sun and the moon. The two languages complement each other in the study of Indian Buddhist texts, reflecting the light of understanding. However, in preserved writings of the life and teachings of Atiśa, the scholar currently only has access to the Tibetan side of the story. As there are currently no surviving, or at least accessible, Indian manuscripts of Atiśa's writings or accounts of his life, the Indian side of the story is not represented in Sanskrit or Old Bengali. Scholars cannot even be sure of the underlying meaning of his nickname, "Atiśa." So, the reader should be aware that the life and teachings of Atiśa are in some ways filtered by the Tibetan accounts of his life and the Tibetan translations of his teachings.

Atiśa's life and teachings are a Tibetan story, and what an amazing story it is. Atiśa's life is guided by dreams, visions, and predictions from buddhas and bodhisattvas, including the savioress Tārā. In the story of Atiśa's life, we enter a world of gold, sailing ships, palm-leaf manuscripts, and mantras, rather than credit cards, automobiles, social media, and cell phones. The story involves transactions in over two million dollars' worth of gold and travels throughout maritime Buddhist Asia. The Tibetans have faithfully preserved what is known of Atiśa Dīpaṃkaraśrījñāna, the vicissitudes of his life, the struggles in his travels, and the spirit and meaning of his teachings.

Calgary, Alberta
August 7, 2018

Acknowledgments

I ESPECIALLY THANK Kurtis Schaeffer for the invitation to contribute to the Lives of the Masters series. At Shambhala Publications, I have benefited from the advice and editorial skills of Casey Kemp and Nikko Odiseos. I acknowledge and thank the scholarly community, whose work has contributed to my understanding of Atiśa. First and foremost I'd like to thank Helmut Eimer, the great pioneer of the scholarly study of Atiśa, whose works provided a foundation for understanding this Indian Buddhist master. Richard Sherburne, Glenn H. Mullin, Dan Martin, Hubert Decleer, Thupten Jinpa, Izumi Miyazaki, Kaie Mochizuki, and Kazuo Kano have also contributed to my understanding of Atiśa's life and teachings. I thank Roger R. Jackson for his editorial acumen in significantly improving my translations over the years.

I would like to thank my parents, Jeanne Bedwell and James Apple, for their support and advice. Finally, but certainly not least, I would like to thank my wife, Shinobu, who, step by step, has supported me throughout the writing of this book.

Selected chapters of this book were originally published as journal articles:

Chapter 4. "Atiśa's Open Basket of Jewels: A Middle Way Vision in Late Phase Indian Vajrayāna," *The Indian International Journal of Buddhist Studies* 11 (2010): 117–98.

Chapter 4. *On the Awakening Mind* and Chapter 5. *Entry to the Two Realities* are excerpts adapted with permission from Wisdom Publications. Readers should consult *Jewels of the Middle Way: The Madhyamaka Legacy of Atiśa and His Early Tibetan Followers* (Apple 2019a) for complete annotated studies of these works.

Chapter 5. "An Early Tibetan Commentary on Atiśa's *Satyadvayāvatāra*," *Journal of Indian Philosophy* 41.3 (2013): 263–329, and "An Early Tibetan Commentary on Atiśa's Satyadvayāvatāra: Diplomatic Edition with Introduction and Notes," *Journal of Indian Philosophy* 41.5 (2013): 501–33.

Chapter 14. "Atiśa's Teachings on Mahāmudrā," *The Indian International Journal of Buddhist Studies* 18 (2017): 1–42.

Atiśa Dīpaṃkara

Introduction

ATIŚA, also as known Dīpaṃkaraśrījñāna (982–1054), is famous for being a master from the ancient Indian Buddhist land of Bengal and for his journeys in Indonesia and Nepal.[3] He is most well known for the last thirteen years of his life in Tibet. Atiśa was one of the most influential Indian Buddhist masters ever to set foot in Tibet. Atiśa's Mahāyāna Buddhist teachings, encompassing instructions on entering the way of bodhisattvas up through the most advanced practices of the esoteric secret way of mantras, came to influence all subsequent traditions of Buddhism in Tibet.

Atiśa lived at a unique juncture in the history of India and Tibet. Atiśa resided in India during a revival phase of the East Indian Pāla Dynasties (760–1142) of Bihar and Bengal. During this time, Bengal was an "international" region with trade routes on land from Assam and Burma passing through to the ancient Buddhist pilgrimage holy sites of Magadha. Buddhist holy places in Magadha included such sites as Vajrāsana, the "Diamond Seat," where Śākyamuni Buddha attained awakening, located in present-day Bodh Gayā, India. The international environment of northeast India also included maritime routes connecting the Bay of Bengal to harbors in South and Southeast Asia.[4] The Pālas ruled over the northeastern lands of Bihar, West and North Bengal, and explicitly claimed to be Buddhist in their inscriptions. They utilized the dharma wheel of the Buddha's teachings on the top of inscribed copperplates and described themselves as "entirely devoted to the Buddha" in the colophons of manuscripts they sponsored.[5] The Pālas supported a perpetual endowment of donations for the Buddhist monastic community and established a network of major monasteries, including the prestigious centers of Vikramaśīla and Somapura. Atiśa, the Princely-Lord, came of age, studied, meditated, and taught during this buoyant time of maritime Buddhist Asia.

The Pāla Dynastic period was permeated with the religious practices of esoteric Buddhism, or Secret Mantra practices. This form of Buddhism was primarily disseminated from master to disciple and based on groups of texts called *tantras*. Institutional monastic esoterism and the esoterism of *siddhas*, accomplished adepts on the margins of society, dominated the Buddhist culture of the time. By the late tenth and early eleventh century, during the lifetime of Atiśa, Buddhist monastic communities and the siddha culture had undergone almost two centuries of blending and accommodation. The accommodation of esoteric Buddhism into monastic communities was influenced, in part, by a highly competitive environment between Buddhists and non-Buddhists seeking patronage and economic support. Esoteric Buddhists lived in a cultural context where Buddhists who did not support esoteric practices, as well as non-Buddhist esoteric practictioners such as the diverse groups of Śaivas, the followers of Śiva, contested for prestige and authority. These groups took part in a whole range of ascetic and ritual practices.

The kings in West Tibet at this time were seeking to rejuvenate Buddhism in order to replicate the order, ethical principles, and stability that Mahāyāna Buddhist ideals had brought to the Tibetan Empire during the seventh to ninth centuries. In seeking out Atiśa as the rejuvenator of Mahāyāna Buddhist ideals, the Tibetans must have initially considered him to be a descendent of the great bodhisattva-scholar Śāntarakṣita, who was also from Bengal. Śāntarakṣita was responsible for establishing the first ordained monks in Tibet and contributing to the translation of texts and the construction of Tibet's first monastery of Samyé.[6] Although Atiśa and Śāntarakṣita may have been from the same region, Atiśa lived in an era of Indian Buddhism different from Śāntarakṣita. Rather than a Mūlasarvāstivāda monk who blended Yogācāra and Madhyamaka philosophies like Śāntarakṣita, Atiśa upheld the Mahāsāṃghika ordination lineage and was a follower of the Madhyamaka tradition of Candrakīrti. Atiśa was also a lineage holder of a number of Yoginī tantras, such as the *Laghuśaṃvara Tantra* and *Hevajra Tantra*, whose practice was only introduced into Tibetan culture in the late tenth century by Rinchen Zangpo (958–1055). Tibetans at this time were not fully familiar with these areas of monastic discipline, Madhyamaka philosophy, and esoteric Buddhism that Atiśa brought with him to Tibet.

Atiśa also brought with him to Tibet fervent devotion to the goddess Tārā, and he is responsible for the extensive worship of the goddess in the Land of Snows. Atiśa revitalized the Tibetan devotion to the great bodhisattva of compassion, Avalokiteśvara, as well. Atiśa introduced a number of ritual practices that were formative in the renaissance of Tibetan Buddhism, such as the ritual recitation of the *Heart Sūtra*. Atiśa's teachings were formative for all Buddhist groups in Tibet. He introduced to Tibetan Buddhists a number of topics and issues, such as the stages of the path, three vow theory, the doctrine of three continuums, the complementary use of Candrakīrti and Bhāviveka's Madhyamaka philosophy, and his understanding of the practice of the Great Seal (Mahāmudrā). Atiśa brought these topics and issues to the attention of scholar-meditators of West and Central Tibet, but not all Tibetans adopted his suggestions. Atiśa's views on a number of issues of Buddhist thought and practice differed from how many later Tibetan sectarian developments such as Sakya, Kagyu, Geluk, or even later Kadam followers came to understand them. Nevertheless, Atiśa's influence on Tibetan Buddhist practices of moral discipline, integrated stages of the path, meditations of the advanced Secret Mantra Vehicle, and practices of mind training are still visible in present-day Tibetan forms of Buddhism.

In coming to Tibet, Atiśa was stripped of the social and ritual institutional duties he had while residing in his Indian monastery of Vikramaśīla. Ironically, when Atiśa arrived in Tibet, because he followed the Mahāsāṃghika-vinaya instead of the Mūlasarvāstivāda-vinaya already established in Tibet, he had no other responsibility than to teach Mahāyāna Buddhism in a purified dogmatic manner. Atiśa did not have any institutional power and did not establish a Mahāsāṃghika-vinaya ordination lineage while in the Land of Snows. While in Tibet, Atiśa was like a prestigious guest lecturer visiting a modern university. A prestigious guest lecturer, rather than assessing student performance and assigning grades, attending committee meetings, or negotiating with administrators and colleagues about administrative or pedagogical duties, ostensively teaches and instructs on just the subject matter at hand. Likewise, while in Tibet, Atiśa instructed on just the Mahāyāna Buddhist practices of the perfection path and the way of the Secret Mantra Vehicle rather than founding and administering monastic institutions and ordaining monks and nuns.

The stories of Atiśa's life are preserved only in Tibetan sources. Helmut Eimer has identified over forty Tibetan sources that provide biographical information about Atiśa.[7] Among these sources, I have primarily followed (unless noted otherwise) two of the oldest, which furnish almost all the information known about Atiśa's life story. I have utilized *The Extensive Biography*[8] attributed to Ja Dülzin Tsöndrü Bar (1091–1166 or 1100–1174) and *The Universally Known Biography*[9] attributed to Chim Namkha Drak (1210–1285). These accounts of Atiśa's life record the vicissitudes of his travels in India, Indonesia, and Tibet. One moment he is seeing rainbows and the next he is living in a cave hungry for food. One moment Atiśa and his entourage cannot find a place to stay and in the next they are staying in the treasury of Samyé Monastery. Atiśa's life story also reveals a contrast between the rejuvenation of Buddhism in West Tibet under Jangchup Ö and the conservative establishment in Central Tibet with the political figure Bodhirāja. The divided conservative establishment in the Central Tibetan provinces of Tsang and Ü, although somewhat supportive of Atiśa and his entourage, were established in the system of the Mūlasarvāstivāda-vinaya and entrenched in clan-based factional disputes for power and authority.

When telescoping back to think about Atiśa's thought in its historical context, one must be careful not to read into his life and teachings later developments in the history of Indo-Tibetan Buddhism, such as the Svātantrika/Prāsaṅgika division in Madhyamaka thought and practice, the "empty of intrinsic existence" (*rangtong*) versus "empty of other" (*zhentong*) debate, or even the Old Translation (*Nyingma*) versus New Translation (*Sarma*) divisions of esoteric Buddhist literature. The Tibetan Buddhist institution of incarnate spiritual teachers, or *tulkus*, had not yet been established either. Atiśa lived in India and Tibet at a juncture when these concepts and their divisions had yet to be discussed and debated.

Atiśa composed over one hundred works throughout his life while in India, Indonesia, Nepal, and Tibet.[10] Recent publication of his collected writings in Tibetan organize his compositions into those related to view, conduct, union of view and conduct, and Secret Mantra practices. The selections of his writings and teachings that follow are found in each one of these areas. *Open Basket of Jewels* (chapter 4), *Entry to the Two Realities* (chapter 5), and the Song with a Vision for the Realm of Reality (chapter 6) are related to Atiśa's teachings on the philosophical view, or vision of reality. *Lamp for the Summary of Conduct* (chapter 7), *Special Instructions on Unique Mindfulness* (chapter 8), *Bodhisattva's Jewel Garland* (chapter

9), and *Middle Way Special Instructions for Cultivating All the Qualities in the Scriptures* (chapter 10) are writings and teachings that center around conduct. The *Lamp for the Path to Awakening* (chapter 11) and *Stages of the Path to Awakening* (chapter 12) are related to both view and conduct. Selections of Atiśa's writings on Tārā (chapter 13) and his teaching on coemergent union (chapter 14) focus on Secret Mantra practices.

One principle that pervades almost all of these writings as well as Atiśa's other works and teachings is the cultivation, increase, and full actualization of the awakening mind (*bodhicitta*). Atiśa is remembered for being the master illuminator of the awakening mind. As the famous fifteenth-century Tibetan crazy yogi Drukpa Künlé explained, "There is no rivaling Atiśa and his sons in terms of the awakening mind."[11] Indeed, Atiśa always recited the following four-lined prayer during his travels:

> I pay homage to the awakening mind,
> Which destroys any rebirth in the lower realms,
> Liberates from all obstructions, and
> Illuminates the majesty of complete buddhahood.[12]

A Note on Tibetan Transliteration

Tibetan proper names of persons and places have been transliterated phonetically in the main body of this book. Wylie transliteration equivalents for these terms can be found in the Table of Tibetan Transliterations section.

The Biography

CHAPTER 1

India

THE BENGALI MASTER Atiśa was born in the Tibetan year of the Water Horse (Western year 982) in the great city known as Vikramapura in the eastern Indian land of Sahor (Tib. Zahor). Today, the area is most likely located in the present-day Mushiganj district of Bangladesh.[13] Traditional accounts emphasize that he was born into a royal family of great wealth and power. His father was King Kalyāṇaśrī and his mother Śrīprabhāvatī. He was born into the same royal lineage as the Indian master Śāntarakṣita (725–788), who established monasticism in Tibet during the eighth century.[14] Atiśa's birth name was Candragarbha. He was the second from among three sons, the oldest being Padmagarbha and the youngest Śrīgarbha. Śrīgarbha would later become the monk Vīryacandra. Atiśa, as the youthful prince Candragarbha, was a prodigy from his childhood and became proficient in math, writing, and grammar at the age of three. His mother, who was a Brahmin, instructed him in the Vedas, and his father introduced him to the way of mantras. He also began studying works of crafts and medicine. Later, when the prince reached six years of age, he could differentiate between non-Buddhists and Buddhists. By the age of fifteen, he could thoroughly refute non-Buddhist tenets.[15]

Atiśa's early education in Buddhist thought and practice begins with his training under numerous Indian masters. Five masters that are prominent in his early education include the brahmin Jitāri, the scholar-monk Bodhibhadra, the contemplative-monk Vidyākokila, and the tantric yogis Avadhūtipa and Rāhulaguptavajra. Atiśa would study under these masters from around the age of ten up to the age of twenty-one.

At ten (ca. 992), not satisfied with the palace life, Atiśa went to the forest, where he met Jitāri (ca. 940–1000). Jitāri was a lay Buddhist scholar and master of tantra who also taught at the monastery of Vikramaśīla in the region west of Vikramapura.[16] Well versed in epistemology (*pramāṇa*), Jitāri received the honor of *paṇḍita* during the reign of Mahāpāla (ca. 977–1027).[17] Atiśa took refuge in the three jewels and received initial teachings on the awakening mind from Jitāri. Atiśa also learned the basics of Buddhist doxography and epistemology under Jitāri. Jitāri then guided the young Atiśa to travel away from Vikramaśīla Monastery to the more distant monastery of Nālandā in Magadha in order to study under the scholar-monk Bodhibhadra.

Around 994, Atiśa met Bodhibhadra upon arrival at the Indian monastic university of Nālandā, where the young Atiśa received novice vows from the scholar-monk. Bodhibhadra instructed the young prince on how to generate the awakening mind, the altruistic resolution for achieving the awakening of full buddhahood for the benefit of all sentient beings.[18] Practices on the awakening mind would permeate Atiśa's life of study and teaching. Bodhibhadra also gave the prince instruction on death and impermanence, encouraging him to renounce his kingdom and become a fully ordained monk. Bodhibhadra then instructed Atiśa to study with Vidyākokila, a monk living in retreat to the north of Nālandā. Atiśa left Bodhibhadra and sought instruction from Vidyākokila.

Vidyākokila was an accomplished master who upheld the Madhyamaka lineage of the great Ācārya Candrakīrti descending from Nāgārjuna.[19] Based on this lineage of practice, Vidyākokila guided Atiśa in the general instructions on the stages of the path and gave specific guidance on the view of emptiness.[20] Vidyākokila instructed the young prince on how to realize nonduality in meditative absorption and then view sentient beings with compassion during post-concentrative activities. Vidyākokila also instructed Atiśa in the cultivation of the awakening mind. After a period of instruction, Vidyākokila advised Atiśa to visit the tantric yogi Avadhūtipa, who lived to the south of the Black Mountain (Kṛṣṇagiri), one of the mountains near the ancient city of Rajgir.[21]

Atiśa then resided with the tantric yogi Avadhūtipa in the forest. Under the tutelage of Avadhūtipa, the youthful bodhisattva received a consecration (*abhiṣeka*), or tantric rite of initiation, that empowered him with a generative force of the awakening mind for advanced Great Vehicle practices. Atiśa studied the Middle Way teachings with Avadhūtipa from the age of twelve until the age of eighteen. Avadhūtipa also taught him the principles of adhering to the karmic laws of subtle cause and effect until one is free from self-grasping. Avadhūtipa had opened Atiśa's heart to the dharma, and Atiśa returned to his home region to ask permission from his parents to renounce the palace life. His father was upset that Atiśa did not wish to govern the kingdom. Atiśa replied that he was unattached to running a kingdom and wished to achieve the path to awakening and achieve liberation. Atiśa's mother was upset as well. She tried to dissuade Atiśa from renouncing the palace life and suggested that he seek out the path at a later time. Despite his parents' efforts to entice Atiśa with the wealth and resources of the kingdom, Atísa bid his parents farewell and returned immediately to stay with Avadhūtipa.

Avadhūtipa then advised the young prince Candragarbha to go train under the tantric yogin Rāhulaguptavajra. Avadhūtipa told Atiśa to go to a Black Mountain temple in the presence of Rāhulaguptavajra, as Atiśa had a special connection with this teacher from previous lifetimes. When Atiśa initially approached the spiritual teacher Rāhulaguptavajra, he saw him speaking about tantra and understood the previous lifetime spiritual connection. When Rāhulaguptavajra saw Atiśa, he was amazed that such a prince was unattached to his kingdom. As soon as Atiśa met Rāhulaguptavajra, he listened closely to his teachings on the way of mantras. Atiśa alone received consecrations into the practice of the tantric deity Hevajra for thirteen consecutive days from Rāhulaguptavajra. Rāhulaguptavajra conferred upon Atiśa the esoteric initiatory name Jñānaguhyavajra.[22] Atiśa engaged in the tantric practice of the awareness observance during this time, a practice where the yogin wears the ornaments of the deity, relies on a consort, and uses code language.[23] Atiśa also heard a number of tantric teachings from *ḍākiṇīs* and had visions of many tantric deities during this phase of his life. From the age of twenty-one to twenty-nine, he received consecrations and special instructions within the four main groups of tantra. Atiśa intended to take up the conduct of Secret Mantra discipline in order to attain the accomplishment of the Great Seal.[24] In a vision of Tārā, however, the goddess asked Atiśa, "Hey paṇḍita, are you proficient in Secret Mantra practices?" Atiśa replied, "Yes, I am." The goddess asked him, "Do you understand this tantric *sādhana*, or how about this sādhana?" Since Atiśa had never seen the esoteric Buddhist texts before, the goddess told him, "The knowledge about Secret Mantra practices in your human realm is not even the mere tip of a horse's hair. Many examples and meanings of Secret Mantra practices are in the hands of ḍākiṇīs." The goddess broke Atiśa's pride about his knowledge of Secret Mantra practices.[25]

In a dream around this time, Atiśa saw Śrī Heruka, the supreme wrathful deity of the Cakrasaṃvara and Hevajra tantras, before him in the sky. Śrī Heruka told Atiśa that *avadhūti* conduct did not lead to the status of a monk who could guide many disciples.[26] On another night, Atiśa had a vivid dream in which Śākyamuni

Buddha himself, surrounded by many monks, directly asked Atiśa, "Why don't you become a monk?" In still another dream, Atiśa was hindered by an elder monk who was, in fact, the bodhisattva Maitreya. The elder stopped Atiśa from approaching a throne in a temple since the place was sacred space for monks. Atiśa understood these dreams as an invitation to renounce the world.[27] Atiśa then went to Rāhulaguptavajra, who encouraged him to quit sporting around in the life of a tantric yogi and become a monk to benefit sentient beings.

With these visions and advice, Atiśa became ordained into the Mahāsāṃghika ordination lineage at the age of twenty-nine years at Mati-vihāra in Bodh Gayā. The preceptor of the Mahāsāṃghika ordination lineage was Śīlarakṣita, who had attained the level of patience in the path of preparation.[28] At that time Atiśa received the ordination name Dīpaṃkaraśrījñāna,[29] a name in the lineage tradition of Devabuddhajñāna. Atiśa then studied the extent of Buddhist knowledge with one hundred fifty-seven spiritual teachers. He trained in all the spiritual teachings found in the sūtras and tantras at the time. In particular, he studied the *Mahāvibhāṣakośa* of Upagupta under Dharmarakṣita at Odantapurī for several years. This work, comprised of eight hundred chapters, provided a complete overview of the seven main texts of Abhidharma.[30] In learning the Abhidharmapiṭaka, Atiśa mastered the scriptures and tenets among the four main ordination lineages: the Mahāsāṃghika, Sthaviravāda, Saṃmatīya, and Sarvāstivāda. During his study with Dharmarakṣita, a member of the Saindhava *śrāvakas*, Atiśa had to change his residence every six days because his bodhisattva discipline did not permit him to spend more than seven days residing among śrāvakas.[31]

Atiśa studied other subjects at this time as well, including the Sanskrit grammatical works of Kalāpa, Candrapa, Pāṇini,

Samantabhadra, and so forth. Atiśa also studied the "science of justificative reasons/evidences,"[32] including Dignāga's *Compendium on Valid Knowledge* (*Pramāṇasamuccaya*) and the seven works of valid knowledge by Dharmakīrti.[33] Atiśa trained in the science of logic and epistemology as part of the five fields of knowledge to refute non-Buddhists and Buddhists.[34] For Atiśa, the science of epistemology and logic was only utilized at the level of conventional reality to refute opponents. He continued his training at Vikramaśīla Monastery, learning dharma in both sūtra and mantra.

During his studies, Atiśa continually thought about the quickest path to reach buddhahood, and one time he went to visit his guru Rāhulaguptavajra, who was dwelling in the caves of the Black Mountain. Rāhulaguptavajra, through his supersensory powers, told Atiśa that even if one has a direct vision of a chosen deity, witnesses many assemblies of *maṇḍala* deities, or attains many common accomplishments, or *siddhis*, one's practice will not go anywhere unless it is based on the awakening mind comprised of love and compassion. Rāhulaguptavajra instructed Atiśa to hold the great compassionate one, Avalokiteśvara, as his preferred deity in order to benefit beings.[35]

On another occasion, while circumambulating the main temple at Vajrāsana, the Mahābodhi Temple in modern-day Bodh Gayā, Atiśa overheard two women speaking about the one method to quickly attain awakening. One woman asked, "What is that one method?" The other replied, "You should train in the awakening mind." Along a stone wall that had been built by Ācārya Nāgārjuna, he overheard an older woman tell a younger woman that if one wishes to attain full awakening quickly, one should train in the awakening mind. Atiśa, having overheard these discussions on the awakening mind, made a commitment to produce this precious altruistic resolution and to expand and increase the awakening mind until he attained full awakening. Atiśa then began to seek out a qualified teacher who completely possessed the special instructions on how to fully actualize the awakening mind.[36]

Sojourn to Sumatra

Atiśa heard from colleagues and associates that the renowned teacher Serlingpa was a master of awakening mind teachings. Serlingpa, "The man of Gold Island," also known as Dharmakīrtiśrī, was the adviser in the field of religion to King Cūḍāmaṇivarman in the capital city of Śrīvijayapura in the kingdom of Śrīvijaya on the Indonesian island of Sumatra.[37] Śrīvijayapura was not only a political and economic power in maritime Southeast Asia, the city was a major center of Buddhist culture as well. Scholar-monks from India and China had traveled to the region for centuries to study and practice Buddhism.[38] Around the year 1012, Atiśa undertook a thirteen-month journey to Sumatra in order to study under Serlingpa. Atiśa went on a ship with a retinue of one hundred twenty-five disciples of the Mahāsāṃghika ordination lineage. During the dangerous journey, the ship and its passengers were challenged by Maheśvara, an emanation of the god Śiva, who took the form of a large sea monster. At first, Atiśa meditated on love and compassion to subdue the monster. However, as this cultivation was not successful, Atiśa and his close disciple Kṣitigarbha called upon the meditational deities Yamāntaka, Aparājita, Acala, Tārā, and then Raktayamāri ("Red Slayer of Death") to overcome the obstacles. When the ship finally arrived in Sumatra, Atiśa and his entourage spent two weeks on the outskirts of the island near a golden reliquary among meditator monks inquiring about Serlingpa.[39]

Atiśa did not initially meet with Serlingpa for twelve months. Atiśa eventually met Serlingpa at a great offering ceremony attended by over five hundred monks. Due to a relation from previous lifetimes, they both knew each other upon meeting. When they met, Guru Serlingpa uttered many blessings and placed his hand on Atiśa's head. Guru Serlingpa asked Atiśa if he was able to train in the awakening mind comprised of love and compassion and emphasized that in three years Atiśa would be able to possess supersensory powers. Serlingpa then asked Atiśa if he would be able to stay for twelve years in Sumatra. Atiśa replied in the affirmative to Serlingpa's questions and then Atiśa received a golden statue of Śākyamuni Buddha as a gift.[40]

Atiśa then trained in all the Mahāyāna trainings he could receive from Serlingpa for twelve years. Atiśa attended lectures in fifteen sessions on the *Ornament for Clear Realization*.[41] Atiśa's study of this work under Serlingpa indicates the high level of scholarship and presence of royal sponsorship in Śrīvijayapura at the time.[42] Atiśa also received instructions for achieving the perfections (*pāramitās*) and received special instructions in the works of Śāntideva, including the guidance for bodhisattvas in the *Compendium of Training* and the uncommon special instructions in the *Introduction to the Practice of Awakening*.[43] Atiśa learned from Serlingpa the pure higher resolve instructions of cultivating the conventional awakening mind through the practice of exchanging oneself and others. In particular, Atiśa learned from Serlingpa the single most important teaching of establishing love and compassion.

Among Atiśa's spiritual teachers, Guru Serlingpa was unmatched and unrivaled in terms of faith and devotion. When Atiśa was among his disciples, he would press his hands together in prayer and utter verses of praise when he heard the name of one of his spiritual teachers. But, when he heard the name Serlingpa, Atiśa would raise his joined hands in prayer above his head and shed tears. Atiśa was one of the four main disciples of Serlingpa; the others were Jñānaśrīmitra, Ratnākaraśānti, and Ratnakīrti.[44] Even though Atiśa had great faith in Serlingpa, they differed as to philosophical view. Serlingpa followed Yogācāra thought, while Atiśa was a

Mādhyamika. Atiśa composed his *Entry to the Two Realities* (see chapter 5) to convert Serlingpa to the Mādhyamika understanding.[45] When Atiśa returned to India, he brought back at least seven manuscripts of Serlingpa's works and various sacred objects. Among the manuscripts was the *Illumination of Points Difficult to Understand*,[46] a subcommentary to Haribhadra's *Illumination of the Ornament of Clear Realization*,[47] which Atiśa would later translate in West Tibet. Atiśa also brought back several of Serlingpa's esoteric Buddhist teachings and ritual texts. These included Serlingpa's practices of venerating the goddess Tārā, as well as manuscripts of the Sādhana of Noble Acala and the rare Sādhana of Wrathful Gaṇapati.[48]

Back to Bodh Gayā and Life at Vikramaśīla

Atiśa returned to India in 1025 around the age of forty-four. Serlingpa had instructed Atiśa to study with one of his former students, Ratnākaraśānti, at Vikramaśīla upon returning to India. Before going on to Vikramaśīla Monastery, Atiśa carried out religious work in the Vajrāsana area.[49] While in Vajrāsana, Atiśa instructed various religious pilgrims, monks, and yogis in the trainings of love, compassion, and the awakening mind. One time, a yogin at the root of a tree saw Atiśa approaching and prostrated his full body on the ground toward Atiśa. The yogin then said, "I pay homage to you, master of Jambudvīpa. I pay homage to you, the life-tree of the Buddha's teaching. Please offer guidance." Atiśa replied, "It is necessary to gather immeasurable accumulations of merit to have trust in the profound dharma of the Great Vehicle. There is not a distinction in the Lesser and Greater Vehicles through philosophical view. They are distinguished according to the practice of compassion."[50]

On another occasion, Atiśa was meditating on love and compassion in an Amitābha temple on the west side of Vajrāsana. While meditating on love and compassion, Atiśa had a direct vision of Avalokiteśvara, who said, "It is good, it is good, holy one. You have understood the secret treasury of all the buddhas of the three times." Avalokiteśvara then predicted, "My realm is in the northern direction from here. Noble Tārā also dwells there benefitting sentient beings. Since many beings are there for you to train, go north!"[51]

At this point in his life, Atiśa was well trained, having received direct transmissions of a number of teaching lineages from various Indian masters. Atiśa upheld lineages of classical Mahāyāna practices and philosophies as well as lineages from the great adepts (*mahāsiddhas*). Traditional accounts mention that he had twelve root gurus. The great adept Nāropa instructed him in the vision of emptiness, Ḍombipa in yogic discipline, Balinācārya in tantric ritual, Mahājana in miraculous abilities, Bhutakoṭi in the worship of Vajravārāhī, Paramaśva in the special instructions of Nāgārjuna, Prajñābhadra in the awakening mind, Ratnākaraśānti in the meaning of the commentaries, and Serlingpa in the stages of mind training. Jitāri, Bodhibhadra, and Dharmarakṣita rounded out the list of twelve.[52] In addition, Avadhūtipa and Kamalarakṣita bestowed the teachings on the Great Seal to Atiśa. Atiśa upheld the lineage of the profound Middle Way, the pure view of emptiness descending from the tenth-stage bodhisattva of wisdom Mañjuśrī, Nāgārjuna, Candrakīrti, Vidyākokila the elder and younger, and Avadhūtipa the elder and younger. Atiśa also held the complete lineage of extensive meritorious deeds descending from the tenth-stage bodhisattva Maitreya, the brothers Asaṅga and Vasubandhu, Ārya Vimuktisena, Bhante Vimuktisena, Paramasena, Vinitasena, Vairocana, Haribhadra, Kusali the greater, Ratnabhadra, Ratna the lesser, and Serlingpa. Atiśa also fully possessed the transmission lineage of blessings from Vajradhara, Tilopa, Nāropa, and Ḍombipa.[53]

In addition to having the oral instructions and embodying the virtuous qualities of all these lineages of sūtra and tantra, Atiśa upheld the three types of vows.[54] Atiśa upheld the *prātimokṣa* vows of a fully ordained monk within his Mahāsāṃghika ordination lineage, the ethical conduct of the bodhisattva vows,[55] and the commitments of the Secret Mantra vows.[56] Atiśa strictly adhered to the vows of conduct and would not break even small vow commitments. For example, Atiśa avoided touching things belonging to women and, according to the rule of Mahāsāṃghikas, he would not accept flour stored in a wine jug.[57] If Atiśa did break a small vow, or have a fault within the precepts, he would immediately purify any downfalls and transgressions through confession. He would not allow an uncleansed transgression to last overnight. In guarding and protecting his commitments in this way, Atiśa was of complete honorable character due to his diligent maintenance of his vows as well as his immediacy in confessing any transgressions.[58]

While carrying out religious work in Vajrāsana, Atiśa may have arrived at Vikramaśīla after being appointed "preceptor" at Vikramaśīla with responsibility also for Uddaṇḍapura under King Bheyapāla, who reigned, according to the Tibetan historian Tārānātha, as the predecessor of Neyāpāla (r. ca. 1027–1043). Other traditional accounts mention that King Mahīpāla I (r. ca. 977–1027) was the predecessor and that this king invited to Vikramaśīla fifty-seven scholars among the four schools of Sarvāstivāda, Sthaviravāda, Mahāsāṃghika, and Saṃmatīya to resolve doubts about Buddhist and non-Buddhist doctrines. The king saw that the venerable Atiśa, by his excellence in knowledge and compassion, far surpassed the other pandits, and he proclaimed him the crown jewel among the gathering.[59] Later sources state that the king gave him the name "Atiśa" at this time, as he was "eminent, superior."[60] Atiśa was held in high esteem at Vikramaśīla, as a painting of Nāgārjuna was hung to the right of the gate of Vikramaśīla's main temple and on the left side was painted Atiśa, indicating that he was considered equal to the Ācārya Nāgārjuna. In addition, on one side of the temple were painted many siddhas and on another side were painted paṇḍitas. Atiśa's image was painted within the murals on both sides.

While residing at Vikramaśīla, Atiśa served in an administrative role related to upholding discipline. Later sources state that he was a supervisor or disciplinarian.[61] The earliest biographies mention that Atiśa was the master of eighteen keys and that a group of twenty monks was established in a residence for each key. Atiśa would expel from a residence any monk who was undisciplined.[62] One particular episode in this regard involves Atiśa's well-known junior contemporary Maitrīpa (986–1063).[63] Maitrīpa was spotted by another monk carrying alcohol as part of the *samaya* substances, or esoteric sacraments, for worshipping Vajrayoginī, and this was reported to the monastic community (*saṃgha*). The community ruled, "Although there is not harm to you, this is harmful to others," and requested Maitrīpa to depart. Maitrīpa declared that it is not suitable for those who transgress saṃgha rules to exit by the main gate and then departed unobstructed, passing through a wall. Atiśa considered whether his own conduct was right or not and prayed to Tārā. When Atiśa fell asleep, he heard a voice say three times, "Your conduct is not good." Tārā appeared in person and told Atiśa that Maitrīpa was a bodhisattva who had produced the initial awakening mind. She stipulated that accumulating transgressions against such a bodhisattva causes serious karmic repercussions. Atiśa asked Tārā about his karmic maturation for this act. Tārā told him that he would be reborn as a sentient being three times as large as Mount Sumeru and would be feasted upon by birds. Atiśa asked, "How can I avoid this karma?" Tārā told him, "To purify the karma you should go north and benefit beings by promulgating the Great Vehicle. You should also cast seven small clay images every day." According to the Tibetan sources, Atiśa perceived this as an influential sign to come to Tibet in order to benefit sentient beings.[64]

Around this time, King Neyapāla of Magadha had a fierce dispute with a brahmin king Karṇa from a region to the west. King Karṇa invaded Magadha and led his armies to Vikramaśīla, where five people—four monks and one layperson—were killed. At the time of transporting goods during the conflict, Atiśa, without an angry heart, entered into a concentration on love and compassion. Atiśa's cultivation had the effect of subduing the violence, and the armies ceased attacking one another. King Karṇa gained great faith in Atiśa and led his troops to the west. Atiśa succeeded in mutually bringing together both kings in agreement and became known as a peacemaker in the region.[65]

Western Tibetan Kings and the Invitation of Atiśa to Tibet

The traditional accounts of Atiśa's life at this point segue to the formative events in West Tibet, leading to Atiśa's invitation and eventual journey there. The revival of Buddhism in West Tibet had been going on for several decades in the late tenth century. A well-developed Buddhist community and monastic institutional infrastructure were in place and prepared to receive teachings from an advanced Indian Buddhist master like Atiśa.[66]

Formative in this regard was the monk-king Lha Lama Yeshé Ö (947–1019/24), a descendent of the royal lineages from the earlier Tibetan Empire of the seventh to ninth centuries. His birth name was Song Nge, and at the age of thirty-one, in 989, in the year of the Earth Ox, he was ordained and received the name Yeshé Ö.[67] Lha Lama Yeshé Ö invited scholars such as Dharmapāla from eastern India to explain the Vinaya and reestablish the Mūlasarvāstivāda ordination lineage in Gugé in West Tibet. This ordination lineage became known as the "Upper Tibet Vinaya."[68] Yeshé Ö, having studied the different vehicles of the noble dharma, perceived a contradiction between the vehicle of mantras and vehicle of perfections. Some practices which were followed in the Vinaya were contradicted in the path of mantra. Some practices in the path of mantra were contradicted in the Vinaya. For Yeshé Ö, the Buddhist teachings of sūtra and mantra became contradictory, like hot and cold.

In the late 970s, Yeshé Ö sent twenty-one sharp-minded Tibetan youths to Kashmir and India in order study and translate Buddhist teachings. The great translator Rinchen Zangpo (958–1055) and the junior translator Lekpai Sherap were the only ones that returned to West Tibet. All the other young Tibetans died from the heat. These two translators became masters of dharma and eventually translated many works that came to be included in the Tibetan Buddhist canonical collections of the Kangyur and Tengyur. The two translators reported to Yeshé Ö that the position and conduct of all Indian masters was that the sūtras and tantras did not have internal contradictions. Yet, Yeshé Ö was still concerned about the tantric teachings that were circulating in his kingdom. In 985, Yeshé Ö issued a decree, "Refutation of False Mantras," that perverted teachings must be refuted and were not competent.[69] In 996, Yeshé Ö supervised the construction of the great Tholing Golden Temple.[70] In a number of traditional histories, Yeshé Ö is said to have sacrificed his own life in order to make the invitation of Atiśa to Tibet possible. However, as these are apocryphal stories, it was most likely the case that the invitation of Atiśa occurred during the reign of Jangchup Ö (984–1078), one of Yeshé Ö's decendents.[71]

Jangchup Ö commissioned Gya Tsöndrü Sengé in the Female Iron Sheep Year of 1031 to make the journey to India to invite Atiśa to Tibet.[72] Gya Tsöndrü Sengé, a layperson and one of the preeminent members of the Gya clan from the Tsang Taktsal area, was given sixteen ounces of gold along with a letter. In the letter Jangchup Ö stated, in part,

> I am a Tibetan king here in the Land of Snows. Although we had former excellence, nowadays our merit has degenerated. Please have compassion for us. I constantly think of you, O Protector, as someone would think about water while in the plains of a desert.[73]

The translator Gya Tsöndrü Sengé along with a retinue of one hundred arrived at Vikramaśīla without any difficulties and delivered the invitation and gold to Atiśa. Atiśa said, "There are two reasons that I would go to Tibet. One is to go with the desire for gold, and I have no need for gold. On the other hand, the awakening mind, which treats others as more important than oneself, would be a reason to go, but I do not have that, so therefore I will not go." Gya Tsöndrü Sengé was devastated and held the corner of his monastic robes and cried. During that time, a great number of the Tibetans among the translator's retinue died from fever and the heat. Atiśa expressed his deep empathy for the Tibetans. Then, the translator Gya Tsöndrü Sengé returned to Tibet and offered the gold back to King Jangchup Ö. He informed the king that the invitation of Princely-Lord Atiśa was not successful. At that time, another Tibetan translator, Naktso Lotsāwa Tsultrim Gyalwa (1011–1064), had asked Gya Tsöndrü Sengé for guidance on the study of the Abhidharma. As Gya Tsöndrü Sengé planned to return to India to study at Vikramaśīla, he told Naktso Lotsāwa that he did not have the time. Gya Tsöndrü Sengé along with a retinue of five then returned to India.[74]

Jangchup Ö observed in Tibet at the time many crude behaviors misrepresented as the practice of the Secret Mantra Vehicle propagated by such figures as the Red Ācārya, Blue Robe extremist teachers, eighteen Arsho bande, and others. Practices such as animal sacrifice and kidnapping were distorted and seen as legitimate esoteric Buddhist rituals.[75] The king prayed to the three jewels and petitioned astrologers for divinations on who could invite Atiśa for the sake of the Buddhadharma that was disappearing in West Tibet. They determined that Naktso Lotsāwa Tsultrim Gyalwa was the person to make the journey.

Naktso Lotsāwa Tsultrim Gyalwa was a monk originally from the Gungthang region of Mangyul. He was regarded as an expert in Vinaya and Abhidharma. At the time that Naktso Lotsāwa was summoned by Jangchup Ö, the twenty-seven-year-old translator was staying in the Golden Temple of Ngari Gungthang. Jangchup Ö sent for Naktso Lotsāwa from the village to come to Ngari. Jangchup Ö venerated the translator and eulogized him for his great competence and discipline.

Jangchup Ö gave Naktso Lotsāwa seven hundred ounces of gold to offer to Atiśa. Around 1033, Naktso Lotsāwa Tsultrim Gyalwa along with a retinue of seven carried the gold and set out on the road to India. Jangchup Ö escorted Naktso and his retinue for some distance and then, before turning back, told them to pray to Avalokiteśvara for protection on their journey. Naktso Lotsāwa and his delegation encountered numerous obstacles on their way through Nepal into North India, including sickness, robbers, poisonous snakes, and extreme fatigue. They finally arrived at Vikramaśīla during the night.[76]

When they arrived near the entrance gates, they called out in Tibetan and Gya Tsöndrü Sengé heard them from a window in the gate tower. Gya Tsöndrü Sengé said, "Hey, where have you venerable Tibetans come from?" Naktso Lotsāwa and his retinue replied, "We are from Upper Ngari." Gya Tsöndrü Sengé warned them to wait outside the gate until dawn. In the early morning, the travelers recited sūtras in Tibetan. Gya Tsöndrü Sengé heard them and was glad that they had not been robbed, and he got up and went to them. Naktso Lotsāwa and his retinue greeted Gya Tsöndrü Sengé with some gold. Gya Tsöndrü Sengé asked if they had come to invite a scholar or to study. Naktso Lotsāwa reported the order of the Tibetan king to invite a scholar who was as significant as Atiśa. Gya Tsöndrü Sengé replied that there were scholars like Tathāgatarakṣita, Vairocanakṣita, Ratnakīrti, as well as others, mentioning over thirty names. Gya Tsöndrü Sengé emphasized that, as only Atiśa could benefit Tibet, they should not speak of any plans of invitation and should quickly register as students by meeting with Ratnākaraśānti, the senior superintendent in Vikramaśīla.[77]

Gya Tsöndrü Sengé and Naktso Lotsāwa then met with Ratnākaraśānti and presented him with a half ounce of gold. Ratnākaraśānti welcomed them to Vikramaśīla and offered his assistance but told them that Atiśa was vital to the administration of the monastic institution as well as a significant authority for the Buddha's teaching. Ratnākaraśānti wished the translators well in their study at Vikramaśīla. The translators settled in the monastery and pursued their studies.

Naktso Lotsāwa did not initially meet Atiśa for several days. One day Naktso Lotsāwa recited the *Heart Sūtra* at one of the gates of the monastery. When he was reciting "form *ha*, feeling *ha*," at a certain point in the recitation, other scholars passed by but did not say anything. However, when Atiśa came near Naktso Lotsāwa, Atiśa stopped and smiled. Atiśa then said, "Thank you, venerable one. But your recitation has vulgar pronunciation. You should say, 'form *a*, feeling *a*.'" Naktso Lotsāwa did not realize that he was speaking with Atiśa but thought to himself, "This kind scholar seems special. He is gentle, humble, clear, and whatever he says is spoken with the wish to be helpful. If I cannot invite Atiśa, then I must invite this scholar to come to Tibet." The next morning, Naktso Lotsāwa was reciting "form *a*, feeling *a*" when Atiśa came by again and smiled. Atiśa said, "Venerable one, even that recitation comes out sounding harsh. This is the speech of the protector Avalokiteśvara. There's nothing wrong with it. It is fine to just say, 'no form, no feeling.'"

As a result of their conversations, Naktso Lotsāwa had strong faith in the kind scholar-monk, and a few days later Naktso Lotsāwa realized the kind scholar-monk was Atiśa.[78]

One evening, the two Tibetan translators went to Atiśa's living quarters, and Gya Tsöndrü Sengé formally introduced Naktso Lotsāwa to Atiśa. Naktso Lotsāwa presented the seven hundred ounces of gold as a gift, and Gya Tsöndrü Sengé reported on the development of Buddhism in Tibet from the time of the religious kings to Lang Darma and then up until the time of Yeshé Ö and Jangchup Ö. They then asked Atiśa to come to Tibet.[79]

Atiśa agreed that Yeshé Ö and Jangchup Ö were bodhisattvas and that, for the sake of his invitation, many people and great treasures had been offered. Yet, Atiśa stated, "I am old and have many duties." Atiśa explained that it was first necessary to examine whether his presence in Tibet could be of use, and then Atiśa returned the gold.[80]

During the night, Atiśa prayed three times to Tārā and asked if his trip to Tibet would benefit the Buddhist teachings, whether he could help the Tibetan king spiritually, and whether his own life would be shortened by the journey. In the dream, the goddess told him to go to a city of non-Buddhists near Vikramaśīla, Mukhena, to question a *yoginī* there at a Buddhist temple. Atiśa went there, met the yoginī, and asked if his journey would benefit the Tibetans. She said the journey would be greatly beneficial, especially for a certain Buddhist layperson, or *upāsaka*. The yoginī also said that Atiśa's life would last ninety-two years if he stayed in India but would last only seventy-two years if he journeyed to Tibet. Since Atiśa received indications that the trip would benefit the Tibetans, his resolve to go to Tibet was strengthened.[81]

Atiśa then went on a pilgrimage to Vajrāsana, and he received from his colleague Jñānaśrīmitra a hint that he would meet there an old woman who was an emanation of Tārā. On the journey,

Atiśa along with the Tibetan translators and others, a group comprised of twelve persons, met a superhuman female figure. Atiśa asked her whether the journey to Tibet in the border area would benefit living beings. This emanation of Tārā advised him to travel without regard for life and limb and said that the journey would be beneficial for others. In Vajrāsana, Atiśa met an old woman, to whom Jñānaśrīmitra had referred. Atiśa questioned the yoginī, who told him that the encounter with the layperson would bring benefits and that in the next life the Great Seal would be achieved. After the pilgrimage, Atiśa called the two translators, Gya Tsöndrü Sengé and Naktso, and told them that he would come to Tibet. But Atiśa then explained that he would have to spend another eighteen months in India for spiritual preparation and fulfillment of his duties. Atiśa told them not to talk about the invitation. The two Tibetans agreed, and Naktso Lotsāwa studied and translated texts with good success.[82]

Gya Tsöndrü Sengé and Naktso Lotsāwa studied under Atiśa during this time and worked together translating works by Atiśa and his disciples. Atiśa's *Entry to the Two Realities* (see chapter 5) and its commentary were translated into Tibetan at this time. The *Open Basket of Jewels* (see chapter 4) was translated into Tibetan at Vikramaśīla around this time as well. The two Tibetan translators also accompanied Atiśa on teaching tours to other monasteries. While Atiśa taught a Madhyamaka course utilizing the *Jeweled Lamp of the Middle Way* (*Madhyamakaratnapradīpa*) and the *Blaze of Reasoning* (*Tarkajvālā*) at Somapura around the year 1034, Gya Tsöndrü Sengé and Naktso Lotsāwa initially translated the works into Tibetan.[83]

Around this time the former abbot of Nālandā Monastery and famous mahāsiddha Nāropa (956–1040) visited Vikramaśīla.[84] Nāropa descended from his transport, with Atiśa supporting him with his right arm and Jñānaśrīmitra supporting him with his left arm. While seated on a lion throne, Nāropa stated that he did not have much longer to live and said to Atiśa, "You, Dīpaṃkara, are now master of the Buddha's teaching." Twenty days after leaving Vikramaśīla in a southernly direction, Nāropa died.[85]

Shortly thereafter, while on pilgrimage in Vajrāsana, Atiśa announced to his companions that he wanted to travel to the outlying Indian district of Tsindhili Krama to consecrate the site for a temple. Ratnākaraśānti sent a retinue of sixty persons. When the temple dedication was completed, Atiśa then said he wanted to go to Svayaṃbhūnātha in Kathmandu, Nepal. Ratnākaraśānti now saw through the plans and realized Atiśa's intentions to go to Tibet. Ratnākaraśānti and Naktso Lotsāwa discussed the plans for Atiśa's journey, and they came to an agreement that Atiśa must return to India in three years. Naktso Lotsāwa then pledged to return Atiśa within the stipulated time frame. The seven hundred ounces of gold that the Tibetans had offered for the invitation were divided by Atiśa into four parts. One part of the gold was offered to Atiśa's teachers, one part for rituals in Vajrāsana, one for the monastic community in Vikramaśīla under Ratnākaraśānti, and one for the king to distribute to his own teachers. Atiśa then transferred his adminstrative duties to Ratnākaraśānti.[86]

Atiśa set out on the journey to Tibet riding on an elephant and surrounded by an entourage of nineteen companions. Atiśa's retinue included his foremost Indian disciple Kṣitigarbha, his youngest brother, Vīryacandra, the Tibetan translators, and attendants. They received a warm welcome from a small monastic community in an outlying Indian district while traveling north. The community expressed concern that Atiśa's journey to Tibet was a loss for India. The Indian monks asked if he could be prevented from leaving India because his absence would lead to the downfall of the Buddhist teaching. Atiśa and his retinue said they would not be diverted from their purpose.[87]

In the frontier lands, Atiśa had debates with fifteen non-Buddhist teachers about their religion, which he knew well, and they gave Atiśa umbrellas as a token of their gratitude for his knowledge and compassion. The non-Buddhists were worried that Buddhism in Tibet would be spread through Atiśa and sent people to kill the teacher. Atiśa banished them with the help of mantras. As they crossed the border country, the entourage faced obstacles against non-Buddhist naked ascetics, who Atiśa subjugated with the creation stage practices of Ārya Tārā. In an abandoned nomad camp, Atiśa found three puppies and took them on the journey. The biographies report that the offspring of the puppies could later be found in Radreng Monastery.[88]

Atiśa and his entourage then arrived in the Kathmandu Valley in 1041. There was a great reception at the Svayambhū sacred site offered by delegates from West Tibet. The Tibetans constructed a hearth for boiling tea, arranged seats in rows, and set out porcelain cups to serve food and drink. Atiśa was offered a throne in the shade of a tree. On his right side were seated Tibetans headed by Gya Tsöndrü Sengé and on his left side were seated Indians, including Vīryacandra. Mahārāja Bhūmi Saṃgha, a royal monk disciple, sat on a central throne seat. Atiśa was then offered tea, a drink unknown in India at this point in history. A group of six main delegates then presented Atiśa with a white horse named "Swift as the Wind"[89] that was steady like a horse-drawn chariot. Its forehead was adorned with pieces of turquoise and gold. The horse's saddle and saddle carpet were soft and adorned with ornaments, and the halter was made of white silk. Atiśa then said, "All of this is extremely auspicious, like a container converging with its contents. But, what is this drink?" The translator replied, "This is called tea (*ja*). It is a drink of Tibetan monks. The tree itself cannot be eaten, but once boiled the juice is consumed. It has many wonderful qualities." Atiśa then said, "This is most certainly established from meritorious qualities of Tibetan monks. It is most excellent."[90]

Atiśa and his entourage then stayed at a royal residence in the Kathmandu Valley, and Gya Tsöndrü Sengé became extremely ill.[91] Atiśa asked him, "What did you do?" Gya Tsöndrü Sengé replied, "I did not do anything other than receive a harmful mantra from a non-Buddhist. I gave him some gold powder from the gold that was left with me, but he was not satisfied. The non-Buddhist told me, 'Melt it into one piece!' I was not able to do so and had a fight with him. Ever since, I have been slightly sick." Atiśa said, "Although, in general, it is not possible to melt it, had you thereafter disclosed the matter to me, I would have used a method leading to a solution," and added, "Depite my blessings, Gya Tsöndrü Sengé has gone beyond the possibility of being saved." Since Gya Tsöndrü Sengé was going to be murdered by the non-Buddhist's harmful mantra in Nepal, the local law sanctioned that, if one died in a house, the householder would take for himself the deceased person's property. Therefore, that night, Atiśa and the entourage camped at the bank of a river on the plain ground. Gya Tsöndrü Sengé died later that night and most of his belongings were brought to Tibet.[92]

At the death of Gya Tsöndrü Sengé, Atiśa exclaimed in grief, "My going to Tibet has no purpose. It is useless as my voice has been silenced!" Naktso Lotsāwa tried to reassure him, pointing out that there were other translators in Tibet, such as Rinchen Zangpo, Lekpai Sherap, Gewa Lodrö, Geshé Khu Lotsāwa, himself, and others. Atiśa replied that it was not up to a student to speak to his teacher in such a way. "In our land of India," Atiśa explained, "yogis consol the grief of paṇḍitas, and the paṇḍitas explain the Buddhadharma to the yogis." However, as Naktso Lotsāwa had traveled through all the hardships, Atiśa said he would be satisfied with learning Tibetan from the translator.[93]

While in Nepal, Atiśa wrote a letter to King Neyāpāla entitled *Letter of Unblemished Precious Jewels* and translated it into Tibetan with Naktso Lotsāwa.[94] In Wölka, in Nepal, Atiśa and his companions stayed with a deaf Sthavira for a month. The monk requested a teaching on the perfections not including the way of mantras. In the teaching, Atiśa emphasized that both mantras along with the perfections lead to awakening. Atiśa then composed the *Lamp for the Summary of Conduct* (*Caryāsaṃgrahapradīpa*), which he translated together with Naktso Lotsāwa (see chapter 7).[95] Atiśa and his entourage next reached the "Plain of Kathmandu Valley" in present-day Tham Bahīl in Thamel, north of old Kathmandu. Atiśa met with a Nepalese king named "Boundless Fame." Atiśa entrusted his elephant mount named "Admirable to See" to the king, as the elephant would not be able to survive in Tibet. Atiśa instructed the mahārāja not to use the animal as a mount or servant. Rather, the king should use the elephant to help construct the building of a monastic complex known as Tham Vihāra. Atiśa and the king then had the complex built to support a saṃgha of both Indian and Tibetan monks to be led by the king's son, Prince Padmaprabha, who became a monk.[96]

CHAPTER 2

Tibet

Atiśa's Arrival in Tibet

ATIŚA AND HIS ENTOURAGE were greeted at Balpo Dzong (modern-day Nuwākoṭ) with a grand welcome party of three hundred Tibetan horsemen that had been sent from West Tibet by Jangchup Ö. The horsemen reenacted the welcome presented, centuries earlier, to the "Abbot Bodhisattva," Śāntarakṣita. The horsemen were wearing only white clothes and were adorned with ornaments. Among the horsemen were four government ministers named Lha Wangchuk, Lha Drodrö, Lha Sherap, and Lha Sidzin. Altogether the horsemen surrounded Atiśa's entourage while on their horses and then sang melodious and pleasing songs along with aspirational prayers welcoming the Indian master and his retinue. The ministers encouraged Atiśa and his retinue to spread the Buddha's teaching in Tibet. The senior minister addressed Atiśa with praises, singing the song "*lo a le ma lo de a lo la lo la.*" Atiśa, his entourage, and the three hundred accompanying horsemen then set out for West Tibet. Atiśa was surrounded by his disciples Parahitabhadra, Vīryacandra, and Naktso Lotsāwa, as well as other monks, totaling thirty-five in number. Atiśa's horse strode gently like a golden swan while Atiśa's pleasant and handsome appearance was beautiful to behold and worthy of worship by the gods. Wearing an ever-present smile, he would utter Sanskrit mantras, often calling out, "*e ma ho, ati ati, pha la pha la, āryatāre, ārya acala, mahākāruṇika, śākyamune.*" [97]

The group came to Gungthang in Mangyul and stayed there for one year as guests in the homeland of Naktso Lotsāwa. When asked about how to perform water offerings,[98] Atiśa required the use of the six kriyāmantras and the six "seals." On the journey to Purang, Atiśa performed water offerings on Lake Mānasarovar for the hungry ghosts.[99]

Atiśa and his entourage arrived in Tholing, the West Tibet seat of Ngari, in the year 1042 when Atiśa was sixty years old. On arrival at Tholing, Atiśa along with his entourage settled in the monastic temple of Jangchup Ling.[100] The royal monk Jangchup Ö then hosted a large reception for Atiśa, and the special trumpets blown were called the "reception trumpets for Lotsāwas and Pandits." Jangchup Ö offered a maṇḍala to Atiśa and made a request. The king said,

> In this northern Land of Snows, our ancestor kings undertook many hardships to disseminate the Buddha's teaching. Now, some, having relied on Secret Mantra practices, despise the Vinaya. Some, through relying on the Vinaya, despise Secret Mantra practices. Some claim that sūtra and mantra are contradictory, like hot and cold. Some practice as they like. Lord Atiśa, compassionate one, for these unruly Tibetans to be disciplined, please teach a profound and marvelous dharma, something wonderful and not known but which maintains the karmic laws of cause and effect.[101]

Atiśa was delighted and said, "The especially profound dharma is only causes and consequences of karmic actions.[102] Other than a direct vision of one's chosen meditational deity,[103] when one attains a firm conviction in the causes and consequences of karmic actions, that itself is the most sublime." Atiśa then spoke on causes and effects, telling the story of a yogi who practiced Yamāri and who had a direct vision of the Highest Yoga Tantra deity. However, the yogi then committed transgressions against the monastic community's possessions and was reborn as a hungry ghost in the form of Yamāri. Another monk at Vikramaśīla maltreated elder monks in the community, and another monk took grain without permission. They both were reborn as hungry ghosts in the next existence. With such teachings on the causes and consequences of karmic actions, the Tibetans called Atiśa the "teacher of causes and effects." Due to his great compassion, he was also called "the bodhisattva practitioner."[104]

The Questioning of Atiśa by Scholars from Central Tibet

Around this time, a great number of Tibetan scholars had come from the Central Tibet regions of Ü and Tsang. They had followed Atiśa to West Tibet and wished to hear his teachings on the Buddhadharma. Some of the Tibetan scholars asked Atiśa a number of questions, such as "What do you assert?" "Do you accept the Madhyamaka and Cittamātra teachings of old?" Atiśa replied that he does not assert anything and that he follows the dharma according to scripture and reasoning. Having said this, a sharp-minded one from Ngari named Losal asked Atiśa, "If you do not assert anything, then how do you teach common to all?" Atiśa explained that as a follower of the Buddha, he teaches according to the inclinations of those to be trained.

Another scholar named Metsun Yönten Sherab asked, "Well, then, what do you assert?" Atiśa said, "I do not assert anything." To this, the scholar asked, "If you do not assert anything ultimately, then how do you assert conventionally?" Atiśa said, "All these things are according to how a person with eye disease sees hair, that is how they abide." Someone then asked Atiśa, "Are appearances cleared away or not?" Atiśa replied, "Appearances are like how hairs appear in cooked rice for someone with eye disease, but you should investigate for yourself." He was then asked whether there are appearances or not in the purview of valid cognition with a reasoning consciousness. Atiśa replied that there are no appearances, for when the object does not appear the subject does not either. Atiśa was asked whether, at the level of buddhahood, a continuum of wisdom exists or not. He replied that a buddha does not have any at all. Atiśa then said, "It is like how an illusionary adept deceives a minister, but you should investigate for yourself. The Buddha, not having a continuum of wisdom, strikes victory from everywhere. You Tibetans will not tolerate the understanding of mind-only in terms of my Madhyamaka view."

Atiśa then asked, "How do you posit the example of an illusion for a Madhyamaka?" When the Tibetan teachers replied, "When casting a spell on a piece of stone or wood, there appears a horse or an elephant," Atiśa frowned and replied that the basis of emptiness in that example is asserted according to the Mind-Only system. Atiśa explained that by casting a spell in the sky there is the appearance of a horse or elephant, but that the mistaken basis of the mere appearance of various things is only conventional and does not really exist.

The Tibetan scholar-yogi Mangnang Gomchen requested an example to understand how ignorance is like suffering from eye disease. Atiśa then gave the example of an old woman and her son in India. Atiśa said,

> At the time of the son's going away on business, he left behind the daughter-in-law to take care of his mother. The son told his wife to take care of the mother and then he left. Then, at that time, the old woman suffered from eye disease, which obstructed her vision. All of her food appeared to

> have hairs in it. The old woman complained to the daughter-in-law. The daughter-in-law became depressed, and when the son returned the old woman made an accusation. The son asked his wife how this could be, and the wife told him she was dutiful but that the old woman suffered from an eye disorder. She added that the son himself had provided the food. The son saw the well-prepared food that he had provided. The old woman spoke, asking if the son would prepare tainted food like that. The son replied that he would not, and that since she was mistaken and disturbed about this food, he was going to summon a skillful doctor. The doctor nourished her eyes by applying internal and external medicine to them. Then, through the natural healing of her eye disease, she understood that the food did not have hairs in it.

Likewise, Atiśa explained, "the dharma teachings of the Three Baskets remove external superimpositions. The special instructions of the excellent spiritual teacher remove internal superimpositions." All the Tibetan scholars of Ü and Tsang were impressed and stated, "We must invite this bearded one for teachings on the dharma."[105]

Meeting with Rinchen Zangpo

The great translator Rinchen Zangpo was honored and revered in Ngari when Atiśa came to West Tibet. Atiśa wished to meet the great scholar and discuss dharma with him. Rinchen Zangpo invited Atiśa to his residence in Tholing, where there was a three-story temple with deities of the Secret Mantra Vehicle on each floor. Atiśa recited mantras for each of the deities among the four classes of tantra, recited four verses of praise concordant with the sādhanas for each of the main deities, and bowed his head. Atiśa asked the translator if he understood this and the dharma concerning the sūtras and tantras. "These I know," the translator replied. Atiśa then thought it was unnecessary for himself to come to Tibet if he had known of such scholars like Rinchen Zangpo.

However, that night, while dwelling in the deity temple, Rinchen Zangpo meditated on the creation and completion stages[106] of the deities of the Guhyasamāja on the lower floor after sunset, meditated on a circle of deities of Hevajra on the middle floor of the temple at midnight, and then meditated on the deities of Cakrasaṃvara on the top floor at dawn. Atiśa was somewhat unhappy and had a number questions for Rinchen Zangpo the next day. Atiśa asked, "Great Translator, you do have great knowledge of the dharma, yet how do you practice these dharma teachings when meditating in a single meditative session?" When Rinchen Zangpo explained that he practiced a sādhana for each individual deity, Atiśa realized that it was necessary for him to come to Tibet. Then Rinchen Zangpo, generating great faith, asked about the manner of practice, and Atiśa stated, "Although there are many teachings of dharma according to the inclinations of those to be disciplined, fundamentally they have the same flavor. It is sufficient to practice all creation and completion stage meditations in one single spot."[107]

Furthermore, Atiśa explained, "In the vehicle of perfections according to the system of Ācārya Asaṅga and his followers, all things are conventionally posited according to the three characteristics.[108] One takes up the three characteristics at the time of practice. The result also has three characteristics: the emanation body is the imaginary nature, the enjoyment body is the dependent nature, and the dharma body is the perfected nature." Atiśa continued,

> According to the noble Nāgārjuna and his disciples, within conventional reality all things are settled according to the two realities. At the time of practice in meditation, ultimate

> reality is free from elaboration, and in the postmeditative time conventional realities are perceived like an illusion. These are the two realities at the time of practice. For the result, the dharma body is the ultimate reality and the form body is the conventional reality; these are the two realities when brought to realization.
>
> In the Secret Mantra Vehicle, conventionally, things are settled by three continuums.[109] At the time of the path, abiding in the meditation of inseperable emptiness and compassion is the continuum of the cause. Meditating on the path of the creation and completion stages is the continuum of means. Completely practicing altogether the path along with the result in one meditative session is the continuum of the result; that is practicing the three continuums. At the time of the result, the three continuums are also manifest: the dharma body, which is inseparable emptiness and compassion, is the continuum of the cause. The emanation body, which performs various miraculous deeds for the benefit of those to be disciplined, is the continuum of method. The enjoyment body, that performs deeds for the benefit of those in cyclic existence through the inseparability of the three bodies and five wisdoms, is the continuum of the result.[110]

"Accordingly," Atiśa concluded, "in terms of one deity, everything is completely practiced. The creation stage for one deity alone completely practices all of the deities."[111] After their discussion, the translator Rinchen Zangpo offered seven ounces of gold to Atiśa and requested the stages of Cakrasaṃvara and the blessing of the venerable Vārāhī. The translator subsequently had many special experiences and realizations. Later, after making offerings to Atiśa with one hundred eight ounces of gold and offering his own texts,

Rinchen Zangpo made Atiśa's Cakrasaṃvara and Vārāhī practice manuals his own principal practices. Rinchen Zangpo would often say that any great knowledge or achievements that he gained were due to the influence of Atiśa. When Atiśa viewed his *Compilation of All the Pledges*[112] that had been translated into Tibetan by Rinchen Zangpo, Atiśa said to Rinchen Zangpo, "I need you as a translator." Rinchen Zangpo replied, "My hair has turned totally white. How can I have any achievement?" Atiśa said,

> Rinchen Zangpo, your achievement in reality is based on the force of immeasurable virtuous and beneficial qualities from your previous lifetimes. You have attained a precious human body. You have met with the Buddha's teaching. You have found the spiritual friend who indicates special instructions. You have gained the medicine of dharma which pacifies the sickness of existence. You have found a lamp of dharma which eradicates the darkness of existence. You have gained the ship of wisdom, the means of liberating from the river of existence. Now, at this time, practice one-pointedly and do not be distracted with bad thoughts.

Rinchen Zangpo took to heart Atiśa's special instructions and nailed them on an iron door of the temple where he practiced. On part of the door Rinchen Zanpo wrote in addition, "If I generate ordinary thoughts within this temple, may the guardians who protect the dharma split my head into a hundred pieces!" Practicing this way one-pointedly, Rinchen Zangpo had a direct vision of Cakrasaṃvara.[113]

In spite of Rinchen Zangpo's age (between 85 and 87) at the time of their meeting, Atiśa and the great translator worked on over twenty translations together.[114] A significant work among these translations was Serlingpa's massive *Illumination of Points Difficult to Understand*, a commentary to the *Ornament for Clear Realization*, which Atiśa had brought with him from Sumatra. This commentary is one of the earliest extant texts of Southeast Asian literature.[115]

Teachings and Advice to Jangchup Ö

Atiśa and Rinchen Zangpo also translated texts that were composed by Atiśa himself. Among the most important was a tantric text on Avalokiteśvara that was specifically composed for the royal monk Jangchup Ö. Jangchup Ö supplicated Atiśa and offered him three hundred ounces of gold for a special practice. Jangchup Ö was devoted to Avalokiteśvara, and Atiśa ingeniously composed a sādhana that placed the high-level bodhisattva at the center of a highest tantra maṇḍala. Atiśa composed a practice manual with Avalokiteśvara residing as the lord in Buddhajñāna's system of the *Guhyasamāja Tantra*.[116] Atiśa's sādhana for Jangchup Ö is one of the earliest examples of royal initiation into a Highest Yoga Tantra in Buddhist history.[117]

Atiśa stayed in Tholing for three years, from 1042 to 1045, composing, translating, and teaching the dharma. One biography conveys how Atiśa's presence and dharma teachings purified the local environment of practitioners. Atiśa stipulates similar immediate karmic repercussions in his *Stages of the Path to Awakening* (see chapter 12, section 54). The accounts mention that King Lhade became a monk. All the monks were set in their vows. All the practitioners of mantra were set in the samaya precepts. The householders were established in one-day precepts (*upavastha*). In additon, spirits were pleased, animals were taken care of, the sick were medically examined, *tormas* or offering cakes were given, and a number of virtuous deeds were accomplished. The royal monk Jangchup Ö even had a direct vision of Avalokiteśvara. Atiśa's mission to West Tibet seemed to be a success.[118]

Naktso Lotsāwa was aware that Atiśa would not be able stay much longer than a year in Tibet and urged the royal monk Jangchup Ö and others, saying, "You should request Atiśa to give an all-inclusive teaching!" Jangchup Ö then made an offering of three hundred ounces of gold and requested, "In this land of Tibet, individuals with wrong ideas and geshés mutually debate one another regarding the Buddha's teaching, the Mahāyāna path. Each one has their own ideas about the practice and meaning of the profound view and the extensive practices. Since there are many who are in discord, I ask that you give a teaching that clarifies their doubts."[119] In addition to this request, the king asked two questions related to both vehicles in common, two questions related to the vehicle of the perfections, and three questions related to the vehicle of Secret Mantra.[120] Some of the questions that were asked included: (1) Is it possible to attain Buddhahood by exclusively cultivating either skillful means (*upāya*) or wisdom (*prajñā*)? (2) Is it necessary to accept bodhisattva precepts in reliance upon prātimokṣa vows? (3) Is it permissible to explain tantras without attaining the Vajrācārya consecration? (4) Is is permissible for those who practice celibacy to receive the two superior kinds of consecration? (5) Is it permissible for those who have not received consecration to engage in Secret Mantra practices?[121] In response to Jangchup Ö's request and questions, Atiśa wrote his *Lamp for the Path to Awakening* (*Bodhipathapradīpa*). The text was then translated into Tibetan by Atiśa and the translator Gewa Lodrö in the Golden Temple of Tholing (see chapter 11).

After Atiśa had completed three years of extensive teaching in Ngari töd, Naktso Lotsāwa kept the pledge that he committed with the elder Ratnākaraśānti. The translator respectfully informed Atiśa that the time to return to India had come. Atiśa agreed to depart and the entourage proceeded to Purang, east of Ngari and on the northwest border of Nepal. The royal monk Jangchup Ö again petitioned for further instruction, and Atiśa responded that all the previous teachings he had given were sufficient. Yet, Jangchup Ö continued on with his request, and Atiśa then gave the following advice:[122]

E ma ho!
O friend, you whose knowledge is high and whose mind is utterly clear,
Though it is inappropriate for me, one of low intelligence and lacking in accomplishments, to offer any advice,
As you, my excellent friend who is so dear to my heart, have exhorted me,
I, a childlike one with small intelligence, offer this suggestion to your heart, my friend.

As one requires a teacher until the attainment of awakening, rely on a sublime teacher, O friend.
As one requires learning until the ultimate mode of being is realized, listen to your teacher's essential instructions.
As the mere knowledge of the teachings does not lead to full awakening, put it into practice, for knowing alone is inadequate.
Distance yourself from those objects that afflict your mind and always reside in places that increase virtue.

As distractions cause harm until one has attained stability, seek solitary forests.
Forsake friends who give rise to afflictions, and seek those who enhance virtue and respect their wishes.
As there is no end to mundane chores, discard them and abide with natural ease.

Throughout day and night, dedicate your virtues and always guard your mind.
As you've received essential instructions, whatever you do, be it meditation or other activities, do so in accordance with your teacher's words.

If you pursue this with great respect, you will reap its fruits before long.
If you act in accord with the dharma from your heart, both provisions and support will be attained as by-products.
O friend, sensual desires are insatiable, like drinking salt water, therefore cultivate contentment.

Despise all thoughts of haughtiness, conceit, and arrogance and be tranquil and tamed.
As distracting pursuits referred to as "merit" are obstacles to dharma practice, relinquish them.
As offerings and honor are Māra's lasso, measure them carefully like the weights of a scale.
As words of praise and fame are tricksters, cast them out like spit or snot.

Since all happiness is the teachers' blessings, repay their kindness.
Since you cannot tame others' minds while your own mind remains untamed, first discipline your own mind.
Since you cannot enhance others if you lack superior cognition, strive well in your meditative practice.
Since you are certain to depart leaving your accumulated wealth behind, commit no negative karma for its sake.

Since this wealth of distractions is without essence, give
charity adorned with gifts.
Since it beautifies this life and leads to happiness in the
future, always observe pure ethical discipline.
Since hatred profilerates in the degenerate age, put on the
armor of forbearance free of anger.
Since you might be left behind because of laziness, ignite the
flame of joyful perseverance like a blazing fire.

Since it is on the road of distraction that one exhausts one's
life span, the time has now come for the endeavor of
concentration.
Due to wrong views one fails to realize the ultimate mode of
being, so inspect well the perfect truth.
O friend, there is not joy in this mire of saṃsāra, so depart to
liberation's dry shores.
Practice well the teachers' instructions and drain the lake of
saṃsāra's suffering.

Keep this advice well in your heart and listen to this
suggestion, for this is not a mere mouthing of words.
If you do this, I'll be happy, and both you and others will
enjoy happiness.
O listen well, dear friend, to these words of advice from an
ignorant man.

Atiśa Meets His Foremost Tibetan Disciple Dromtönpa Gyalwai Jungné

The goddess Tārā had previously given a prediction to Atiśa that coming to Tibet would bring great benefit to the dharma in relation to a special Tibetan layperson. While translating, teaching, and traveling in West Tibet, Atiśa would repeatedly say to himself, "Layperson quickly appear!" and question, "Is Tārā's prediction for the appearance of a beneficial layperson false?"[123]

The special person that Atiśa had been anticipating was Dromtönpa Gyalwai Jungné (1005–1064), an ambitious layperson who had studied under Setsun Wangchuk Shönu and Smṛtijñānakīrti at Danma in East Tibet in the region of Kham.[124] Dromtönpa had taken the precepts of a layperson in the Mūlasarvāstivāda lineage tradition under Shang Chen po of Gyal, also known as Shang Nanam Dorjé Wangchuk (976–1060), one of the "four pillar" disciples of Lumé Sherap Tsultrim of the Eastern Vinaya tradition. At the age of thirty-eight, with the encouragement of his teacher Setsun Wangchuk Shönu, Dromtönpa traveled west to meet the great Indian master Atiśa he had heard about. Along the way to West Tibet, Dromtönpa gathered patronage and support for a future monastery.

Meanwhile, in Purang, Atiśa kept wondering if the prediction to meet with a special layperson was false or not. In a dream, Tārā came and told Atiśa that a great layperson would arrive in three and a half days. Atiśa then set out a vase for consecration and blessed it with mantras. At noon on the fourth day, Atiśa pondered if Tārā had spoken falsely and then went to teach dharma in the countryside. While Atiśa was traveling on the road, Dromtönpa was following behind him in the entourage of attendants. Atiśa encountered Dromtönpa on the road in the countryside, and they both mutually seemed to know each other. After a brief conversation, Atiśa placed his hand on Dromtönpa's head and spoke many verses of praise. Then, later that evening, in the residence hall of the temple in Gya shing, Atiśa placed the vase for consecration on Dromtönpa's head and blessed him. They did not sleep and discussed dharma throughout the night. Atiśa explained how his goddess Tārā had predicted Dromtönpa's arrival and that Atiśa would bestow his lineage of oral teachings upon Dromtönpa.[125]

Next, Atiśa and his entourage gradually journeyed to the village of Kyirong in Mangyul. Atiśa gave many dharma teachings in the Āryadeva temple there. Atiśa traveled to the forest of an auspicious mountain to the north of the village and disseminated the Buddha's teaching while residing in that forest. Then, Naktso Lotsāwa, who was in charge of leading Atiśa back to India, had gathered information on the local conditions and determined that the passage through Nepal was blocked by a great war taking place at the border. The entourage would not be able return through the planned route. The group waited while the roads through to India were closed. During this time, Atiśa consecrated a "white deity temple"[126] that had been constructed in Mangyul.

Journey to Central Tibet

Dromtönpa, with high hopes, made repeated requests for Atiśa to travel to Central Tibet. Dromtönpa encouraged Atiśa to visit the numerous temples in Lhasa, Samyé, and other areas, as well as to see the Sanskrit manuscripts preserved in Samyé brought by the late eighth-century scholars Śāntarakṣita and Kamalaśīla. Dromtönpa emphasized that there were hundreds of well-disciplined monks that resided in Central Tibet. The proposal pleased Atiśa, as he remarked that many hundreds of monks were rare in India. Atiśa agreed to go to Central Tibet if he received an invitation from the Buddhist community in Ü and Tsang. Dromtönpa then sent a letter through Shang Wangchuk Gön for delivery to Geshé Kawa Shākya Wangchuk. The letter consisted of nineteen verses and addressed the Buddhist dignitaries of Central Tibet to invite the Indian master to the region.[127]

During this time, as they were unable to journey back to India due to the warfare at the border, Naktso Lotsāwa worried about what to do, but Atiśa told Naktso Lotsāwa that he should not be upset, as there was no one at fault due to the situation. Pleased with Atiśa's response, Naktso Lotsāwa also invited Atiśa to Central Tibet. Accordingly, messengers were sent to India to convey the news that Atiśa was unable to return to India, as the battle occurring in Nepal prevented the traveling party's return.[128]

The messengers delivered a copy of Atiśa's *Lamp for the Path to Awakening* on three sheets of paper. The Indian scholars then realized that this text would not have been composed, even with great effort or encouragement, if Atiśa had stayed in India. Thus, they praised the news that Atiśa would stay in Tibet, and the elder Ratnākaraśānti as well as other scholars were satisfied. Atiśa also was pleased to stay in Tibet, as he could benefit many people there. During this time, Atiśa finished composing his autocommentary to the *Lamp for the Path to Awakening*.[129] Naktso Lotsāwa was greatly relieved. The moutainous burden of maintaining the pledge he had made to the elders of Vikramaśīla of safely returning Atiśa to India had been lifted.[130]

Travels in Central Tibet: The Region of Tsang

Atiśa and his entourage then journeyed onward to the central provinces of Ü and Tsang. Dromtönpa's letter had been received by officials in Central Tibet and they prepared for his arrival. Atiśa and his entourage focused on traveling through Ü and Tsang by horseback and preserving their resources. The traveling group arrived in the region of Tsang in 1046. When the Tibetan scholars started off on their journey to receive Atiśa in Central Tibet, Khutön Tsöndrü Yungdrung (1011–1075), a powerful dignitary from Yarlung, complained that his name was not mentioned in the letter. He quickly traveled ahead of the group to meet Atiśa. Khutön, like the other primary early disciples of Atiśa, had studied in Kham under Setsun Wangchuk Shönu and was ordained in the Lower Eastern Vinaya tradition from Lumé. He was considered a master of Abhidharma and the perfection of wisdom. Atiśa also met around this time Ngok Lekpai Sherap (eleventh century), a monk in the Eastern Vinaya tradition who had been ordained by Dring Yeshé Yönten and who had also received his monastic education in East Tibet under Setsun Wangchuk Shönu. Ngok Lekpai Sherap had followed Khutön to Central Tibet a year after Dromtönpa went to meet Atiśa.[131]

When the Tibetan teachers from Central Tibet traveled to meet Atiśa, they were wearing nice clothing and hats and rode on ornamented horses. Atiśa could immediately see them from a distance. Atiśa initially thought that a herd of Tibetan demons were coming, as their heads were covered. Then, as they arrived in front of Atiśa's entourage and the ministers descended from their horses, the three robes of a Buddhist monastic along with the golden rosaries adorned on the Tibetan teachers became clearly visible. Atiśa was delighted and saluted with his hands. Atiśa remarked that the good food and resources for Tibetan monks was much greater than that of Indian monks.[132]

While the entourage traveled along the upper plains, Atiśa met Gönpawa Wangchuk Gyaltsen (1016–1082). Gönpawa had left his home region of Dokham to meet with the Indian master. Gönpawa would study with Atiśa for nine years and was known for his meditative abilities and insight. The entourage gradually arrived in the area of Sakya, and Atiśa made a prediction that many emanations of Mañjuśrī would appear in this location. Setön Drachan Dzin, after following Atiśa and his entourage for seven months, requested and then received teachings on the view of Madhyamaka.[133] While gradually traveling, they arrived in the area of Narthang, and Atiśa predicted that many emanations of noble elders would appear in that place.[134] In Upper Nyang, Atiśa met Marpa lotsāwa Chökyi Lodrö (1012–1097). Marpa lotsāwa attended a few sessions of Atiśa's teachings. Atiśa asked Marpa to serve as his translator, but Marpa respectfully declined, as he was on his way to India.[135] While traveling through in the morning, they reached rock caves in the Zhalu district of Tsang. After that they visited a marketplace. At that time they were invited by the great teacher Keg, and having journeyed to the Shang district of Tsang, Atiśa taught a short commentary on the *Perfection of Wisdom Sūtra*.

Upon receiving an invitation from benefactors along the upper Myang River in Tsang, Atiśa and his entourage stayed for three months during the summer retreat season. The faithful heard many dharma teachings. At that place a throne was built for Atiśa. Based on the reverence and material offerings he had received, Atiśa taught the perfections for his public teachings and gave secret teachings of tantric empowerments and hymns to the geshés that lead to a direct understanding of the Buddhadharma. These disciples received many cycles of teachings on the peaceful and wrathful forms of the Great Compassionate One, Avalokiteśvara. The disciples gained direct visions of both Avalokiteśvara and Hayagrīva within six months.[136] Dromtönpa requested a great blessing that was easy to practice, and Atiśa then taught eleven-faced Avalokiteśvara. Naktso Lotsāwa requested teachings for those of great power and Atiśa taught the cycle of teachings on Yamāri. In addition to these teachings, Atiśa received further requests for a teaching that was easy to accomplish and he gave teachings on Tārā (see chapter 13).

Around this time, the great yogin Amé Jangchup Rinchen (1015–1078) came to meet Atiśa. Amé Jangchup, also known as Geshé Naljorpa, was born to a wealthy family in lower Dokham[137] and came to see the Bengali master after becoming a monk. Amé Jangchup had traveled in Ü to meet with a perfect spiritual teacher and to receive teachings. As soon as Amé Jangchup met Atiśa, Atiśa bestowed to him the esoteric deity Array of the Three Pledges.[138] Atiśa instructed him to recite the mantra eight hundred thousand times to have a direct vision of the chosen deity. Amé Jangchup became a close disciple of Atiśa.[139]

While journeying through the valleys of Tsang, the traveling party was not able to find a suitable place to stay, as the houses in the region were small and narrow. Dromtönpa requested Atiśa to sit and rest as a larger residence was built. An extensive maṇḍala was then offered to Atiśa. Atiśa was pleased with his faithful Tibetan disciples and thought, "If only there were disciples like these in India." Some of the faithful Tibetan students made extensive material offerings that included horses and showed great reverence for Atiśa. While traveling and residing for one year in the area of Tsang, Atiśa then taught the monks how to meditate through integrating emptiness and compassion.[140]

Travels in Central Tibet: The Region of Ü

Atiśa along with his retinue then traveled along the plains and arrived on the banks of a river in Yarlung in Tsang. At that time Atiśa said, "I see in the sky above Lhasa clusters of rainbows on top of each other and many sons of the gods continuously making offerings. We should go up there." While traveling through Üntrana, Atiśa covered his head. When he was asked why he hid his head this way, Atiśa explained that the precious gems in the mountains were a cause for selfishness.[141]

When they reached Chingru, a young bride offered to Atiśa her headdress, and she was reprimanded by her parents. The young woman then jumped into the Tsangpo River and drowned. Later in Zhung, Atiśa learned that the girl had drowned and expressed his empathy. In Nyamogur the people said they could not take care of the scholars and translators and shut their doors in front of the traveling entourage. Atiśa and his companions then stayed for five days in the caves of Takkar in Zhung. Atiśa constructed a maṇḍala for the deceased and cast many small clay statues (*tsa tsas*) for them.[142] Geshé Āryadeva invited Atiśa to the village of Nonda. In the village, Atiśa blessed a temple of Āryadeva and also consecrated the temple's statue of eleven-faced Avalokiteśvara. Then, having been invited by an innkeeper in Drachi tsongdu, Atiśa blessed a small reliquary in the area.[143]

Atiśa and His Entourage Arrive at Samyé Monastery

In 1047, in the year of the Water Pig, Atiśa and his entourage arrived at the great monastic complex of Samyé, the first monastery built in Tibet. When he toured inside the main temple, Atiśa said that there was no difference between the statue of the great awakening in the Samyé temple and that of the Mahābodhi in Bodh Gayā. When proceeding into the Jangchup Ling, the temple of Great Awakening, Atiśa prayed and focused on generating the awakening mind. In an inner sanctuary, Atiśa wiped away the dust from the statue of the lotus-eyed Buddha Padmanetra.

Atiśa took residence in the Treasure-Chest Temple of Pekar,[144] where the temple treasury was located. One night, Atiśa requested to read Āryaśūra's *Garland of Birth Stories* (*Jātakamālā*) under the light of butter lamps. When Atiśa was asked why he wanted to read birth stories of the Buddha's previous lives, Atiśa said that his faith had lessened and that he needed to refresh his faith.

While Atiśa was in residence, the royal monk ruler Bodhirāja of Ü provided economic and material support for the performance of a ritual of Nāgārjuna's *Five Stages*. During this time, Atiśa and Naktso Lotsāwa undertook translations of multiple texts. Atiśa and Naktso Lotsāwa translated ritual manuals of the *Buddha Skull Tantra* and the

Sādhana of Vajrapāṇi Who Wears a Blue Robe. Moreover, they also translated the *Explanation of the Five Aggregates* of Candrakīrti along with several works composed by Atiśa, including the *Eight Branches of Medical Cures*, the *Instructions on the Compendium of Discourses*, the *Bodhisattva's Jewel Garland* (see chapter 9), the *Brief Instruction on Bodhisattva Practice*, and the *Supramundane Sevenfold Ritual.*[145]

Atiśa proceeded to the Kachu temple near Samyé, and based on the request of both Khutön Tsöndrü Yungdrung and Ngok Lekpai Sherap, Atiśa taught on the "six texts of Madhyamaka reasoning."[146] At the hermitage of Chimphu on the northeast edge of Samyé Monastery, Devarāja, Nāgarāja, Gargewa, and Naktso Lotsāwa requested the special instructions of the great brahmin Saraha,[147] but they were prohibited from receiving the teachings by Dromtönpa. Atiśa bestowed upon Dromtönpa a number of special instructions of the Secret Mantra Vehicle at this time, including rituals of consecration—*Homavidhi*, *Gaṇacakravidhi*, *Heroic Feast*—as well as the ritual manuals for the "conduct of Samantabhadra," the "conduct which is victorious in all aspects," the "conduct of the skullcup," the "Avadhūtipa conduct," the "conduct of madness," and the "conduct of eating, sleeping, and defecating."[148]

On another occasion while Atiśa was residing at Samyé, many Tibetans from Ü and Tsang gathered in the Treasure-Chest Temple of Pekar. Atiśa performed a great ritual for the awakening mind. The Tibetans were joyful and proud. People proclaimed that many in attendance had become bodhisattvas. Atiśa pointed out, however, that the conferral of the rite did not always lead to the goal.[149]

After teaching for a while at Samyé, Atiśa viewed the Indian manuscripts in the Treasure-Chest Temple. Atiśa noticed many manuscripts he had not seen before and told his disciples that many of the Indian manuscripts contained teachings given by ḍākiṇīs. Atiśa also saw texts that did not even exist in India at the time, including Kamalaśīla's *Illumination of the Middle Way* and the *Flower Garland*

Scripture (*Avataṃsaka Sūtra*). Atiśa had the manuscripts copied and sent to India.[150]

A number of Tibetan scholars came to Atiśa while he was at the Pekar temple in Samyé. They asked him to calculate the year of the Buddha's nirvāṇa. Atiśa calculated the Buddha's nirvāṇa to a monkey year that is equivalent to 2137 BCE.[151] The Tibetan teachers made an offering and requested that Atiśa give teachings on Haribhadra's *Illumination of the Ornament for Clear Realization*. Atiśa considered the request but questioned the disciples about a suitable location for extended teachings on this commentary to the *Eight Thousand Line Perfection of Wisdom Sūtra*. Khutön Tsöndrü Yungdrung proposed his monasteries in Yarlung as a suitable location.

Teachings in Yarlung

Khutön Tsöndrü Yungdrung persuaded Atiśa that Yarlung was a pleasant country and especially auspicious since it was a place where the previous great Tibetan religious kings had worked. Khutön explained that Atiśa could live during the summer in Khutön's monastery of Lhading, spend the winter in his monastery of Sölnak Tangboché, and it would be of great benefit to beings. Atiśa accepted the invitation to come to Yarlung to give teachings on Haribhadra's commentary to the *Perfection of Wisdom*. Dromtönpa, however, was concerned about the pride of Khutön. He sent a message to Bangtön Jangchup Gyaltsen, a religious companion[152] who had previously studied under Setsun and Dromtönpa. Dromtönpa suggested to Bangtön that he should invite Atiśa and his entourage from Yarlung to Samyé and then offer invitations to Nyethang with a calvary escort.

In the meantime, Atiśa and his entourage went on to Yarlung. On the journey to Khutön's monastery in Yarlung, at a temple near Tsetang in the Yarlung Valley at Chasa, Atiśa blessed many old religious objects. Then, having arrived at Sölnak Tangboché, Atiśa resided at the Ratshigkhang temple. At that point Khutön offered one hundred ounces of gold to Atiśa. Atiśa then gave many teachings on Haribhadra's *Illumination of the Ornament for Clear Realization* and on the *Unsurpassed Continuum*,[153] the *Distinguishing Dharma and Dharmatā*,[154] and other works, including the Yamāri sādhana of Kamalarakṣita.[155]

However, during the time that Atiśa and his entourage resided and taught at Sölnak Tangboché, Khutön stayed in Lhading. Khutön told his attendants that any guest services provided for the people of India and Nepal should be limited. Atiśa and his companions got into trouble and could not support themselves with food and resources while at Sölnak Tangboché. The Indian master and his entourage moved to Lhading. The entourage and their livestock had been starving for seven days. Dromtönpa communicated to Bangtön to quickly fetch Atiśa with horse riders based on their previous plans. Dromtönpa emphasized that Atiśa and his disciples were not sufficiently supplied with resources because of the pride of Khutön.[156]

Khutön was envious of Atiśa's elder disciple Dromtönpa and had contempt for the younger pupil Amé Jangchup. Khutön also treated Atiśa contemptuously and did not want to provide any services to Atiśa and his entourage in spite of Khutön's request for teachings. Dromtönpa asked Amé Jangchup for assistance, as Atiśa needed trusted helpers for the performance of the tantric rites. Dromtönpa explained that Atiśa was already over sixty years old and had white hair. As there was a karmic connection between Atiśa and Amé Jangchup, Amé Jangchup promised to serve Atiśa until the end of his life. Amé Jangchup discussed with Dromtönpa the differences between the situation of Atiśa and his retinue of followers and that of Khutön. Khutön had a thousand pupils around him, while Atiśa had only about three hundred.

Atiśa told Dromtönpa that he wanted to go back to Samyé and that there were too many hindrances at Lhading. Atiśa thought that while he himself was a simple man, Khutön lived like a world ruler. Khutön possessed wealth like the deities of the Heaven of the Thirty-three Gods, while Atiśa himself was living as if he were a hungry ghost. Atiśa and his retinue were upset, some were crying, and the group thought about Dromtönpa's plans of going to Nyethang. Atiśa and his entourage prepared to leave during the night and they left early in the morning.[157]

The next day Khutön became infuriated when he was told that Dromtönpa had kidnapped Atiśa. Khutön called for his horse Chanak, but the horse had been let loose and had to be captured first. Khutön and his attendants started on horseback in pursuit of Atiśa and his entourage. Khutön gave the order to knock down Dromtönpa. Meanwhile, Atiśa and the entourage were boarding a platform ferry from 'On. The accompanying cattle were transferred to the boat. Dromtönpa asked to be taken across the river first, otherwise he would be beaten. Dromtönpa and several attendants were allowed to go ahead. Atiśa and the others followed after Dromtönpa had crossed. Atiśa hovered several feet over the floor of the platform ferry while they were being transported across the river.

Khutön and his pursuers had fallen into a storm and were late arriving to the river. When the pursuers arrived at the river bank, Khüton rode out into the river on his horse and he almost drowned in the water. Khutön wanted to justify his behavior and called out to Amé Jangchup and said, "A guest must act as a guest." Ngok Lekpai Sherap said, "I don't want to be included as your guest." Khutön asked Atiśa to come back again. Atiśa then said, as the ferry was approaching the riverside, "Great Scholar! Please do not make a request from way over there. Here now, have this as an offering!"

Atiśa then threw his paṇḍita hat across the river. Khutön and his retinue returned home.[158]

Return to Samyé

All of the traveling party could not spend the night together in 'On, so Dromtönpa moved to Kachu and Atiśa moved to the ancient temple of Lha khang Ke ru 'On. Lha khang Ke ru 'On had been founded by the Tibetan religious king Trisong Detsen (r. 755–797).[159] In the locale of the ancient temple, an old woman gave fifteen *khal*[160] of pure barley as an offering. Atiśa stayed for a month at the temple and gave lectures on the dharma and performed effective tantric rites. Afterward, Atiśa and his entourage returned to Samyé again.[161] Geshé Garmi Yontan Yungdrung provided material support that summer for Atiśa to teach on the *Eight Thousand Line Perfection of Wisdom*.

While residing at Samyé, Atiśa was asked about his royal benefactors in Tibet. Atiśa avoided comparing the royal monk Bodhirāja in Central Tibet and the royal monk Jangchup Ö of West Tibet. The royal monk Bodhirāja was very much devoted to spiritual study at this time, and this displeased a local noblewoman, Jomo Chimmo, who wanted to have Bodhirāja as a husband. While Atiśa was at Samyé, Jomo Chimmo asked a local minister if he would retrieve a deer that had been hunted. The minister replied that this was not possible as long as Atiśa was residing at Samyé. Jomo Chimmo taught the local childern to recite verses mocking the Indian master and the translators. When Atiśa heard the children singing the verses of ridicule, he decided that it was time to leave Samyé. Dromtönpa sent communications for Bangtön to bring horsemen to eventually travel to Nyethang.

Meanwhile, Shangtrang Khaber Chung, an important Shang patron from the noble family of Khaber, sent an invitation for

Dromtönpa to teach. Dromtönpa replied that he could not come now because he had to feed the aged, sick Atiśa. Atiśa sent Shangtrang Khaber Chung two poems of eighteen verses each on which to meditate. Fearing that Shangtrang Khaber Chung might change his mind for patronage and support, Dromtönpa addressed prayers to Mañjuvajra, his chosen deity. Dromtönpa then wrote a letter saying that he would stay with Atiśa until his death and would come later. Bangtön was late to arrive with the horsemen because the Indian royal lay disciple Sai Sangga was always in trouble. Atiśa scolded the upāsaka Sai Sangga (a.k.a. Mahābhūmi Saṃgha).[162]

At Samyé, Atiśa gave more instructions on the awakening mind. Atiśa stated, "When one pays homage to whoever has the precious jewel of the awakening mind, an immeasurable amount of merit arises." While Atiśa and Naktso Lotsāwa were translating this instruction, Naktso Lotsāwa spilled ink on the manuscript and was expelled from the room. As a similar incident had occurred in Ngari, Atiśa taught him that one should not be resentful.[163]

Around this time, Bangtön arrived with a calvary of two hundred horsemen and the entourage moved to Samyé Phu. The cattle that Atiśa had acquired were brought over the La'o che Pass. A number of disciples thought Atiśa should have sold the cattle, but he did not, as he had grown to see the cattle as like old parents. Atiśa and his retinue resided in Gyaphip for only a half-month and then journeyed onward toward Nyethang.[164]

A Visit to Lhasa

While on the journey to Nyethang, Atiśa and his entourage went to the Trulnang Tsuglakhang temple in Lhasa at the invitation of Ngok Lekpai Sherap. When the traveling group was in the vicinity of Lhasa, a certain white solitary man was seen about. Atiśa immediately descended from his horse and joined his hands in salutation to him. He also recited some sūtras. Accordingly, members of the retinue asked Atiśa, "Why did you do that?" Atiśa said, "Did you see this white solitary man?" "We saw him," they replied. Atiśa told them, "He is my chosen deity, the Great Compassionate One, Mahākāruṇika Avalokiteśvara, and I wished to salute him."

When the entourage arrived at the temple in Lhasa, Atiśa thought that there is no greater wonder than seeing the deity, the Great Compassionate One, Avalokiteśvara, at the Trulnang Tsuglakhang temple. Atiśa said, "This is actually the Great Compassionate One!" and he made many offerings. Seeing the great Jowo statue of Śākyamuni, Atiśa remarked that the image was an actual emanation body and a support for one's practice.[165]

Ngok Lekpai Sherap, having negotiated with the authorities in Lhasa, requested Madhyamaka teachings, and Atiśa taught the *Special Instructions on the Middle Way* and revised the translation of Bhāviveka's commentary the *Blaze of Reasoning on the Heart of the Middle Way* in preparation for the lectures.[166] Tibetan scholars asked if there was a general confession for the Sarvāstivāda tradition, and Atiśa gave the text written by Devaśānti and left it for translation. Atiśa remarked that one should confess any transgressions, whether they were carried out unconsciously or due to forgetting the rules, with the help of a confessional text according to one's own ordination lineage.

In relation to ordination lineage rules, Atiśa suggested that he establish his own ordination school, the Mahāsāṃghikas, in Tibet. Dromtönpa was resistant to the suggestion and did not allow for it. Atiśa protested in frustration and explained that if he was not allowed to introduce the teachings of this school, then there was no possibility of instructing on tantric vows and teachings or on any of the *Dohā* songs for immediate realization, and that his coming to Tibet was pointless. Atiśa pointed out that while the Vinaya rules of Dromtönpa's ordination lineage do follow the basic conditions for the observance of vows, in special cases there is a deviation from the Mahāsāṃghikas regarding regulations for the appropriate ingestion of meals. Atiśa also spoke about the thirty-four offenses due to alcohol.[167]

Around this time, Dromtönpa, along with several Tibetan teachers, requested instruction on the practice of circumambulation. Atiśa explained that there is no greater conditional merit for roots of virtue than circumambulation. The practice of circumambulation, Atiśa explained, involves virtuous karmic action of body, speech, and mind. He noted that practitioners in India attained great accomplishment by circumambulating holy cities, temples, and holy places in the forest.[168] Atiśa suggested that similar places in Tibet were just as meritorious.

While residing in Lhasa, Atiśa saw miraculous signs, *arhats*, as well many yoginīs. Atiśa asked about burial traditions and practices in Tibet. He then wrote the *Explanation of the Eight Cremation Grounds* as these places are particularly suitable for tantric rituals.[169]

Teachings in Yerpa

Atiśa spent the summer in Yerpa to the east of Lhasa at the invitation of Ngok Jangchup Jungné. Ngok Jangchup Jungné and six other men asked for teachings on the creation and completion stages, a sādhana of Tārā, and several other teachings. Nätan Dadpa Lama built a house for Atiśa, where he stayed one day; later the small house was called Zimkhang (*gzims khang*). A person from Yerpa named Shangtsun Ögür Bar had great reverence for Atiśa and requested instruction. Atiśa said, "Son of good family, life is short, objects of knowledge are many. Since the measure of a lifetime is only ignorance, you should meditate. Realization is abundant through meditation. There is not much realization through study. You should make essential exertion for accomplishment in meditation."[170]

During the summer in Yerpa, Dromtönpa went to the district of Jang to acquire gold. Geshé Namkha Lama entrusted his property to Dromtönpa because his parents had died. Likewise, the local faithful people offered much wealth in support. When Dromtönpa returned, he presented the gifts on the slope at the heart of Mount Yerpa[171] near Lhasa. Although Atiśa was not pleased about the situation, he made an offering maṇḍala with gold dust along with one hundred ounces of gold, offerings of many animals (including an offering of twenty-one horses), and an offering of various types of utensils that had been received. The Tibetans believe that no greater reverence and amount of offerings in one day had been made in Tibet before. Atiśa gave instructions related to the essence of the stages of the path and gave empowerments and teachings on the seven deities and the sixteen seminal drops.[172] While in Yerpa, Ngok Lekpai Sherap offered a maṇḍala to Atiśa and Dromtönpa and reverentially asked for an uncommon special secret teaching concerning both of them. Atiśa elucidated the previous lifetimes of Dromtönpa and these teachings became later known as the *Book of Kadam*. After having spent one summer in Yerpa, Atiśa and his entourage went along the route proceeding to Nyethang and quickly passed through the Tölung Valley.[173]

Atiśa's Final Years in Nyethang

At the time of the invitation to Nyethang, Bangtön along with his calvary were short of resources. They received help from wealthy patrons when mentioning Atiśa's name and established resources for Atiśa's stay in Nyethang. Atiśa had great faith in Nyethang as a place to stay. Once Atiśa settled in, all the great men of Ü and Tsang congregated and requested many dharma teachings.[174] Lhatsunpa ordered a tax for Atiśa from all monks in Tibet, and the offerings were handed in to a handsome man named Götongtsan Namkha. Also, a wealthy noblewoman offered all her jewelry.[175]

On one occasion, Khutön Tsöndrü Yungdrung came to Nyethang. He found Atiśa's living quarters locked. Khutön accused Dromtönpa and became very angry. Meanwhile, other Tibetan teachers came to Nyethang and requested that Atiśa give teachings on the *Eight Thousand Line Perfection of Wisdom*. Atiśa wanted to know if he should emphasize the meaning or the words when teaching on the scripture. When Atiśa strictly followed the words of the text, the teachings did not turn out well.[176] Naktso Lotsāwa became upset and threw barley flour on Khutön, as Khutön claimed that while Atiśa was especially well versed in daily routine ceremonies of taking refuge and the awakening mind, he himself was proficient in the texts. Khutön said he knew the *Perfection of Wisdom* texts well. Dromtönpa thought that Khutön possessed the qualities Atiśa considered important and consulted with other Tibetan teachers. Everyone then requested that Atiśa give a new teaching on the *Perfection of Wisdom*. Atiśa then gave a series of lectures on the non-dual *Perfection of Wisdom* based on the eight topics of the *Ornament for Clear Realization*.[177] These teachings were very successful, and Chakdar Tönpa took notes and made a record of these lectures. These teachings became known as the "Perfections According to the Method of Kham" and were considered significant.[178]

Shang Nachung Tönpa, Dangjang Tönpa, Gyura Tönpa, and Chakdar Tönpa asked Atiśa about the tenets of philosophical schools. Atiśa said, "There are many philosophical systems of various teachers; some have tenets such as the 'five entrances of non-Buddhists' and the 'single entrance of Buddhists.' All of these are conceptualizations. As there is no time to spare in this life, now is the time to take up the most essential." Shang Nachung Tönpa then asked, "How does one seek what is most essential?" Atiśa replied, "Generate the awakening mind pervaded with compassion for all sentient beings. For their sake, strive to gather the two accumulations for supreme awakening and dedicate in common all the roots of virtue that arise from this toward the benefit of all sentient beings. Make sure to realize that all external and internal things are like dreams and illusions. In this way you should seek the most essential."[179]

Dromtönpa offered his realization of Candrakīrti's system of the Middle Way to Atiśa. Atiśa, placing his hands in prayer toward the eastern direction, said Candrakīrti's system is the only one upheld in India now. Atiśa told Dromtönpa, "With great bodhisattvas like you in Tibet, the merit of Tibetans is not small." Dromtönpa replied, "Although it is not necessary, please give more special instructions." Atiśa himself asked some questions to Tibetan teachers. Atiśa asked one teacher about Yogācāra tenets: "How do you accept the storehouse consciousness (*ālayavijñāna*)?" When the Tibetan replied, "All of space is completely pervaded by the storehouse consciousness," Atiśa said, "Even the non-Buddhists do not accept such a coarse philosophical doctrine."[180] Atiśa asked, "How do you accept the two vehicles of Mantra and the Perfections?" Without thinking to ask others, Shang Nachung Tönpa replied, "My guru teaches they are near and far at the time of the path. There is no difference in quality at the time of the result." Atiśa stated, "If they occur near and far at the time of the path, then how can there be no difference in the result? You must unmistakenly understand that all things for insider Buddhists are cause and effect. Your guru has received few teachings. I will give you an analogy: there are some who tell lies with respect to selling food. For you in Tibet, there appears to be many merchants who trade in dharma, teaching dharma for honor and gain. For me in India, there are many merchants who trade goods." When asked which of the two pleased him, Atiśa said, "Those who trade in dharma, teaching dharma for honor and gain are those who sell unripened fruit. At least the merchants who trade in goods have all sorts of ripened fruit." Atiśa's analogy demonstrates that, for him, the path of the Secret Mantra Vehicle takes the result as the path. Atiśa commented further that "there are not actual non-Buddhist *tīrthikas* here in Tibet, but there are some who are similar." When asked who are similar, Atiśa said, "The elder monks with crumbling permanent residences."[181]

One night in Nyethang, two venerable Indian monks who possessed the twelve "virtues of purity" requested teachings from Atiśa.[182] When Atiśa taught them personal selflessness, they listened with the palms of their hands joined in prayer. When Atiśa taught the "essencelessness of all things" they covered their ears and asked Atiśa not to speak. When they covered their ears while hearing the recitation of the *Heart Sūtra*, Atiśa was saddened about it. This is because these monks had not made the extraordinary effort for the accumulations of merit and wisdom impelled by love, compassion, and the awakening mind. As the two monks only guarded the precepts, they were not able to achieve anything.[183]

On another occasion, Indian disciples came to Nyethang to visit Atiśa. They brought gifts and told him about a yogi who, after twelve years, obtained the "great seal" of Mahāmudrā. Atiśa said that when he left for Tibet, a "perfected adept" appeared daily in East India. Dromtönpa said that there will be miracle stories about Atiśa in India even after his death.[184]

Geshé Gönpawa Wangchuk Gyaltsen resided, practicing concentration, in Nyamgamo in Bur, the valley of present-day Ratöd near Nyethang. Occasionally Atiśa would visit him there. One night, a large scorpion came out of the earth making noises, and Gönpawa made fervent prayers to Atiśa. The creature then disappeared. Atiśa came out from Nyethang the next morning to visit Gönpawa and asked what had happened. Atiśa then bestowed to Gönpawa the cycle of teachings on Acala as a protector of yoga. Naktso Lotsāwa and Dromtönpa were astonished.

While visiting in the valley of Bur, Atiśa was pleased and showed reverence to all the empty monasteries, as they were suitable for meditation. Atiśa was told that people were not in the monasteries because they were meditating. Atiśa asked if the Tibetans were disturbed by demons in meditation because of sloppy morality. Atiśa commented that in India yogis meditate in the midst of demons. Atiśa emphasized that his disciple Puṇyamati found peace, despite any presence of demons, through meditation on emptiness (*śūnyatā*). Atiśa was displeased that many who were possessed by demons occasionally lived alone.[185]

Gompa Gyamon asked Ngok Lekpai Sherap if he accepted the five small outer tantras of the Secret Mantra Vehicle in the Old Translation school but did not want to perform the creation and completion stages. He then asked, "Well then, is it suitable or not to explain that Heruka really resides in the Princely-Lord Atiśa?"

Ngok Lekpai Sherap went to Atiśa and Atiśa said, "Although one does perform the creation and completion stages, the Tibetan stages are ineffective. With great faith, Tibetans are disciples who are suitable as vessels of the Secret Mantra Vehicle. However, no one appears able to bestow the Ācārya consecration. Even if not performing the stages, if there is a steadfast awakening mind, then all of these Secret Mantra teachings are suitable to hear."

Later in the day, when Atiśa was on the throne, he explained what he had said and Ngok Lekpai Sherap later realized the way of the Secret Mantra Vehicle and gained conviction in this teaching bestowed by Atiśa.[186] Someone else came to Atiśa requesting teachings and Atiśa said, "The only thing that counts is faith."

Atiśa was asked about the tantric practice of extracting the essence. Atiśa said, "I extract the essence of the awakening mind." Atiśa later stated, "If there is not mindfulness at the time of following the Buddha when sleeping in the middle watch of the night wearing monastic robes, a fault occurs. What account of the Vinaya do you Tibetans monks uphold?"[187]

Many people came from the regions of Ü, Tsang, and Kham, some requesting to take refuge, some seeking blessings, some requesting teachings on the awakening mind, and others on the stages of the path. The group seeking teachings on the awakening mind had provisions for requesting the dharma but did not have offering materials. Moreover, the group from Kham who were requesting blessings kept smiling and paying attention to Dromtönpa. Atiśa then instructed Dromtönpa on how to bless and consecrate various offering materials.[188]

Atiśa and his disciples translated a number of texts while he resided at Nyethang based on the requests of patrons and students. Dromtönpa translated the Sādhana of the Land of Maitreya, the *Twenty-One Praises to the Venerable Tārā*, the *Eight Thousand Line Perfection of Wisdom*, and other texts. Naktso Lotsāwa translated innumerable works. At the request of Bangtön as the leader, along with Amé Jangchup and Trichok, Naktso Lotsāwa translated works composed by Atiśa, including the *Praise of Wrathful Acala*, the *Wish-Fulfilling Jewel Ritual* and the *Medicine Guru*, formerly translated in Purang.[189]

At the request of Kawa Shākya Wangchuk, Garmi Yungdrung, Darjang sel, Santen Gyelwa, and others, Atiśa and Naktso Lotsāwa translated the Sādhana of Arapacana Mañjuśrī of Serlingpa, the Sādhana of the Blessed One Śākyamuni, and at the request of Dromtönpa, the Sādhana of the Three-Faced, Six-Armed Avalokiteśvara[190] that Atiśa had directly seen in a forest in India, and the *Ritual Manual for Purifying Karmic Obstructions*, among others.[191]

Amé Jangchup asked for the Acala ritual with special instructions, and Atiśa and Naktso Lotsāwa did the translation. At the request of Bangtön, Dromtönpa, Amé Jangchup, Trichok, Ngok Lekpai Sherap, and others, Atiśa and Naktso Lotsāwa translated the *Inquiry of Avalokiteśvara on the Seven Qualities.*[192] They also translated Atiśa's own *Manual for Generating the Awakening Mind* and the *Commentary to the Chapter on Moral Conduct* written by Guṇaprabha.[193] After a great amount of activity translating texts, Naktso Lotsāwa asked Atiśa to retire to Chimphu for a while. Naktso Lotsāwa received the permission only after repeated requests. In his absence, Atiśa transferred the task of translating to Dromṭönpa. Atiśa stayed in Chimphu for three months.[194]

After three months, the teacher Ronpa Tönpa, Gargewa, the teacher Nyangro, and many other teachers arrived. Dromtönpa requested to Naktso Lotsāwa, "Quickly bring back the Ācārya!" and Atiśa returned. The teacher Gargewa requested the *Coemergent Yoga of Śrī Heruka* composed by Ācārya Ratnākaraśānti and the commentary on Ḍombi Heruka called *Light Rays of Ambrosia* written by Atiśa himself. Atiśa and Naktso Lotsāwa also translated many texts on Cakrasaṃvara and the Sādhana of Śrī Mahāmaya.

At the request of Yorpo, Tsangpa, and Urupa, the *Bodhisattva Stages*, the *Ornament of Mahāyāna Sūtras*, and the *Lamp for the Path to Awakening* were taught by Atiśa, and Naktso Lotsāwa translated these texts.[195] In the summer, Atiśa preached the *Compendium of Training*,[196] the *Compendium of Sūtras*,[197] the *Introduction to the Practice of Awakening*, and the *Lamp for the Path to Awakening*. When Atiśa advised Dromtönpa that he would give teachings on the *Compendium of Training* and the *Introduction to the Practice of Awakening* according to the system of Serlingpa, Dromtönpa replied that he had already studied these texts under Setsun Wangchuk Shönu.[198]

Atiśa and his disciples translated and studied scriptures and treatises composed in India. However, on one occasion several Tibetans brought textbooks written in Tibet to Atiśa, but Atiśa was not pleased with most of them. The only one that Atiśa accepted was the *Entering Great Vehicle Yoga*[199] written by the yogi Aro. Atiśa said that the work was poetic, meticulous, and profound. Someone asked whether it was to be used for ceremonies, and Atiśa agreed after a close look.[200]

Up to this point, Atiśa had spent seven years and five months in the Tibetan region of Ü, and from then on he seldom preached the dharma. The only teachings Atiśa would give were based on songs such as the Song with a Vision for the Realm of Reality (see chapter 6), the Song of the Liberation of the Mind from Cyclic Existence, the Song of Six Blisses, the Song for the Awakening Mind, and several others.[201] At night, in the assembly of dākiṇīs, Atiśa perceived the profound meaning of the mantras in songs such as A Song for Practice, The Diamond Song, and A Song of Vajradharma.[202] Atiśa was requested to bestow all of these teachings, and Naktso Lotsāwa translated them.[203]

Atiśa performed a great amount of worship and made extensive offerings during his final years in Nyethang. When he directly witnessed his chosen deities (*yidam*) in visions, his sickened body became vividly clear and bright. This happened quite often. In general, during the time Atiśa resided at Nyethang, he had many direct visions of his chosen deities. In particular, during the waning of the full moon, he directly saw the buddhas and bodhisattvas of the past, present, and future. Every evening he would have visions of his chosen deities.

One evening, when there was a strong winter storm, Atiśa made maṇḍalas and got cracked hands. Tārā appeared to him and asked why he was taking such trouble.[204] On another evening, in a dream, Atiśa woke up hearing musical instruments, a rattling sound like women's jewelry, but he did not look. Then, Tārā, who had appeared in full adornment in the sky, asked him why he did not look at his mother. Atiśa thought that he was seeing Tārā as his mother in a dream, but he was witnessing Tārā directly before him. Atiśa later said that he had dreamed of Tārā as his mother and that she was also present in the current moment while he was pointing to a painting of the goddess protecting from the eight great fears.[205]

One day, in Nyethang, Amé Jangchup called out to Atiśa in his residence for dinner. Atiśa was looking back and forth to heaven, saying "Maitri, Maitri," but did not come out. A little later Amé Jangchup called again, and Atiśa still had not come out. Dromtönpa told Amé Jangchup to not let the food get cold, that the teacher had a vision of Maitreya, but that they, the students, could not see it. When the food was almost cold, they brought it to Atiśa, and he said, "*mai tri bhri kho li*."[206] As a result, the food became warm, and Atiśa told them that he had heard a discussion on the Mahāyāna in the morning from Mañjuśrī and Maitreya and that he also saw Vajrapaṇi holding back hindrances and other gods taking notes. Atiśa drew a sketch of Maitreya as he had seen him and, together with gold, sent it to Vikramaśīla Monastery with instructions to paint a scroll painting. Atiśa also requested that images of Nāropa and the six syllables (*oṃ ma ṇi pad me huṃ*) be painted.[207] Atiśa taught that the color of all buddhas was gold, so he painted the five families of the victorious ones, the esoteric buddhas of the five families, uniform golden yellow to make it easy for students.[208]

Atiśa gave his last will and testament and said, "*dharmān āloka-yāmaḥ*," "May the dharmas be illuminated." When asked about the meaning, he answered that now was time to practice dharma. Atiśa then added, "This path of the Mahāyāna Secret Mantra Vehicle is a blissful path, but it has great risks, benefits, and harms, like placing a snake in a bamboo tunnel or hanging a sword on an elephant's trunk. Since the tantric way is very dangerous, Tibetans should not perform all four classes of tantras. Yoga tantras are suitable for Tibetans."[209]

Atiśa entrusted Dromtönpa with the Buddhist teaching. Dromtönpa asked Atiśa why he had been entrusted with the teaching, as Atiśa had also taught other disciples in the way of mantras. Atiśa responded that this was true, but said that apart from him no other disciple was suitable. Atiśa told him, "You are kindhearted; without the awakening mind, hearing, contemplating, and meditating on a great amount of dharma teachings—including the creation stage and completion stage and meditating on the vision of Madhyamaka—reciting mantras and so forth has no benefit. All spiritual practice that does not embrace the awakening mind and any spiritual practice which harms the awakening mind is demonic activity."[210]

One time Dromtönpa went to visit Atiśa, who had been confined to his bed in his residential quarters. When Atiśa stepped out of the locked quarters, passing through a wall, Dromtönpa asked about this miraculous ability. Atiśa said he was known for this in India. At the time Atiśa passed away, everyone saw that he hovered about an inch above the ground. Atiśa heard the sound of bells, supplicating prayers by his students in India, and the playful sounds of gods worshipping. Atiśa said that ḍākiṇīs went around him, his teachers were in Tuṣita Heaven, and that he would soon go there. Dromtönpa was saddened and asked Naktso Lotsāwa to come quickly from Chimphu, where he had been for six months. Dromtönpa told Naktso Lotsāwa about the marvelous things occurring in Nyethang.[211]

At the time of inviting the benefactor Dhogabharo, Paṇḍit Jñānākara, a disciple of Nāropa, was in Nepal. Naktso Lotsāwa heard that Jñānākara wanted to leave for India and reported this to Atiśa. Atiśa asked Naktso Lotsāwa to go to Jñānākara to hear from him a series of teachings on the *Guhyasamāja Tantra* according to the tradition of Nāgārjuna. Atiśa said that he himself could no longer travel and that in ten months he would go to Tuṣita Heaven to receive teachings from Maitreya. Atiśa's pronouncement saddened Naktso Lotsāwa. Atiśa told him, "You have escorted me here to Tibet.

You have understood all my teachings on internal awareness, and although it is not suitable for you to go to Nepal, you must go, as there are many hindrances to hearing Mahāyāna teachings. From now on, continously make offerings and prayers for me." Then, Naktso Lotsāwa arranged extensive offerings and supplicated in prayer. Jangtsun Darma Jangchup and Tri tri Sakya lodrö visited for one month and they both offered riches to Atiśa. They said, "Since our spiritual teacher Gyalrin is now in Nepal, we came quickly, as he wishes to return to India."[212]

Atiśa made another pronouncement, saying, "I will go to Tuṣita Heaven and take rebirth as Stainless Space, the son of a god (*deva-putra*). You should paint an image of my body. I will consecrate it from inside Tuṣita. Pray, and I will come from Tuṣita." The scholars stayed for one more month and prayed, and for a half-month more they continued to worship and pray. After that, all the Tibetan disciples of Atiśa gathered and came quickly to be near the venerable Atiśa. Naktso Lotsāwa asked, "Who will uphold the tradition of Atiśa since all good qualities arise from the teacher?" Dromtönpa, as the close servant to Atiśa, also inquired, but a consensus was not established. A number of people thought it was correct to name Dromtönpa as the upholder of Atiśa's tradition.[213] Atiśa then told Naktso Lotsāwa that he should now go to Nepal. Naktso Lotsāwa supplicated to Atiśa, "Oh, guru, I pray that you look upon me from Tuṣita Heaven." Atiśa assured Naktso Lotsāwa that he would do so.[214] Dromtönpa also gave a garland of advice, and then Naktso Lotsāwa left.

Amé Jangchup thought, "Since I have little merit, I am not meditating due to respectfully serving Atiśa." Atiśa told Amé Jangchup that it is not necessary to search for other objects of meditation when one is bound in service to the spiritual teacher with one's body, speech, and mind. Atiśa told the other disciples that it was necessary for Amé Jangchup to have a little bit of the gold that had been offered and placed in front of Atiśa. Dromtönpa gave Amé Jangchup thirty ounces of gold. Amé Jangchup, thinking he would not meet with Atiśa again, cried thoughout the night, and both of his eyes swelled shut.[215]

A number of treasures of gold and other offerings that had accumulated at Nyethang were successfully delivered to Vikramaśīla, although three previous attempts failed due to a number of obstacles. Atiśa gave his last will and testament that he would die. Trichok asked Atiśa, "Should I explain the dharma?" Atiśa said, "Cut off the spread of negative actions." Trichok then asked Atiśa, "Well then, should I meditate or not?" Atiśa said, "Cut off the spread of negative actions." Trichok asked, "Well then, how should I do that?" Atiśa said, "Renounce this life. Stay in solitude." Then, Atiśa advised Sherab Dorje and Lodrö bar, saying, "Be kindhearted. You must be kindhearted, for without that, even study, contemplation, and meditation will be without purpose." Geshé Gönpawa asked, "How should that be done?" Atiśa said, "Abandon your worldly mind. For the remainder of your life, do not be separated from Dromtönpa."[216]

Dromtönpa had a dream during the full moon, where all the buddhas bestowed their reassurance and the guru and all the buddhas became essential drops. The essential drops dissolved into the heart of Dromtönpa. After some time, they took form as emanation bodies. Then, a stony mountain in Yerpa tumbled down. All the spiritual disciples of Dromtönpa appeared at the base of the mountain asking questions to Atiśa. At the end of the dream, the master Atiśa and his disciple Dromtönpa transformed into an indivisible essential drop and then manifested again individually. Dromtönpa understood the dream as a sign to carry on Atiśa's lineage of teachings.[217]

Atiśa died at the age of seventy-two in the year of the Wood Horse (1054) on the eighteenth day of the constellation of Aśvinī.[218] When

Atiśa died, he appeared as a form body that dissolved into the realm of reality (*dharmadhātu*), and with a boundless miraculous display his continuum took rebirth in the "Pleasant Doctrine-Bearing Joyous Place"[219] of Tuṣita Heaven as the devaputra Stainless Space. His bodily relics remained to conform with the notions of disciples to be educated. When Atiśa died, all of Atiśa's close disciples did not act in a sorrowful manner. They cleansed away the sorrow of the other Tibetan teachers with compassion.[220] Following his earlier instructions to Dromtönpa, Atiśa's body was cremated in a mortuary *stūpa* according to the *Noble Sūtra of the Buddha's Final Nirvāṇa*[221] that had been constructed in a large meadow at Nyethang.[222]

Dromtönpa gathered Atiśa's bodily remains in a vessel filled with perfume. Dromtönpa did not know how to distribute Atiśa's relics or property and became displeased. The venerable Tārā came to him in a dream and told him, "I will take care of all your troubles." Then, three days passed, and on the morning of the fourth day, Kawa Shākya Wangchuk arrived with packing mules riding on a horse. Kawa Shākya Wangchuk wept and cried at the passing of Atiśa and told Dromtönpa that he intended to help with the passing of his master. This eased the mind of Dromtönpa, and all the keys were offered to Kawa Shākya Wangchuk. Kawa Shākya Wangchuk entrusted Atiśa's relics and property to Dromtönpa, Khutön Tsöndrü Yungdrung, and Ngok Lekpai Sherap. Kawa Shākya Wangchuk asked Dromtönpa how to build a reliquary. As the bones of the spiritual father are necessary for the son, the relics of Atiśa were saved by Dromtönpa. Kawa Shākya Wangchuk also told Dromtönpa, "You should bear the silver parasol of Guru Serlingpa. Since Atiśa's Indian manuscripts need to translated, you should save them." Khutön Tsöndrü Yungdrung was pleased to be offered the golden statue of Śākyamuni that Guru Serlingpa had bestowed upon Atiśa in Sumatra. The six syllables consecrated by the three yogis were offered to Amé Jangchup. Gönpawa was offered an Acala statue that was the preferred deity of Atiśa, which later resided in Radreng. Eight small reliquaries, a silver parasol, and a gold statue of another one of Atiśa's preferred deities, Venerable Tārā, were given to Ngok Lekpai Sherap. After the dispersal to the immediate disciples, eight reliquaries, a Śākyamuni statue, a statue of the Medicine Buddha, and many cast tsa tsas were deposited in a village near Nyethang.[223]

In the following Sheep Year of 1055, all the disciples made extensive offerings to complete Atiśa's wishes. Dromtönpa taught the *Eight Thousand Line Perfection of Wisdom*. Trichok taught the *Introduction to the Practice of Awakening*. All the other disciples taught their individual dharma teachings. At that time, many of the faithful offered gifts and hospitality in a single location managed by Kawa Shākya Wangchuk. The faithful followers and disciples offered the necessary provisions for building a temple at Atiśa's seat in Nyethang. After the passing of Atiśa, four of Atiśa's lead disciples established monastic centers that received support from among the four clan-based groups of Lumé, Ba, Rak, and Dring. Khutön, with support from the Lumé group, established the Lhading or Sedur monastic center of Dren in Yarlung. Bangtön established the monastic center of Nyethang Ö with the support of the Ba and Rak groups. Ngoktön, supported by the Dring group, established the monastic center of Sangphu, including the seat of Gyaphip. In 1056/57, Dromtönpa, along with Amé Jangchup and Bangtön, established Radreng Monastery as a spiritual base for the continuity of Atiśa's teaching.

CHAPTER 3

The Buddhism of Atiśa Dīpaṃkaraśrījñāna

ATIŚA DĪPAṂKARAŚRĪJÑĀNA lived in northeast India during the flourishing Pāla Dynasty support for Buddhism in the late tenth and early eleventh century. As evident in his biography, Atiśa came of age as an esoteric Buddhist yogi in a noninstitutional setting. Atiśa received a thorough education in the best institutions of his time in northeast India and in Sumatra. He then received an excellent education in mainstream Buddhist monastic law and Indian philosophy while studying and teaching in the monastaries of Vajrāsana, Vikramaśīla, and Odantapurī. Atiśa's monastic education included being trained in esoteric meditation and ritual practice as well as learning the classics of Indian Mahāyāna Buddhism. While in India and Indonesia, Atiśa became thoroughly versed in Mahāyāna Buddhist classics, such as the works of Nāgārjuna, Śāntideva's *Introduction to the Practice of Awakening*, and the textual traditions of Maitreya and Asaṅga.

Atiśa practiced and taught the classical Mahāyāna Buddhism of the bodhisattva path blended with advanced meditative practices and rituals in the way of the Secret Mantra Vehicle.[224] The historical context of Atiśa's Mahāyāna differentiated between the Common Vehicle of the Perfection Path[225] and the more advanced way of the Secret Mantra Vehicle. As far as it is currently known, the practices of the Perfection Path, as well as Middle Way philosophy and epistemology, were taught in classroom settings. The practices of meditation and secret mantra were given in a direct lineage of transmission from teacher to disciple.[226]

Atiśa's biography provides a rare example of the life of a Mahāsāṃghika monk in the history of Buddhism. He left behind a considerable amount of evidence for his understanding of Buddhism in his writings, translations, teachings, and transmission record of Sanskrit manuscripts. Atiśa's numerous writings include advice for practice,[227] manuals of deity visualization,[228] manuals for the performance of rituals, and summaries of subtle philosophical thought.

One way to think about the form and content of the Mahāyāna Buddhism practiced and taught by Atiśa is to compare Atiśa with his esteemed colleagues at Vikramaśīla. Most of Atiśa's colleagues there followed various forms of Yogācāra thought and worked with the philosophical traditions of epistemology based on the texts of the seventh-century Buddhist thinker Dharmakīrti.[229] Atiśa's colleagues at Vikramaśīla were also holders of diverse monastic ordination lineages.

Atiśa's colleague Jñānaśrīmitra, a prominent scholar who initially upeld Saindhava śrāvaka views, advocated a form of Yogācāra thought that asserts that cognitive images (*ākāra*) are real. Jñānaśrīmitra also formulated a sophisticated theory of exclusion based on complex epistemological arguments.[230] Jñānaśrīmitra was well versed in Sanskrit metrics and wrote on this topic as well.[231] Atiśa's senior colleague and teacher Ratnākaraśānti was ordained in the Sarvāstivāda school at Odantapurī. Ratnākaraśānti composed numerous works on subjects such as valid cognition, the *Perfection of Wisdom Sūtra* (*Prajñāpāramitā Sūtra*), Yogācāra, Tantra, as well as Buddhist verse metrics (*cansaḥśāstra*) and riddles.[232] Ratnākaraśānti wrote an independent work on valid cognition, *Justification of Intrinsic Entailment*,[233] a digest where he outlined the formal structure of Buddhist epistemology and formulated the position of "intrinsic entailment" (*antarvyāpti*). Ratnākaraśānti also composed two extended commentaries on the *Perfection of Wisdom*, the *Supreme Essence* and the *Pure Mindedness.*[234] In terms of his view, Ratnākaraśānti articulated a middle way based on Yogācāra principles that incorporated the theory of the three natures (*trisvabhāva*) with an emphasis on self-awareness (*svasaṃvedana*) as equivalent to luminosity (*prakāśa*).[235] Atiśa's junior colleague Ratnakīrti followed a nondual consciousness (*citrādvaitavāda*) understanding of Yogācāra and articulated sophisticated arguments against the Nyāya school's God-like being called "Īśvara."[236]

In contrast to all of his known Vikramaśīla colleagues, Atiśa followed a lineage of Madhyamaka based on Nāgārjuna and Candrakīrti that was transmitted through his teachers Avadhūtipa, Bodhibhadra, and Vidyākokila, with whom he studied under in his youth. Atiśa's understanding of Madhyamaka may have been a source of conflict with his teachers and colleagues at Vikramaśīla.[237] Although Atiśa was familiar with Sanskrit grammar and poetics, he only composed treatises on Buddhist thought and practice. As we saw in his biography, Atiśa gave a number of lectures on the *Perfection of Wisdom Sūtra* while in Tibet, but he did not compose any extensive commentaries on it or on the *Ornament for Clear Realization*. Nor did Atiśa write commentaries on other classical Mahāyāna scholastic works such as the *Ornament of Mahāyāna Sūtras*. Rather, Atiśa focused his writings and teachings on essential practices and integrative meditative cultivations leading to the nondual realization of full buddhahood.[238]

Atiśa composed several works focusing on essential practice. Atiśa's works of essential practice include the *Essential Summary*, the *Essence Clearly Explained*, *Lamp for the Summary of Conduct* (see chapter 7), and *Bodhisattva's Jewel Garland* (see chapter 9).[239] In these works Atiśa emphasized cultivation of the awakening mind, moral conduct, and practices for generating merit.

As mentioned in his biography, after Atiśa first arrived in West Tibet, as his teachings focused on the consequences of karmic conditioning, he was called the "Teacher of Cause and Effect." Atiśa strictedly adhered to the Buddhist cosmological worldview of repeated birth and death (*saṃsāra*) as perpetuated by karmic actions and mental afflictions (*kleśas*). Atiśa followed the principles of karmic actions as outlined in texts such as the *Sūtra on the Classification of Acts*,[240] which he translated with Naktso Lotsāwa. Atiśa taught the basic principles of cause and effect found in the *Treasury of Abhidharma* (*Abhidharmakośa*) in his *Stages of the Path to Awakening* (see chapter 12). On another level of advanced Madhyamaka, Atiśa taught a sophisticated theory of karmic causation based on Maitreya's *Ornament of Mahāyāna Sūtras* and *Separation of the Middle from the Extremes* (*Madhyāntavibhāga*).[241]

Atiśa's prescriptive teachings had their basis in the maintenance of moral discipline (*śīla*) through taking vows. Atiśa's major writings, such as his *Lamp for the Path to Awakening* and his *Stages of the Path to Awakening*, stipulate that the basis of the path is found in one of the seven types of vows of moral discipline (*prātimokṣa*). One also must undergo a series of preparations, such as taking refuge in the three jewels, and accumulate stores of merit through the performance of the Sevenfold Supreme Worship in the tradition of Śāntideva.[242] Atiśa also emphasized confession for mitigating against any transgressions or lapses in the guarding of vows.[243]

The vows of moral discipline served as the basis for bodhisattva vows as well as the vows of Secret Mantra practice. As a foundation for bodhisattva vows, Atiśa outlined the moral discipline of the prātimokṣa and the vows of a bodhisattva in his *Open Basket of Jewels* and in his *Commentary to the Lamp for the Path to Awakening*. In his *Commentary to the Lamp for the Path to Awakening,* Atiśa discusses monastic discipline according to the Sarvāstivāda commentators in congruence with the Tibetan monastic environment of his patrons.

Atiśa explicitly mentions two hundred fifty-three rules that must be confessed by a fully ordained monk. However, this does not tally with any known, currently extant Vinaya.[244]

Atiśa explains the general principles of bodhisattva discipline based on Asaṅga's "Chapter on Conduct" and then provides specific points on bodhisattva discipline according to Śāntideva's *Compendium of Training*. Atiśa references additional comments from his teacher Bodhibhadra's *Commentary on "Twenty Verses on the Vow."*[245] In both the *Open Basket of Jewels* and *Commentary to the Lamp for the Path to Awakening*, Atiśa differentiates bodhisattva vows based on what stage of the path the aspirant bodhisattva has reached.[246]

A fundamental concept and practice prevalent in Atiśa's Buddhism throughout his life and teachings is the awakening mind. The awakening mind is the key point in his teachings, as it permeates the stages of the path from the level of the beginner bodhisattva to the most advanced Secret Mantra practices. Atiśa was the master illuminator of the awakening mind. He learned the theory and practice of the awakening mind from lay and monastic masters in India and Indonesia. Serlingpa was Atiśa's most important teacher for his understanding and practice of the awakening mind.

Cultivation of the awakening mind, for Atiśa, is the entrance gate to the Mahāyāna way of the bodhisattva. Broadly defined, the awakening mind is the intention or resolution to attain full and complete buddhahood for the benefit of oneself and all sentient beings. Atiśa stipulates that love, the wish to repay the kindness of sentient beings, and compassion must first be cultivated as preliminaries to developing the awakening mind. Sanctions for practicing the awakening mind must be ritually conferred by a spiritual teacher. Atiśa composed the text the *Ritual Order for the Awakening Mind and Vows*[247] explicitly for this purpose. In fact, a commonly recited daily Tibetan prayer for increasing the awakening mind is found in this text. The prayer in verse states,

I go for refuge to the buddhas, the dharma, and the supreme
community until I attain awakening.
Through my practicing generosity and so forth,
May I attain buddhahood for the benefit of all sentient
beings.[248]

Once the awakening mind is initially cultivated, as the awakening mind goes through phases of development and expansion, various classifications are applied in the stages of the path. Among all the different types of the awakening mind, there is a basic division between the conventional awakening mind and the ultimate awakening mind. The ultimate awakening mind, in brief, is described by Atiśa as the realization of the fusion of compassion and emptiness that he calls "the emptiness endowed with all excellent features" (see chapter 4).

In regard to the conventional awakening mind, Atiśa prescribes numerous practices and meditations and applies various divisions and classifications. Two fundamental types of the conventional awakening mind that Atiśa mentions in both his *Open Basket of Jewels* and *Commentary to the Lamp for the Path to Awakening* are the aspiration (*praṇidhāna*) and engaging (*prasthāna*) awakening minds. Atiśa follows various Mahāyāna sūtras and tantras as well as the textual traditions of Maitreya, Asaṅga, and Śāntideva in outlining his theory and practice of the awakening mind.

Atiśa prescribes the cultivation of concentration (*samādhi*) and meditative absorption (*dhyāna*) based on the foundations of the awakening mind and moral conduct. Atiśa explains concentration, only in a brief manner, based on his teacher Bodhibhadra's *Chapter on the Equipment of Concentration*.[249] Concentration is necessary for the development of quiescence (*śamatha*). Quiescence leads to the achievement of supersensory perception (*abhijñā*) and then special insight and wisdom. Atiśa emphasizes that the development of supersensory knowledge is necessary for a bodhisattva to swiftly complete the two accumulations of merit and pristine awareness that culminates in buddhahood. Supersensory perception includes powers such as clairvoyance, clairaudience, and telepathy.[250] These powers, qualified as mundane in Buddhist texts, are advocated by Atiśa as necessary abilities in the service of achieving awakening for the benefit of others. Atiśa follows the tradition of Śāntideva's *Compendium of Training* in the bodhisattva's cultivation of these powers.

Atiśa's accounts of concentration, meditative absorption, and quiescence are brief, as he emphasized that meditation, as well as instruction on insight, should be learned directly from a qualified spiritual teacher. Atiśa explicitly stated that he will not give detailed instructions about meditation, for as he explained,

> Instruction in meditation is the kind which relies upon the personal instruction of an experienced holy teacher. And that is because details of the teaching on quiescence and insight must be explained, and because of the difficulty of learning meditation just from reading books.[251]

Wisdom and skillful means must be integrated and perfected to accumulate the equipments of merit and pristine awareness necessary for achieving buddhahood. Skillful means signifies for Atiśa the implementation of the first five perfections of the bodhisattva path—that is, the perfections of giving (*dāna*), moral discipline (*śīla*), patience (*kṣānti*), energetic diligence (*vīrya*), and meditative absorption (*dhyāna*). Skillful means, in brief, is the gathering of all virtue based on these practices. Wisdom, or insight, is the understanding that all things are undifferentiated (*asaṃbhinna*). Atiśa will articulate in his stages of the path three different understandings of the undifferentiated state. These include the realization that cause and effect and emptiness are undifferentiated, that skillful means and wisdom are undifferentiated, and, on an advanced level, that appearances and emptiness are undifferentiated.

Wisdom may be either innate or cultivated gradually through the three wisdoms of learning, reflection, and meditation.[252] Atiśa outlines the cultivation of wisdom within the context of meditative equipoise and postmeditative[253] states construed through the purviews of conventional and ultimate realities. Atiśa's understanding of wisdom and its cultivation are based on the *Perfection of Wisdom* and the teachings of Nāgārjuna, Candrakīrti, and Śāntideva. As Atiśa explained to Rinchen Zangpo,

> For the followers of Ācārya Nāgārjuna, first, in the context of conventional reality, one ascertains all things by means of the two realities; in the context of practice during meditative equipoise, ultimately, one is free from all elaborations; and in the postmeditative state one construes objects to be like illusions. At the time of the result when the two realities are actualized, the form body is conventional reality and the dharma body is ultimate reality.[254]

Atiśa was an adherent to Madhyamaka thought and practice with a basis in the works of Nāgārjuna. Madhyamaka thought and practice underlies Atiśa's understanding of advanced bodhisattva practices within both the Perfection and Secret Mantra Vehicles. Atiśa called his understanding of Madhyamaka, or the Middle Way, "Great Madhyamaka."[255] Atiśa's classification of Great Madhyamaka, in brief, represents his effort to differentiate the meaning of the *Perfection of Wisdom* as taught by Nāgārjuna as opposed to its meaning taught by the Yogācāra scholar Asaṅga.[256] Atiśa consistently upheld a Madhyamaka view over and against Yogācāra ontological tenets. Along these lines, Atiśa rejected the utilization of epistemological cognitions for the realization of emptiness. As Atiśa states in his *Entry to the Two Realities* (see chapter 5),

> Direct perception and inference are the two valid cognitions accepted by Buddhists. The deluded whose vision is narrow say that emptiness is understood by these two.[257]

For Atiśa, the science of epistemology and logic[258] was a secular science that was common to Buddhist and Indian non-Buddhist schools. Cognitions derived from epistemological warrants were,[259] for Atiśa, only utilized at the level of conventional reality to refute opponents.[260] Atiśa also disparaged the practice of debate:

> Neglecting one's hard-to-tame mental stream while practicing argument in order to learn debate, or engaging in the explanation of the teaching in every moment of the day and night for worldly things such as fame and so forth, life quickly passes on without purpose and one degenerates from the supreme path.[261]

However, although Atiśa did not advocate the practice of debate, this does not mean that he rejected the use of reasoning (*yukti*). Reasoning for Atiśa is an essential method that leads to the direct realization of insight. Reasoning for Atiśa signifies an "internal" Buddhist form of critical analysis that is different from the "external" epistemological devices used to defend Buddhist dharma and defeat non-Buddhist opponents.

Atiśa states the four great reasons for the cultivation of insight in meditation in his *Commentary to the Lamp for the Path to Awakening*. These are: the reason refuting production according to the tetralemma, the diamond-splinters reason, the reason of being neither one nor many, and the reason consisting in dependent arising.[262] Atiśa understands reasoning to be a conventional process that dissolves itself at the end of a procedure that seeks to establish the existence of an object. Once reasoning consumes the fuel of conceptual thought, as metaphorically described by Atiśa, the fire of reasoning itself dissipates and one comes to rest in nonappearance.[263]

Atiśa did not differentiate Madhyamaka into separate schools. Rather, he utilized the texts of various Madhyamaka authors for pedagogical and soteriological purposes. Atiśa introduced his students to the thought and practice of Madhyamaka with the works of Bhāviveka. On advanced levels of understanding, Atiśa closely followed the works of Nāgārjuna, Candrakīrti, and Śāntideva.

In Atiśa's Madhyamaka all appearances are based on ignorance and comprised of ignorance. Appearances are not nonexistent but rather false, erroneous, and mistaken. The synonyms of the conventions of mere appearance in Atiśa's nominalistic Madhyamaka are mere name, mere word, mere convention, and mere imputation. For Atiśa, the subjective perceiver, the appearance of the cognition, and the appearance of the mind which is like an illusion are only imputedly established.

A key Madhyamaka classification that structures Atiśa's thought and practice is the bifurcation of all things in the universe into the categories of two realities—that is, ultimate reality and conventional reality.[264] As Atiśa states in his Song with a Vision for the Realm of Reality (see chapter 6), ultimate reality is a purified appearance of nonappearance like the center of space, known through individually intuited knowledge. For Atiśa, the "ultimate" is a conventional expression, also embodied by the phrase "realm of reality" (*dharmadhātu*), consisting of selfless nonappearances that are realized with nonconceptual pristine awareness (*jñāna*). The realm of reality, for Atiśa, is a naturally pure object of realization that is the ever-present real state of things that may be cognized in meditative equipoise but is not completely actualized until full buddhahood.

Conventional realities are appearances that arise due to causes and conditions. All conventional realities are false and deceiving, but they are not nonexistent. Rather, they are mere appearances[265] subject to the principle of cause and effect imputed through dependent arising. In Atiśa's system, conventional realities are classified as mistaken or correct from different perspectives in relation to the cognitive understanding of ordinary individuals or the realizations of those who have reached the path of vision.[266]

Mistaken conventional realities are appearances of ignorance that impute impermanent and empty things as either existent or nonexistent. Mistakes are impermanent and cause suffering, and they are also deceptive and false. Mistaken appearances are like the hair that is perceived by someone suffering from eye disease.

Correct conventional reality for the yogi, according to Atiśa, occurs only after the path of vision. Correct conventional realities are considered nondeceptive, nonerroneous, and trustworthy in that, from this perspective, appearances are realized to be unproduced like an illusion, and objects are cognized as essenceless entities. Although correct, they are conventional due to arising through causes and conditions and are considered illusions of pristine awareness. Correct conventional realities are nonerroneous illusions and are imputations conducive to purification since the causes of purification have nondeceptive individual results. This accords with appearances of "purified worldly knowledge"[267] mentioned by Bhāviveka in his *Heart of the Middle Way* and *Blaze of Reasoning*.[268] Atiśa refers to correct conventional reality, following Bhāviveka, as the stairway of correct conventional reality.[269] Atiśa's understanding of correct conventional reality offered him an avenue for upholding the conventional practices of moral virtue that eventually lead to realizing ultimate reality.

Based on these factors of Madhyamaka thought and practice, Atiśa outlines a program of bodhisattva training that integrates the cultivation of wisdom and compassion with the developing awakening mind at both the ultimate and conventional levels. The ultimate awakening mind—the birthless, luminous, nonconceptual realm of reality equated with emptiness—is cultivated during meditative equipoise. The conventional awakening mind is cultivated during postmeditative practices. In this program of training, the two levels of the awakening mind are integrated and stabilized, having the essence of emptiness and compassion.[270] A snapshot of instructions for this integrated cultivation is found in the *Open Basket of Jewels*. Atiśa states,

> Regarding the training, first the mind did not come from anywhere and will not go anywhere at the end. The mind does not abide anywhere and is without color and without shape. The mind does not arise from the beginning nor does it cease at the end. The mind is empty of inherent existence and has the nature of clear light. One should recall this again and again.
>
> On the other hand, one should stabilize through accustoming the awakening mind to love and compassion. One should completely purify [the mind] and stand firm, being continuously mindful of each moment of thought with mindfulness, awareness, thoughtfulness, and conscientiousness.[271]

The *Open Basket of Jewels* then discusses how the integrated awakening mind is protected and increased while the bodhisattva advances through the ten stages as outlined by the *Sūtra of the Ten Stages*.[272] In the course of the training, the bodhisattva alternates between cognizing the nonconceptual space-like realm of reality in meditative stabilization and then viewing things as illusions in the postmeditative state. The alternation, however, ceases at the stage of buddhahood.

At this point, for Atiśa, based on numerous citations from the hymns of Nāgārjuna, the purified realm of reality directly and constantly fuses with the dharma body (*dharmakāya*), without any mental element or gnosis existing at all. In brief, Atiśa strictly followed an Indian Madhyamaka understanding based on the works of Nāgārjuna, Candrakīrti, and Śāntideva, whereby buddhahood does not have any mind or mental functions. This understanding of buddhahood *would not* be followed by a majority of Tibetan scholars, particularly after the time of Chapa Chökyi Sengé (1109–1169).[273]

Atiśa was a fully trained practitioner, scholar, and ritual specialist in the ways of the Secret Mantra Vehicle. As the story of his life illustrates, Atiśa engaged in advanced-level Secret Mantra practices as a youthful nonmonastic yogi and then later as a fully ordained Mahāsāṃghika monk. For Atiśa, the rituals and techniques of the Secret Mantra Vehicle were advanced forms of Mahāyāna bodhisattva practice. Atiśa considered these practices only suitable for aspirants with sharp faculties and properly cultivated altruism grounded in trainings of discipline and the awakening mind. The purpose of these practices, according to Atiśa, was to quickly achieve the immutable bliss of buddhahood for the benefit of oneself and others. Atiśa advocated that the advanced Secret Mantra practices offer the bodhisattva a rapid method to acquire the stocks of merit and pristine awareness necessary for buddhahood and the concomitant acquisition of supersensory perception to benefit others.

First and foremost, the way of the Secret Mantra Vehicle for Atiśa is secret and not for the uninitiated. Atiśa stipulated that one must enter a maṇḍala and receive an empowerment or consecration into the practice from a qualified guru. Atiśa stressed that an aspirant should request a vajra master (*vajrācārya*) consecration to engage in Secret Mantra practices. Atiśa famously instructs, in both his *Open*

Basket of Jewels (see chapter 4) and the *Lamp for the Path to Awakening* (see chapter 11), that bodhisattvas at the level of the creation stage and who hold full monastic vows practicing celibacy should not receive higher-level consecrations.[274] The initial levels of consecration provide access to practices for deity visualization, the muttering of mantras, and studying esoteric Buddhist literature. When the bodhisattva aspirant has taken consecration and received permission to engage in Secret Mantra practices, then the aspirant must protect vows and commitments that have been oathed at the time of consecration.

Once initiated into the practices related to ones's chosen esoteric Buddhist deity, Atiśa outlined two stages of practice: the meditation practices of the creation stage followed by the more advanced completion stage practices of dissolution. The creation stage practices focused on "deity purification,"[275] where the practitioner transforms their ordinary identity into that of an esoteric deity constituted by awakened forces of wisdom and compassion. The more advanced completion stage leads to awakening in this lifetime and the attainment of the Great Seal.[276]

Atiśa upheld a number of esoteric Buddhist lineages based on his writings and the biographical accounts of Atiśa's life. Atiśa had a mastery of a vast amount of esoteric Buddhist literature which he classified within seven categories. These categories included Action, Performance, Practice, Dual, Yoga, Great Yoga, and Highest Yoga classes of tantra. This differs from the Tibetan division of four classes accepted by scholars such as Rinchen Zangpo.[277] Atiśa had four primary chosen deities:[278] Hevajra, Trisamayarāja, Avalokiteśvara, and Tārā. Two additional deities, Acala and Cakrasaṃvara, are also predominant in a number of Atiśa's writings and teachings.[279] Atiśa composed over thirty sādhanas related to the cultivation of the illusory body in deity yoga. He also wrote six texts on the advanced practices related to clear light (*prabhāsvara*) (see chapter 14). Atiśa also composed over thirty short works on mental training within the Secret Mantra Vehicle, including ritual manuals and praises.[280]

Atiśa was familiar with the noble tradition of the *Guhyasamāja Tantra* system, as he cites from Nāgārjuna's *Five Stages*, Āryadeva's *Lamp that Integrates the Practices*, and Candrakīrti's *Illumination of the Lamp Commentary* throughout his *Open Basket of Jewels*.[281] Atiśa knew Buddhajñānapāda's system of the *Guhyasamāja*, as he places Mañjuvajra as the central deity in his *Open Basket of Jewels*.[282] Atiśa also upheld the Cakrasaṃvara practice tradition of Vikramaśīla and its accompanying system of commentarial exegesis. While traveling in Nepal and Tibet, Atiśa had with him a small collection of Sanskrit manuscripts which included such esoteric Buddhist works as the *Guhyasamāja Tantra*, *Kṛṣṇayamāri Tantra*, and the *Hevajrapañjikā*, among other works.[283]

Atiśa was well versed in the couplets (*dohā*), performance songs (*caryāgīti*), and diamond songs (*vajragīti*) composed by such figures as Saraha and Tilopa in the Apabhraṃśa dialect of Atiśa's native northeast India. In fact, Atiśa was the first person to bring Saraha's *Treasury of Dohā Verses* to Tibet.[284] Atiśa composed his own *Diamond Song of the Diamond Seat*.[285] As the biography indicates, he was not allowed by Dromtönpa on multiple occasions to teach the *dohā* verses. The dohā verses and their underlying background of Yoginī tantras were controversial at this time in Tibet. Not only were the practices involved with such teachings problematic for Dromtönpa, but Atiśa advocated dohās as teachings for achieving sudden awakening, a long-standing controversial issue in the history of Tibetan Buddhism since the Samyé debate in the late eighth century. In brief, Dromtönpa restricted the teachings of this literature to just a few disciples within Atiśa's inner group.

Atiśa also transmitted oral lineages of esoteric Buddhist teachings. At the time of the Tibetan scholar-meditator Mokchok Rinchen Tsondru (1110–1170), a disciple of Khyungpo Naljor, there circulated a set of nine esoteric Buddhist teachings transmitted from Atiśa. These teachings included: (1) the *Oral Transmission of Ḍākiṇī*, (2) the *Great Vision and Meditation*, (3) a set of uncommon teachings, (4) the *Precious Rosary*, (5) *Vārāhī*, (6) *Single Heroic Cakrasaṃvara*, (7) *White Tārā*, (8) *Coemergent Union*, and (9) the *Four Conditions*.[286]

As briefly mentioned in the biographies, Atiśa was a lineage holder of Great Seal teachings. The attainment of the Great Seal is often regarded as the crowning achievement of esoteric Buddhist practice in Indian and Tibetan forms of Buddhism. Atiśa received Great Seal instructions from Ḍombi Heruka in a lineage stemming from Tilopa. Atiśa's exegesis of Great Seal-related thought and practices reflects influence from his institutional environment of Vikramaśīla Monastery. Atiśa's teachings on the Great Seal focused upon realizing the clear light coemergent nature of the mind. In a series of early writings composed in India known as *Vision and Meditation*, Atiśa brings together a variety of sūtras and tantras that emphasize the vision of clear light. Atiśa's exegesis accentuates the importance of the coemergent mind as the hidden nature of reality. Atiśa inherited a mode of exegesis at Vikramaśīla that emphasized gnostic awareness in the practice of the Great Seal. Atiśa's exegesis focuses on the nondual unity of clear light and uncontaminated virtuous qualities. Atiśa's system represents a fully domesticated esoteric contemplative tradition, emphasizing gnosis and vision that are internalized to an advanced degree. Atiśa's instructions point out the coemergent nature of one's own mind that is equivalent to the realm of reality. Atiśa's *Coemergent Union* (see chapter 14) illustrates how the practice of meditating on the clear light allows one to recognize the natural clear light at the time of death. The meeting of the natural clear light[287] and the clear light of meditation,[288] according to Atiśa, is the attainment of the Great Seal.

Atiśa's greatest contribution and legacy were his synthesis and reintegration of the interrelationship of the three vows[289] together with the teachings of sūtras and tantras into a coherent system of Buddhist practice. Atiśa's well-known *Lamp for the Path to Awakening* (hereafter referred to as the *Lamp*; see chapter 11) and his important but lesser known *Stages of the Path to Awakening* (hereafter referred to as *Stages*; see chapter 12) are long-standing testaments to his innovative and dynamic system. Atiśa began to formulate teachings that integrate sūtra and mantra in his early writings on Cakrasaṃvara. Atiśa's *Analysis of Realization*[290] articulates the "stages of the path of the essential meaning."[291] The stages of the path, as far as it is currently known, was initially formulated by Atiśa based on these advanced stages of esoteric Buddhist teachings.

Atiśa further developed his stages of the path system under the urging of Jangchup Ö while he was in West Tibet. Atiśa's *Lamp* was the result of Jangchup Ö's patronage and inquiries, and the treatise became a model for subsequent generations of Tibetan scholars in their understanding and practice of the Buddhist path. The *Lamp* was an imperially sanctioned public teaching that influenced Tibetan Buddhists for over nine centuries. The *Stages*, on the other hand, written at the behest of Dromtönpa, was a secret teaching that was transmitted among early followers of Atiśa until the time of Pakmo Drupa (1110–1170).

Although the *Stages* has not been widely studied (or even recognized) among later traditional and modern scholars of Tibetan Buddhism, its impact was just as great as the *Lamp*. This is because the *Stages* contains within it all the major topics found in later stages of the path literature that the *Lamp* does not mention. The *Stages* clearly outlines the practices and realizations of the individuals of small and middling capacity. The *Stages* outlines such topics as taking refuge, meditations on death and impermanence, the elimination of wrongdoing, and recollecting the sufferings of cyclic existence. The *Stages* elucidates these topics interspersed with principals of the Secret Mantra Vehicle as well. For example, the practice of viewing one's guru as the Buddha is derived from Secret Mantra texts and practices.[292] The topics found in the *Stages* and the sequence in which they are presented impacted all subsequent stages of the path literature in Tibet.

Atiśa was a charismatic, creative, and dynamic Indian Buddhist master whose teachings on essential practice and works on the integration of the path influenced Tibetans in their understanding of the theory and practice of Mahāyāna Buddhism for succeeding generations. The themes within Atiśa's teachings focusing on the primacy of ethics, the significance of ritually taking and properly maintaining vows, the focus on generating and increasing the awakening mind and implementing an orderly and harmonious system of practice in which the Perfection Path and the ways of the Secret Mantra Vehicle are complementary have shaped the beliefs and practices of Tibetan Buddhists up to the present day.

The Teachings

CHAPTER 4

On the Awakening Mind, from *Open Basket of Jewels*

The Open Basket of Jewels[293] *is one of the primary works among Atiśa's collected writings and perhaps the most extensive of his extant writings composed in India. After preliminary instructions, Atiśa's provides a detailed discussion of the awakening mind under thirteen subject headings. The selection also includes a brief discussion on conduct. Atiśa cites sūtras and tantras in his discussion that provide one of the most thorough overviews on the awakening mind in Indian Buddhist literature.*

Open Basket of Jewels, Special Instructions on the Middle Way

In the Indian language: *Ratnakaraṇḍodghāṭamadhyamakopadeśa*
In the Tibetan language: *Dbu ma'i man ngag rin po che'i za ma tog kha phye ba*

Homage to the venerable Mañjuvajra!
Homage to the three jewels!

1 Preliminary Instructions

I will write the special instruction of the lineage of Ācārya Nāgārjuna.

As for this, an individual who remembers the suffering of

beginningless saṃsāra, of oneself and other beings without exception, should not be attached even to an object the size of a mere sesame seed, entirely discarding like a drop of spit all activities and objects of the world. First, one who keeps the pure uncorrupted three vows of morality that have been pledged, who possesses the wisdom of hearing and reflection, who has compassion naturally, who disregards his own life and body for the sake of the holy dharma, should search for a holy individual having the special instruction of the lineage of Ācārya Nāgārjuna, and please him for a long time. Since one is a beginner, one should reside where it is easy to obtain a livelihood, in a great, vast land, or great city, or isolated place at the edge of a mountain rock, and so forth. Sitting on a soft and smooth seat in front of the images of the three jewels, one should reflect as follows: "When I survey the five types of sentient beings—those born from an egg, those born from moisture, those born miraculously, those possessing form and those not possessing form, and those possessing consciousness and those not possessing consciousness—I see that they are all my mothers. These mother-like sentient beings produce and accumulate polluted actions on account of their own selfish purposes, and with the maturation of those actions, experience much suffering."

Ācārya Nāgārjuna states:

> The intelligent, having seen the sufferings of the three realms caused by the faults of conceptual thought and habitual tendencies, should pull out from the abode that is saṃsāra.[294]

Ācārya Nāgārjuna also says:

> As I have brought suffering upon sentient beings living in the prison of existence who are tormented by the fire of the

afflictions, since all of them previously were dear friends and parents who provided great benefit, now it is suitable to make them happy.[295]

By understanding their kindness, generate the awakening mind with the four immeasurables,[296] thinking, I will "liberate them from suffering, set them free, relieve their sufferings, and make them reach nirvāṇa."[297] For this purpose accumulate the two collections of wisdom and merit.

The immediate sphere of space before one, not separate from the dreamlike mind, is filled with the three jewels like a heap of mustard seeds. Remembering the seven mental perceptions and the seven holy things, utter words of remembrance, and by means of the six antidotes,[298] having made the proper posture of body, prostrate, make offerings, confess transgressions, rejoice, request the wheel of the teaching to be turned, make supplication,[299] go for refuge, generate the awakening mind, offer the body, take the vow, make firm the promise of the vow to remain in the path of the Mahāyāna, and dedicate all of these to great awakening. All of this turns into the realm of reality, the place of offering, the assembly of offerings—all of these. Now, first of all, when one examines where these come from and where they go, one realizes that they do not go anywhere and they do not come from anywhere. Since all inner and outer things are exactly like that, all of them appear as a false emanation of illusion in one's own mind. These things with false appearance belong to the body and also belong to the mind. The mind is without color, without form, by its own nature clear light, and unarising from the beginning. The wisdom of individual analysis[300] itself turns into clear light. Amidst that, consciousness does not absolutely exist, does not at all abide, is not at all established, is unproduced in any aspect, and is totally pacified of elaborations.

One should reside as long as one is able in the appearanceless diamond concentration (*vajrasamādhi*), like the sky from which all signs of dust are gone, like the midday sky with a noontime autumn sun. If the mind becomes distracted through the force of not being used to regular practice, stand firm through summoning suchness. In other sessions one should do the same. Many sessions should be done for a short time. At the time of becoming accustomed, when the practice becomes a bit more firm, one should do longer and longer meditative sessions. One should pacify with the individual antidotes to the five obstacles of śamatha,[301] and after that open the eyes, saying, "*E ma ho!* The dharmadhātu, without anything existing, appears everywhere. This is amazing. These things, the nature of one's own mind, an illusory emanation, appear like an unreal apparition and are as false as they appear. Appearances are exemplified by the eight similes of illusion[302] and are not intrinsically real." Then, having offered prayers of aspiration, release slowly from the sitting position and take to molding statues and so forth, doing as much virtuous activity as one can. Accordingly, one should make effort to accumulate the two collections in six sessions of cultivation. Meditate on śūnyatā at the time of sleep and go to sleep in the sphere of that. After that, at the last session, think to wake up with the awakening mind arising from love and compassion. These above activities generate the ultimate awakening mind. Food should be divided into four portions.[303]

Again, Ācārya Nāgārjuna states:

> The ultimate awakening mind should be produced by the power of cultivation for a bodhisattva who does the activity by way of Secret Mantra.[304]

In this way, when one strives with devotion for a long time and without stopping, it will automatically produce compassion toward sentient beings. Ācārya Nāgārjuna states:

> Accordingly, when yogis cultivate emptiness, the mind no doubt will become joyful for the welfare of others.[305]

Moreover,

> The ultimate, birthless from the beginning, when deeply realized by the mind, will effortlessly produce compassion for those sinking in the mud of saṃsāra.

Likewise, when the yogi internalizes this cultivation and cultivates the ultimate awakening mind, then through cultivating the conventional awakening mind one will stabilize both awakening minds, the two minds each having the essence of great compassion and emptiness. The *Complete Enlightenment of Mahāvairocana Tantra* states:

> Awakening, the characteristic of which is similar to that of space, is the abandonment of all conceptual thought.

The *Verses That Summarize the Perfection of Wisdom* says:

> There is not even a mere particle of something to be obtained. One should not apprehend awakening as real. This should be demonstrated to beginners.[306]

The *Perfection of Wisdom in One Hundred Thousand Lines* states:

> I have completely awakened in the essence of awakening without obtaining anything at all.

The *Perfect Gathering of Qualities Sūtra* states:

> In this regard, what little desire of a bodhisattva is there? He is one who does not desire even awakening. What is the satisfaction? He is one who does not excessively long for the awakening mind.

This meaning is indicated in many other precious sūtras as well as tantras of Secret Mantra. The *Guhyasamāja Root Tantra* states:

> Due to the sameness of the essencelessness of things, one's own mind—free of all entities, without aggregates (*skandhas*), elements (*dhātus*), sense spheres (*āyatanas*), and subject and object—is unproduced from the beginning, the very nature of emptiness.[307]

The *Perfection of Wisdom in Eight Thousand Lines* says:

> Śāriputra, whatever is thought, that is no thought; thought by its nature is clear light.

As Ārya Nāgārjuna has indicated:

> The mind has not been seen, and will not be seen, by all buddhas. What will one see of something that has the nature of having no nature?[308]

The venerable Āryadeva states:

> When one becomes accustomed to ascertaining the mind with wisdom, then the mind will not be seen.[309]

The *Perfect Gathering of Qualities Sūtra* states:

> Devapūtras! Moreover, even the desire to understand the awakening mind is the activity of Māra. Apprehending the mind as real while seeking out the illusionary mind is to be confessed by whomever produces the mind of unsurpassable awakening.

One who has been accustomed to the Great Vehicle for innumerable previous lives, and has a well-purified mental continuum and sharp mental faculties, knows the conventional awakening mind itself as producing the ultimate awakening mind, and since that mind has both great compassion and emptiness, one stands firm in the emptiness endowed with all excellent features.[310] Intending this meaning, Ācārya Nāgārjuna states:

> The buddhas teach that the awakened mind is not obscured with notions of a "self," "skandhas," and so forth, but has the characteristic of being empty of such notions.[311]

Well then, if someone asks, "How is the awakening mind produced?" the reply is: One should produce it conventionally, like a magically created individual or emanated individual arousing the awakening mind. As is said in the *Inquiry of the Nāga King Sāgara Sūtra*:

> King of Nāgas! Due to one dharma, bodhisattvas will be quickly awakened in unsurpassable fully complete awakening! What, one may ask, is that one dharma? It is the awakening mind that does not let go of all sentient beings.[312]

This sūtra teaches that it is necessary to generate the awakening mind.

2 The Awakening Mind

Regarding the awakening mind, one should be knowledgeable about the (1) cause of arising, (2) condition, (3) nature, (4) aspect, (5) training, (6) apprehension, (7) guarding, (12) increasing, (13) benefits of, (8) cause of dropping, (9) fault of relinquishing, (10) benefits of causing the arising in another, benefits of rejoicing in the arising in others, and (11) bad fault of causing interruption in the arising of the mind in others.

2.1 The Cause of the Awakening Mind

In this regard, the cause is having the sign of the excellent lineage (*gotra*). As the *Sūtra of the Prophecy Spoken Truthfully* states:

> (1) With admiration for the extensive, one is without admiration for the inferior. (2) By having great compassion naturally, one possesses virtuous qualities. (3) By abandoning polluted friends, one is nourished by the spiritual friend. (4) By doing whatever one says, one is undeceitful. (5) By pleasing the buddhas wandering in the world, one has joy. (6) By being without low activities of body, speech, and mind, one abandons sin. (7) By this faultless superior thought, one has trust in the sacred vow. (8) By nonattachment to one's own tastes, one has the nature of pleasing everyone. (9) One is free from the empowerments of Māra. (10) By accumulating roots of virtue, one performs activities well. (11) Since it is in the sphere of great compassion, one has compassionate love for sentient beings. (12) By freely giving necessary things, one has little attachment to anything.[313]

Ācārya Ārya Asaṅga states:

There are four causes: lineage, a spiritual friend, compassion, and enduring the suffering of saṃsāra. [314]

2.2 The Conditions for the Awakening Mind

As for the conditions of generating the awakening mind, there are two: (1) the condition of application (*prayoga*) and (2) the condition of thought (*āśaya*).

The Condition of Application

In regard to that, the conditions of application are that one should: (1) accumulate the provisions of merit, (2) purify the mental continuum, and (3) perform the superior going for refuge in the three jewels.

Accumulating Provisions

(1) To accumulate the provisions, one should perform the seven-limbed *pūjā* three times during the day and three times during the night; memorize, read, and recite the profound *Perfection of Wisdom Sūtra*; make extensive offerings to the three jewels; make gifts and feast offerings for the saṃgha; give ordinary feasts; give great, extensive charity to the protectorless; and give great extensive sacrificial cakes to spirits.

Training the Mental Continuum

(2) Train the mental continuum as before: read, recite, and memorize the profound sūtras, perform the seven-limbed pūjā, recite the *The Sūtra of the Three Heaps*,[315] and confess transgressions with texts such as the *Purification of Karmic Obscurations Sūtra* and the *King of Glorious Sūtras Called the Sublime Golden Light* and so forth.

Superior Going for Refuge

(3) The superior going for refuge is distinctively noble in seven excellent aspects: (1) excellence of the individual person, (2) excellence of the three jewels as objects of refuge, (3) excellence of time, (4) excellence of thought, (5) excellence of application, (6) excellence of advice, and (7) excellence of benefits.

In this regard—the excellence of the three jewels as refuge objects—the object of refuge of the Inferior Vehicle is mentioned in the *Treasury of Higher Knowledge*:

> One who goes for refuge in the Three Jewels goes for refuge in the qualities of the Buddha, the saṃgha, and the dharma, and likewise one takes refuge by going for refuge in the qualities of nirvāṇa.[316]

Here, the distinction of the three jewels is in three aspects: (1) the three jewels of ultimate truth, (2) the three jewels in front of oneself, and (3) the three jewels of realization.[317] One should ask a spiritual teacher for the extensive meaning of this.

Still, I will describe only the excellence of the advice. By means of remembering the excellence of the three jewels and their good qualities, one does not relinquish the three jewels even for the sake of one's life and body. By means of going for refuge over and over again and remembering their great kindness, one should, always or from time to time, offer even as much as a full bowl of pure water, as well as offer the first portion of food and so forth. Whatever you do, whatever your purpose, make requests to the three jewels but abandon other worldly methods. One should perform activities in this manner for other sentient beings as well. As for advice of the Common Vehicle: since one goes to refuge in the Buddha, one should not make homage and so forth to worldly deities; one should follow this advice for each of the three jewels.

The Conditions Necessary for the Awakening Mind to Arise

The *Sūtra on the Samādhi That Is the Seal of the Gnosis of the Tathāgatas* and the *White Lotus of Compassion Sūtra* state:

> Of (1) the mind generation for the awakening of a buddha, (2) the mind generation at the time of the destruction of the holy dharma, (3) the mind generation when one has seen the suffering of sentient beings, (4) the mind generation of bodhisattvas, (5) the mind generation when one has made good offerings and worship, (6) the mind generation when one has seen other deities, and (7) the mind generation when one has seen the body of a tathāgata, the first three are the actual awakening mind.[318]

The *Ten Dharmas Sūtra* also states:

> There is (1) the mind generation when one has been urged by buddhas and bodhisattvas and so forth, (2) the mind generation when one has seen the good qualities of the awakening mind, (3) the mind generation when one has seen the suffering of sentient beings, (4) the mind generation when one has seen the excellence of the buddhas and bodhisattvas.[319]

Five Conditions for the Awakening Mind

From the *Ornament of Mahāyāna Sūtras*:

> There are five conditions: (1) the power of friend, (2) the power of cause, (3) the power of the root, (4) the power of

hearing, and (5) the power of being accustomed to virtue. Some of them are firm and some are not firm.[320]

Four Conditions and Four Powers

Ācārya Asaṅga speaks of four conditions and four powers.[321] The four conditions are: the mind generation when one has seen the excellence of the Tathāgata, the mind generation when one has seen the benefits, the mind generation at the time of the destruction of the holy dharma, and the mind generation when one has seen the suffering of sentient beings. The four powers are: the power of cause, the power of activity, one's own power, and the power of others.

In this way, when one thoroughly accumulates the causes and conditions, one will thoroughly generate the awakening mind.

2.3 The Nature of Arising

The nature of arising: the wish, the desire, and the aspiration are synonyms.[322] As Ārya Maitreya states:

> Generation of mind is a desire for perfectly complete awakening for the sake of others.[323]

The essential nature is to perceive the distinctive object of consciousness, which is an intelligence that possesses similarity with compassion and wishing. Like the good foundational earth that produces without exception the crops of virtuous white dharmas, the wish is the awakening mind that is like earth.

2.4 The Distinctive Aspect

The distinction or the particularity of the aspect itself is that it is not even covered by any kind of fault, like deceiving and so forth, and is stainless. For example, like the pure gold that is without the faults of rust, stones, earth, and so forth, that mind itself is a pure thought, like gold. As for the extensive meaning of this, *The Teaching of Akṣayamati* states:

> Venerable Śāradvatiputra: Regarding the awakening mind, what are the aspects of generating the mind like that? Bhagavān: Kulaputra, by being unmixed with the Inferior Vehicle, that mind arises in the aspect of purity.[324]

Thus it is taught extensively and so forth in the sūtras.

2.5 Training the Mind

Regarding the training, first the mind did not come from anywhere and will not go anywhere at the end. The mind does not abide anywhere and is without color and without shape. The mind does not arise from the beginning nor does it not cease at the end. The mind is empty of inherent existence and is of the nature of clear light. One should recall this again and again.[325]

On the other hand, one should stabilize through accustoming that awakening mind to love and compassion. One should completely purify the mind and stand firm, being continuously mindful of each moment of thought with mindfulness, awareness, thoughtfulness, and conscientiousness.[326]

2.6 Keeping the Awakening Mind

As for keeping the awakening mind, this consists of: (1) the four ways of not letting go of sentient beings, (2) the eight thoughts of a holy individual, (3) the ten masteries of the inner method, (4) the six masteries of the outer method, including the exchange of self and other, as well as equalizing self and others, and (5) dedicating with the "Ten Great Blessings of the Vajra Banner"[327] and the *Vows of Good Conduct*.[328]

Not Giving Up on Sentient Beings

In this regard, not giving up on sentient beings entails: (1.1) not letting go of the mind of beings who are beneficial to oneself, (1.2) not letting go of sentient beings who harm oneself, (1.3a) directly suffering, (1.3b) not giving up the cause of suffering and so forth, and (1.4) not giving up on sentient beings in general.

Not Letting Go of Those Who Benefit Oneself

Regarding that, not letting go those who benefit oneself means to not let go of the mind that knows the kindness of beings and repays their kindness. As Ācārya Nāgārjuna states:

> Sentient beings—who have resided in the prison of existence suffering with the fire of the defilements since beginningless saṃsāra—were previously my parents. Since they provided great benefit, I need to make the same repayment. They have been made to suffer by me, now it is suitable to make them happy.[329]

One should look at the sūtras for the extensive meaning of this. One needs to understand the benefits that the father, mother, relatives, friends, and so forth, of this life have provided and repay their kindness. Accordingly, if one will not do so, the downfall of "not to repay a good turn"[330] will occur.

Not Letting Go of Beings Who Do Harm to Oneself

Not letting go of sentient beings who do harm to oneself means to not mentally relinquish one's control over one's actions. As it is said,

> When answered politely, the supreme individual of the Jambudvīpa continent responds politely, and even when receiving a rude response answers in a considerate manner.

The *Perfection of Wisdom in Eight Thousand Lines* states:

> A bodhisattva, even when faulted by others, does not become disturbed in mind, does not harm them, and does not fight with them. Even in the case of killing, one does not become hostile. One does not have hatred toward any sentient being. Bodhisattvas should firmly produce this disposition.

As is further taught:

> Bodhisattvas should perceive all sentient beings as mother, father, sons, and daughters. As one wishes happiness for oneself, one should apply happiness to other beings as well. One should liberate from suffering all beings without exception, not giving up on any sentient being. Even if they cut one's body into one hundred pieces, one produces love and compassion and does not have malice toward them.[331]

From the venerable Āryadeva:

> When fierce harm occurs, one should understand that as one's own previous karma.

If it is the case that one will not do so, rudimentary downfalls and faults will occur, such as

> "not listening to another's confession," "striking out in anger," "blaming others," "abandoning confession through discussing others' faults," "disdaining those who are angry," "abusing with abusive replies," and so forth.[332]

Not Letting Go of Beings Who Suffer

One does not let go of beings who are certainly suffering from heat, cold, hunger, thirst, and so forth, the immediate suffering of heinous actions,[333] and so forth, and degenerate vows. When seeing them tormented with various sufferings, one does not relinquish the mind of compassion. As the venerable Āryadeva states:

> I have heard that an iron wheel twelve *yojanas* long revolves on the head; as soon as the awakening mind arises, it is dispelled.[334]

Ācārya Aśvaghoṣa says:

> Just as a mother produces anguish for a son tormented by illness, likewise a bodhisattva's love exists especially for those who are inferior.[335]

Ācārya Bhāviveka also states:

> At the time of seeing the sorrowful who are overwhelmed with grief, compassion arises from the bottom of the heart and one provides benefit to them.[336]

One should look in the sūtras for the extensive meaning.

Not Letting Go of Beings Who Have Been the Cause of Suffering

Not letting go of sentient beings who have been the cause of suffering and so forth means to not let go of the mind that has loving compassion. Undermining precepts, performing heinous actions, cutting life, and committing various transgressions—one should do the opposite from these. The *Close Placements of Mindfulness Sūtra*[337] states:

> Whoever, having received good conduct, does not protect it well: that person's flesh and bones will certainly burn in the destructive hell of Memarmu.

And:

> The ārya who obtains and stands firm in desirable qualities, when seeing the breaking of morality, sheds tears, thinking, "What rebirth will come of this?"[338]

Also, Ācārya Nāgārjuna says:

> May I always dissuade all at once all beings of any world who intend to engage in negativity, without doing them any harm.[339]

Not Letting Go of Sentient Beings in General

Generally, not to let go of sentient beings means not to relinquish the mind of love. The *Inquiry of Pratibhānamati Sūtra* states:[340]

> Bodhisattvas should view all sentient beings like a son. One should view them like one's own body.[341]

The *Ornament of Mahāyāna Sūtras* says:

> Like a pigeon who has supreme love for her young, embracing them closely to herself, a bodhisattva has love like that for sentient beings who suffer.[342]

The *Great Tantra of Supreme Knowledge* also states:

> Bodhisattvas do not desire their own happiness, are not even bothered by their own sufferings, and suffer because of the sufferings of others. If others are happy, then bodhisattvas are joyful.

The *Śrī-Vajraḍākiṇī Tantra* and the *Śrī-Pāramādibuddha* state:

> For as long as he can, the best wise person bestrides existence, and for that long he accomplishes unequaled good for sentient beings, without passing beyond suffering.[343]

One should look in the sūtras for the extensive meaning of this point.

Eight Special Thoughts of a Holy Individual

The eight special thoughts of a holy individual: (1) Alas! If possible, may I be able to make sentient beings be without the suffering of birth, and likewise (2) without the suffering of aging, (3) the suffering of sickness, and (4) the suffering of death. (5) I will deliver beings who are not delivered and (6) free those who are not free. (7) I will free them from powerful suffering, and (8) I will lead to nirvāṇa those who have not yet reached nirvāṇa. One should continuously be mindful, moment by moment, thinking these thoughts.

Mastery of the Inner Method

Mastery of the inner method: Make others' suffering one's own and clear away the suffering of others with one's own suffering. Exchange others' suffering with one's own happiness; always grieve on account of others' suffering. As the *Great Tantra of Supreme Knowledge* states:

> Bodhisattvas are not attached to their own happiness; they are not even bothered by their own sufferings. Their minds suffer with others' suffering; when others are happy, bodhisattvas are joyful.

One confesses others' transgressions as one's own, rejoices in others' virtue as if it were one's own, rejoices through making one's own virtue the virtue of others, and dedicates having made one's own virtue the virtue of others.

Mastery of the Outer Method

The mastery of the outer method includes the four means of gathering disciples,[344] the five objects of knowledge,[345] the ten masteries, the six perfections, the four immeasurables, and so forth. The following activities mature all sentient beings without exception: nurturing, terrifying, seducing, conquering, building, and pleasing with presents.

Dedication with Recitation

One should avoid relinquishing beings by reciting the "Ten Great Blessings of the Vajra Banner," the *Vows of Good Conduct*, the *Twenty Aspirational Prayers* composed by Ācārya Nāgārjuna, and the eleven verses that occur in the *Salty River Sūtra*, and so forth. As the *Kāśyapa Chapter Sūtra* states:

> Even for the sake of one's life, without speaking lies, one should stand firm with the superior thought that is undeceiving to sentient beings. One should generate the perception that individuals who have the awakening mind are teachers. One should mature sentient beings who are ready to become established in unsurpassable awakening, but not śrāvakas or *pratyekabuddhas*.[346]

Likewise, the *Inquiry of Avalokiteśvara on the Seven Qualities* states:

> Kulaputra, bodhisattvas who immediately generate the awakening mind should train in seven qualities and should not have sexual enjoyment even with mental perception, not to mention joining together the two sexual organs. One should not take up with a nonvirtuous friend even in dreams. With a mind like that of a bird, one should be completely without grasping. With mastery in skill and wisdom, without grasping at pride and the "I," abandon conceptions of existence and nonexistence, and firmly cultivate the samādhi of emptiness. Pacifying erroneous conceptuality, do not take joy in saṃsāra. In brief, a mind in accordance with mindfulness and introspection will not be separate from conscientiousness.[347]

And:

> Befouled by offences due to the fault of lacking awareness, conscientiousness does not stay in the memory of a mind that lacks awareness, like water in a leaky jar.[348]

Again:

> Through mindfulness, awareness, and mental introspection,
> one does not separate from conscientiousness.[349]

This is taught by Ācārya Śāntideva.

Through not forgetting in each moment of thought and by having continual mindfulness, one should apprehend the awakening mind. In the case where one has not acted appropriately—

> not giving wealth or dharma; being stingy to suffering, protectorless beings; not offering dharma to those who seek dharma; neglecting to do service for the sick; not being a friend in need; doing little for the purpose of sentient beings[350]

—that is how major transgressions and faults will occur.

2.7 Protecting the Awakening Mind

Completely protecting the awakening mind: One should guard against forgetting, undermining, and giving up the awakening mind. As the *Kāśyapa Chapter Sūtra* states, these include:

> Causing those without regret to have regret; deceiving the preceptor, teacher, and objects of generosity; not having the superior thought in abundance; deceiving and agitating sentient beings; and insulting individuals who have generated the mind of awakening.[351]

As *The Absorption That Encapsulates All Merit* states:

> Son Without Desire! With these four qualities one will forget the awakening mind: excessive conceit, not respecting the

> Dharma, disregarding the spiritual friend, and saying bad words; and four further: making acquaintance with śrāvakas and pratyekabuddhas, admiring the Inferior Vehicle, having anger toward and slandering bodhisattvas, and pretending not to know the dharma; and four further: being deceptive to someone else, deceiving with one's own faults, being duplicitous to the guru, and having great attachment to profit and honor; and four further: not understanding evil action, being obscured with the obscurations of karma, having no fortitude for the altruistic attitude, and being without skillful means and wisdom. These will cause one to forget the awakening mind.[352]

The *Inquiry of the Nāga King Sāgara Sūtra* states:

> King of Nāgas! That wisdom of all-knowledge is free from the twenty-two bad paths and wrong paths: (1) not being free from the mentality of śrāvakas and not being free from the mentality of pratyekabuddhas, (2) having pride and excessive conceit, (3) deceiving others and self-deception, (4) conversing with nihilists, (5) engaging in erroneous practice, (6) being frightened by birth, (7) being swollen with pride, (8) engaging in argument, (9) having passionate attachment, (10) having hatred, (11) being ignorant, (12) encountering obstacles of karma, (13) encountering obstacles of powerful dharmas, (14) praising oneself and demeaning others, (15) not wanting to share the dharma, (16) being forgetful, (17) consorting with sinful friends, (18) having a hateful attitude to the spiritual teacher, (19) not being harmonious with the six perfections, (20) having the extremes of nihilism and permanency, (21) performing the four means of conversion

> with nonmastery of skillful means, and (22) not separating from all sins. With these one will forget the awakening mind.

Also, the *Gaṇḍavyūha* states:

> Hey! Sons of the Victorious One, I do not see a greater karmic retribution than negative thoughts occurring among bodhisattvas.

Likewise, one should look in sūtras that speak extensively on this, such as *The Seal of Engagement in Kindling the Power of Faith*.

2.8 The Causes for Downfalls to Occur

The causes for downfalls to occur: being without a lineage, having little compassion, not being frightened by the misery of saṃsāra, being under the influence of evil friends, thinking that highest awakening is far away, being overpowered by Māra, serving an individual of the Inferior Vehicle, making effort in the texts of the Small Vehicle, abandoning sentient beings, uttering insults and having hostility toward bodhisattvas, and not abandoning a position unharmonious with the awakening mind. Furthermore, being without awareness, without conscientiousness, without humility, and having many defilements.

2.9 The Negative Consequence of Letting Go

The negative consequence of letting go: If the sentient beings of the trichiliocosm became arhats and one were to kill all of them and also perform the five heinous actions, the sin of letting go would be even greater. Moreover, the number of dust particles that pervade the limits of space is known by the Buddha, but the measure of this sin—just this—cannot be known by the Buddha. One should look in the sūtras, *Introduction to the Practice of Awakening*, and so forth, for the extensive meaning of this.

2.10 The Benefit of Causing the Arising in Another of the Generation of the Awakening Mind

As for the benefit of rejoicing in the generation of the mind of awakening in others, there is this from the *Perfection of Wisdom in Eight Thousand Lines*:

> The measurable number of all the world realms is knowable, but as for the benefit of making others enter into generating the awakening mind...

—one should look at Mahāyāna sūtras and the *Introduction to the Practice of Awakening*.[353]

> Even the buddhas and bodhisattvas of the ten directions are not able to cognize this. The measure of merit made by rejoicing in the generation of the awakening mind in others is unknowable.[354]

One should look in the sūtras for the extensive meaning.[355]

2.11 The Negative Consequence of Interrupting Others' Generation of Mind

As for the negative consequence of interrupting others' generation of mind, the *Obtaining the Roots of Virtue Sūtra*[356] states:

> Śāradvatiputra, a person who desires to interrupt the generation of mind or causes interruption . . . will have no opportunity for nirvāṇa.

Likewise, the *Perfection of Wisdom in Eight Thousand Lines* states:

> It is a greater sin than performing the five heinous actions and killing as many arhats as there are sands of the Ganges River in three thousand world systems.

Also, the *Introduction to the Practice of Awakening* states:

> Whoever interrupts and hinders the merit of generating the awakening mind becomes inadequate for the purposes of sentient beings; limitless are the bad migrations of that person.[357]

One should look in the sūtras for the extensive meaning.

2.12 Increasing the Awakening Mind

Increasing of the awakening mind: That mind itself, the awakening mind, increases in three aspects: the awakening mind increases by way of the discipline of vows, the discipline of collecting virtuous dharmas, and the discipline of effecting the aims of sentient beings. For example, like the gradual increase of the waxing moon, this mind will also increase.

> Moreover, since it is superior by virtue of its vast and extensive purity, causes great benefit, and is virtuous itself, the pure thought is the superior thought.[358]

This is taught in the *Ornament of Mahāyāna Sūtras*. The superior thought is like the beginning of the moon and is also called the engaging awakening mind.

Three Aspects of Conduct

The "Chapter on Conduct" in Asaṅga's *Bodhisattva Stages* states that conduct has three aspects: naturally endowed conduct, accustomed conduct, and conduct based on accepting vows.

Naturally Endowed Conduct

Regarding naturally endowed conduct: All sentient beings have a single lineage, possess the essence of the tathāgata (*tathāgatagarbha*), and possess the Mahāyāna lineage. Although one may have the fortune to succeed when practicing, nevertheless, the lineage remains covered with four types of faults. As the *Ornament of Mahāyāna Sūtras* states:

> Briefly, the fault of lineage is expressed in four aspects: being accustomed to defilements, having bad friends, being destitute, and being under the power of another.[359]

This said, the individual who possesses the lineage naturally has great compassion and naturally possesses in the mental continuum the virtues of the perfections called "naturally endowed conduct."

Accustomed Conduct

Accustomed conduct has three aspects: from a past life up to this life, one has great familiarity with the Great Vehicle, has moderate familiarity, or has been accustomed from immeasurable previous lives. For this reason, Maitreya states:

> Venerating the buddhas, producing roots of virtue under

them, being protected by the spiritual friend: this is the vessel who hears the teaching.

Engaging in proper worship and respect of the buddhas, and practicing giving, morality, and so forth: that one is understood by the holy ones as a vessel.[360]

Conduct Based on Accepting Vows

In this regard, there is the discipline based on properly accepting vows: the preceptor, having examined well by way of three examinations, should bestow discipline according to the level of the vessel. For the aforementioned individual, the preceptor should give the vows related to the four great basic downfalls of the prātimokṣa, along with the accompanying lesser restrictions, the four similar downfalls of the Mahāyāna, and the forty-six minor downfalls. For the moderate individual [i.e., an individual with moderate familiarity with Mahāyāna], one should bestow the vows of that moderate individual. On top of that, one should bestow vows related to the eighteen root downfalls of the *Ākāśagarbha* and so forth, and the fourteen faults mentioned by Ācārya Śāntideva. For the third individual, in addition to these, the four hundred disciplines that are taught in the *Saptaśatikā* and the precepts of the bodhisattva path of accumulation that are taught in the Mahāyāna sūtras should be maintained. As for one on the path of accumulation, the discipline of vows is foremost. For the person on the path of preparation, the discipline that collects virtuous qualities is foremost. For the person who is beyond the worldly path, the discipline that achieves the purpose of sentient beings is foremost. If you calculate in the continuum of a single individual, the individual at the time of the small path of accumulation should make effort in the precepts of the first type. The individual at the time of the moderate path of accumulation should make efforts in the precepts of the moderate individual. The third individual should make effort in the precepts of the third type. Intending the aforementioned accustomed discipline, the *Cultivating Faith in the Mahāyāna Sūtra*[361] states:

> The bodhisattva-follower with predispositions for faith in the Mahāyāna follows in this way: whether moving, sitting, sleeping, sick, drunk, or crazy, one will always have faith in the Mahāyāna. The bodhisattva, adhering faithfully to the Great Vehicle in this life as well as future lives, will—even if one has forgotten the awakening mind in those lives—not be in an inferior situation or have a mind that has inferior fortune. The bodhisattva will not even be tempted to identify with pratyekabuddhas, śrāvakas, and evil friends. How can one be tempted by other tīrthikas? When one comes across even a small condition for faith in the Mahāyāna, one will swiftly and continuously produce strong faith in the Mahāyāna for that purpose. Therefore, inclinations to faith in the Mahāyāna will increase in later lives, up until unsurpassable fully complete awakening.[362]

2.13 The Benefits of the Awakening Mind

In this regard, the benefits of the awakening mind have two aspects: (1) the benefits of aspiration and (2) the benefit of engaging.

The Benefits of Aspiration

The benefits of aspiration are limitless. In brief, the awakening mind does not cut off the continuous lineage of the three jewels in the world. It is the seed or cause of all virtuous actions, destroying sin, uplifting from downfalls, and rendering nonexistent all interruptions, epidemics, devils, and so forth. The *Obtaining the Roots of Virtue Sūtra* states:

> Śāradvatiputra, firstly, the heap of merit of the awakening mind is not merely a common or minor matter. Accordingly, one is not able to proclaim the merit even in a hundred, a thousand, or a hundred thousand eons. How could one know the measurement of the merit of bodhisattvas' generation of the mind of awakening?

The *Perfection of Wisdom in Eight Thousand Lines* states:

> The merit is greater in someone generating the awakening mind for one day, half a day, or a finger snap than in someone possessed of substantialist views creating for an eon the roots of merit equal to the sands of the Ganges River.

Also, the *Introduction to the Practice of Awakening* states:

> If those who are bound in the prison of saṃsāra generate the awakening mind for one moment, they will be proclaimed a Son of the Sugata, and will be venerated by gods and men in the world.
>
> Seizing this impure form, the awakening mind transforms it into the priceless image of the Buddha-gem. Grasp tightly the supreme elixir, the awakening mind, which must be thoroughly transmuted.[363]

The Benefit of Engaging

The benefit of the engaging mind is stated in the *Introduction to the Practice of Awakening*:

> Although the result of the mind that aspires for awakening is great within the cycle of existence, it is not a source of uninterrupted merit like the mind that engages.[364]

And further,

> From that moment on, an uninterrupted stream of merit, equal to the sky, constantly arises, even when one is asleep or distracted.[365]

Regarding the benefits of both of these, one should look for the extensive meaning in the *Introduction to the Practice of Awakening*, the *Gaṇḍavyūhasūtra*, the *Bodhisattva Stages*, and so forth, as well as in the sūtras.

CHAPTER 5

Entry to the Two Realities

Atiśa based his teaching of Madhyamaka thought and practice on the two realities, conventional reality (saṃvṛtisatya) and ultimate reality (paramārthasatya). Entry to the Two Realities *succinctly lays out in twenty-eight verses a general exposition on the two realities. Atiśa composed this work between 1012 and 1025 while residing in Sumatra and studying under Serlingpa. Serlingpa inquired about Atiśa's philosophical views in a letter and Atiśa composed this set of verses as a response. Atiśa wrote* Entry to the Two Realities *in order to change the philosophical view of Serlingpa from a Yogācāra position to that of the Madhyamaka. Atiśa's introductory text on Madhyamaka presents his understanding based on the synthesis of a number of previous Indian Madhyamaka thinkers.*[366]

In the Indian language: *Satyadvayāvatāra*
In the Tibetan language: *Bden pa gnyis la 'jug pa*

Homage to the Great Compassionate One!

1. The dharma taught by buddhas perfectly relies on two realities: the conventional reality of the world and ultimate reality.

2. The conventional has two aspects: one that is mistaken and one that is correct. The former is twofold: the moon reflected on water and the conceptions of bad doctrines.

3. Something that is pleasing only as long as it is not examined, that arises and ceases to exist, and that is capable of causal efficiency is held to be correct convention.

4. The ultimate is one only. Others maintain that it is twofold. How can the nature of reality, which cannot be established as anything, be two, three, and so on?

5. The ultimate is defined as nonarising, noncessation, and so forth, according to the formula given by treatises. Because of the way in which different ultimates do not exist, there is neither a subject nor its property for inferential reasoning.

6. There is not any differentiation in emptiness. When cognized in a nonconceptual manner, it is conventionally designated that "emptiness is seen."

7. It is said in the very profound sūtras that the state of nonseeing is seeing ultimate reality. In that (ultimate reality), there is neither seeing nor seer, but peace without beginning or end.

8. Reality is devoid of entity and nonentity, free from conceptions, free from objects, without support, without basis, without coming or going, unexemplified.

9. It is ineffable, invisible, unchanging, and unconditioned. If a yogi realizes that, the afflictive and cognitive obstructions are eliminated.

10. Direct perception and inference are the two valid cognitions accepted by Buddhists. The deluded whose vision is narrow say that emptiness is understood by these two.

11. If it were, it would follow that even tīrthikas and śravakas would understand the nature of reality, not to mention the proponents of representation-only, and the Mādhyamikas would be no different from them.

12b. This being so, all tenets would also agree because they understand reality through valid cognition.

12cd–13. Because all reasonings are not in agreement, would not the nature of reality that is understood through valid cognition become manifold? Direct perception and inference are useless. In order to refute tīrthikas, Buddhist masters have composed digests on valid cognition.

14. The master scholar Bhavya stated clearly in scripture that the ultimate is not realized by either conceptual or nonconceptual consciousness.

15. Who has understood emptiness? Nāgārjuna, who was predicted by the Tathāgata and saw the truth of the nature of reality, and his disciple Candrakīrti.

16ab. Ultimate reality may be understood by means of the lineage of special instructions from them.

16c–e. The articles of dharma are said to number 84,000. All of them are inclined toward and lead to this ultimate reality.

17ab. One is liberated by understanding emptiness. All meditational development is for this purpose.

17c–f. But if one has contempt for the correct conventional reality and meditates on emptiness, the conventional cause and effect, virtue and evil deeds, and so on, will deceive one in the next world.

18. Those who rely on a bit of learning without understanding the meaning of discrimination and do not create merit—such despicable persons are destroyed. Wrongly perceived emptiness will destroy people of little wisdom.

19. The Ācārya Candrakīrti has stated as follows: "Conventional reality functions as a means, and ultimate reality functions as the goal. Those who do not understand the difference between the two have a bad understanding and get a bad rebirth."

20. The ultimate cannot be understood without relying on the conventional. Without the stairway of correct convention, a wise man cannot ascend to the top of the palace of reality.

21. When the conventional that appears is analytically examined just as it is, nothing whatsoever is found. The unfindable is itself the ultimate and the nature of reality abiding from the beginning.

22ab. The conventional that appears just as it is is established by being produced by causes and conditions.

22cd. If it were impossible to establish it, by whom would the moon in water and the like be produced?

23. Therefore all appearances are established as being produced by various causes and conditions. If the continuance of conditions is interrupted, they do not arise even conventionally.

24. So if one is not deluded with views and one has extremely pure conduct, without following a mistaken path, one will go to the place of Akaniṣṭha.

25. Time is short and things to be known are manifold. But since the span of time is only as long as ignorance, one should select what one prefers, just as a goose extracts milk from water.

26. Although those with narrow vision are not able to ascertain the two realities, this presentation on the two realities of Nāgārjuna's tradition was given relying on the statements of authoritative teachers.

27. If people of today have faith in this demonstration composed under the auspices of the king of Sumatra, it should be accepted after thorough analysis, not just by faith and not just out of reverence.

28. After the king of Suvarṇadvīpa, the Gurupāla, sent the monk Devamati to me, and under his auspices, I composed this *Entry to the Two Realities*. It should be examined by present-day scholars.

CHAPTER 6

The Song with a Vision for the Realm of Reality

After seven years and five months in Central Tibet, Atiśa gave teachings based on songs. This song on the dharmadhātu, or realm of reality, provides a summation of Buddhist and non-Buddhist philosophical views on reality in a little over one hundred forty verses. Atiśa discusses the realm of reality in the first twenty-five verses, fourteen of which are based on the work of Nāgārjuna. Atiśa then summarizes Buddhist views (verses 26–96), beginning with Madhyamaka and descending to Vaibhāṣika tenets, follows this with non-Buddhist philosophical tenets (verses 97–142), and then provides concluding verses (verses 143–147).[367]

In the Indian language: *Dharmadhātudarśanagītiḥ*
In the Tibetan Language: *Chos kyi dbyings su blta ba'i glu*

I pay homage to the Omniscient One!

I bow to the realm of reality
That resides in all sentient beings.
Being totally ignorant about it,
One roams in the three spheres of existence.
In due order, I will describe
Those who perceive the realm of reality and the others who do not.

That which is profound, peaceful, suchness free from reference points,
Unconditioned luminosity,
Is unborn, unceasing, and primordially pure,
Its nature is nirvāṇa.

One should perceive the realm of reality, which is without middle or end.
It is beheld by subtle, nonconceptual mental eyes
Without the blur of dullness and agitation.

Having purified that which serves as the cause of saṃsāra,
This very purified state is nirvāṇa; likewise it is also the dharma body.

Just as the essence of butter is not visible when mixed with milk,
Likewise, the realm of reality is not seen when it is mixed with afflictions.

Just as through the purification of milk, the essence of butter becomes purified,
Similarly, through the purification of afflictions, the realm of reality becomes purified.

Just as a lamp placed in a vase does not shine with any sparks of light,
Likewise, when stuck in the vase of the afflictions, the realm of reality does not shine forth.

Wherever holes are made in a vase,
From these very places issues forth the nature of light.

When the thunderbolt of concentration smashes the vase of afflictions,
Then that realm of reality illuminates everything up to the ends of space.

The dharmadhātu is unborn and never disintegrates.
It is without afflictions in all the three times
And is stainless in the beginning, middle, and end.

A lapis-lazuli jewel
Radiates all the time,
But when residing in its ore
Its light does not shine forth.

So, too, although the realm of reality is stainless,
When covered with afflictions,
Its light is not seen in the world.
When liberated, its light shines forth.

Just as unthreshed rice covered with chaff
Is not considered to be rice,
Likewise, when covered by afflictions
This realm of reality is not considered "Buddha."

Just as when released from the chaff
Rice becomes manifest,
Likewise, when liberated from the afflictions
The dharma body becomes manifest.

Just as the child in
A pregnant women's womb is unseen,

Similarly, being covered by the afflictions,
The realm of reality also is not seen.

Since the realm of reality is neither a self,
Nor woman, nor man,
Free from anything to be apprehended,
How, then, can it be conceived as a subject?

The mind is purified by these three:
Impurity, impermanence, and suffering.
The best teaching for the purification
Of the mind is essencelessness.

The sūtras that teach emptiness,
Which were taught by the Victorious One,
All dispel the afflictions
But do not destroy the element.

Just as horns on a rabbit's head do not exist and are only imagined,
Likewise, all things do not exist and are only imagined.

As they are not made of solid atoms,
The horns of an ox do not exist either.
Just as before so it is after,
What is to be imagined there?

Since arising is a dependent occurrence,
And cessation is a dependent occurrence,
There is not one single thing that exists—
How could the childish think that there is?

The nature of the realm of reality is like space.
Like this element of space, it has no causes or conditions.
Birthless, ageless, unabiding, unceasing,
It is unconditioned.

It is inseparable from the Buddha's qualities
The attainment of the lineage by its very nature.
Since its qualities lack deception and delusion,
It is primordial, natural peacefulness.

As it is like the ocean,
Words, examples, and the intellect
Cannot find its depth or end.
Therefore, it is extremely profound.

As the realm of reality has no distinctions,
Differences in view are not possible.
However, due to the difference in intellect
I speak a little bit about different views.

Those who follow the Middle Way
Assert its meaning according to two realities:
The conventional and the ultimate.

Those who know the distinction between the two realities are not
Deluded about the words of the Sage. They, having accumulated
The collections in their entirety, accomplish their own and others' welfare
And go definitely to the perfect other side.

Conventional reality is the elaboration
Of "I" and "mine," permanence and nihilism,

Affliction and purification, cause and effect,
And subject and object.

That which is emptiness, selflessness, and peaceful,
Which is not agitated by elaboration,
Without any differentation, and lacking conceptualization,
That is ultimate reality.

Through correct and incorrect,
Enumerated and unnumerated,
The two realities are separately distinguished.

Mere imputation, entities of sight and sound,
Nominal, deception, illusion,
Are synonymous with conventional reality.

Emptiness, reality limit,
Signlessness, the ultimate,
And the realm of reality are synonyms.
As it obscures, it is conventional,
As it is unchanging, it is the ultimate.

Because there are two consciousnesses,
Correct and incorrect, there are two realities.
If someone objects, "There is no correct consciousness,"
It's true; it exists only conventionally.

To those who seek reality, at first, one should state,
"Everythings exists." When they have understood reality and
Have become detached, one then later declares things as isolated
(*viviktatā*).

The two realities are neither one nor different
Because four faults are stated for each.
Whoever conceptualizes them as one or different
Engages in an improper approach.

If you accept entities,
Desire and hatred will endlessly arise.
On upholding a horrible view,
Quarrels will arise.

One who cognizes objects
Has neither attainment nor realization.
When not even a similitude of receptivity is obtained,
What can be said about nirvāṇa?

If their view of emptiness is wrong,
Those of little wisdom will be hurt.
Like a wrongly held snake,
Or a spell wrongly cast.

All the victorious ones taught that emptiness
Is the removal of all views.
Those for whom emptiness is a view
Are said to be incurable.

Those who perceive entities and nonentities
Due to own nature and other nature
Do not perceive the essence
Of the Buddha's doctrine.

Nonexistence presupposes existence.
Existence presupposes nonexistence.

Therefore, nonexistence should not be discussed
And existence should not be imputed.

Realists attain the happy realms;
Nihilists go to lower realms;
Because of understanding reality as it is,
Those who do not rely on either of the two extremes attain liberation.

Riding the horse chariot of the two systems,
Holding the reigns of reasoning,
They, for that reason,
Become followers of the Great Vehicle in its true meaning.

For all things, ranging from
The appearance of forms and so forth to the Sugata
Should be contemplated as the very Middle
Like the horns of a rabbit and an ox.

Reality (*tattva*) that is free from the four extremes—
Neither existent, nor nonexistent, nor both existent and nonexistent,
Nor even neither existent nor nonexistent—is known by the
Mādhyamika.

While the middle is free from extremes,
The middle also does not exist, as it is devoid of extremes.
The view that is without extremes and middle
That is the perfect view.

That is the unsurpassable view.
The wise always meditate on it.

Whoever enters that view
Will attain omniscience.

Vijñānavādins accept
Three natures: The imaginary, dependent, and perfected.
Respectively, they are imputed, arising from causes, and are unchanging.

By whichever conceptual cognition,
Whatever thing is conceptualized,
That has the imaginary nature
Which does not exist.

The dependent nature is conceptual,
As it arises from conditions.
The perfected nature is that which precedes it
And is perpetually unchanging.

Since the extremes of existence and nonexistence do not exist,
The perfected nature is neither different nor not different from the dependent nature.
This is explained as impermanent and so forth.
Through the examples of the lapis lazuli and crystal,
The three natures should be understood.

Each, respectively, has two divisions:
Imputations as self and phenomena,
Pure and impure,
Changeless and unmistaken.

All those who are wise
Make effort for introspection.

The consciousness which is free from
Subject and object ultimately exists.

There is nothing that originates,
Nor does anything cease.
It is only the cognition
That originates and ceases.

Nonexistent things appear
But they do not arise from matter, nor from other things,
Nor from nonexistence, since that has two faults.
Therefore, they have the nature of mind.

Consciousness arises as something
Opposite from the nature of matter.
What is immaterial in nature
Is accepted here as self-cognizability.

Space, earth, wind, sun
Oceans, directions, and waterfalls
Are parts of real internal consciousness
That appear as externally existent.

Since it appears as the nature of luminosity
Its relation to that is not hidden.
One who knows that relation
Thereby recognizes the knowable.

If the mind abandons its self-grasping,
Which is like the blade of a sword or fingertips,
As it said in the *Saṃdhinirmocana Sūtra,*
its self-luminosity will not be lost.

Therefore, the defining characteristic of mind
Is established as reflexive awareness.
Since it is difficult to realize,
Its nature cannot be analyzed.

Reflexive awareness, because of its subtlety,
Can only be subtly perceived by the buddhas.
Although it resides in one's own body,
Fools like me cannot see it.

Since clarity and mind have a relation
Of identity, they are of mere mind.
The nature of the mind is real,
But the mental images are false and mistaken.

Since the mind is confused by images,
Oneness is a dualistic appearance.
Why are they not thoroughly known
From the distinctions of subject and object?

Since the image of the perceived is immovable,
It appears as if it were an external thing.
But since the image of the apprehension is animate,
It appears as if it were inside.
Having eliminated that phenomenal sign,
One should cultivate pristine wisdom, which is like space.

The nature of the mind is uncontaminated.
As long as the contaminated seeds are not destroyed
That is the state of the storehouse consciousness.
When it is destroyed, it becomes the uncontaminated element
(*dhāturanāsrava*).

The liberated body
Is always like the sun and its rays.
Since it is the abode of Buddha qualities,
It is the dharma body of the protectors.

Those who have entered the vehicle of śrāvakas,
The aggregates, sense powers, sense spheres,
Five bases, and the three times
Are devoid of self and mine.

All the existents that are to be apprehended
Are grasped with the object.
Both are accepted as ultimately existent.

It is said that the afflictions are eliminated
Through seeing and meditating on the truths.
The truths are of four kinds:
Suffering, as well as origin,
Cessation, and path.
Their sequence is according to their realization.

Suffering is the appropriated aggregates.
The origin of suffering is karma and the afflictions.
Cessation is the two cessations.
The path is the thirty-seven aspects.

Residing in moral conduct, one who has heard the teachings
And reflected upon them should practice meditation.
The way of training in virtue (*śrāmaṇya*) is the stainless path.
Its result is both conditioned and unconditioned.

There are eighty-nine paths of liberation
Along with their cessations.
The four results are established
Since five causes are possible.

There are four kinds of śrāvakas:
Those who are emanations, those who will be awakened,
Those on the way to peace, and those who uphold tenets.
The schools may be divided into two, four, or eighteen types.
The two are the Vaibhāṣikas and the Sautrāntikas.

A Vaibhāṣika is one who asserts that knowledge of objects such as form
Is through a cognition without cognitive images.
A Sautrāntika is one who asserts that knowledge of objects
Is through the experience of cognitive images that are
Causally supported by the objects.

The four are the Mahāsāṃghika, Sarvāstivāda, Sthaviravāda, and the Mahāsaṃmitīya.
The eighteen are as follows:
Pūrvaśaila, Aparaśaila, Haimavata, Prajñāptivādins, and Lokottaravādins
Are the five ordination lineages (*nikāyas*) of the Mahāsāṃghika.

The Mūlasarvāstivāda, Kāśyapīya, Mahīśāsaka,
Dharmaguptaka, Bāhuśrutīya, Tāmraśāṭīya, and Vibhajyavāda
Comprise those of the Sarvāstivāda.

The Jetavanīyas, Abhayagirivāsins, and the Mahāvihāravāsins
Comprise the Sthaviras.
The Kaurukulla, Āvantaka

And the Vatsīputrīya are considered to be the three types of
Saṃmitīyas.
These are the eighteen different kinds of ordination lineages
In accordance with their differences in place, purpose, or
teachers.

One who seeks the awakening of a pratyekabuddha
Eliminates the conceptions of a cognitive object
But has not eliminated the conceptions of the cognitive subject.
Thus, the path which is like a rhinoceros is their support.
They will reach awakening
By meditation at the end of a hundred eons.

Dependent arising has
Twelve links in three divisions.
Two in the beginning, two in the end,
And eight in the middle complete the set.

Ignorance is the phase of afflictions in a previous life.
The compositional factors are the
Actions in a previous life.
Consciousness is aggregates at conception.
Name and form are the aggregates from this moment on,
Until the arising of the six sense spheres.

That appearance of the six sense spheres are the five aggregates
Until the coming together of the three: the sense-faculty, object,
and consciousness.
Contact until the moment when the capacity of distinguishing
the cause
Of pleasure, suffering, and so forth is acquired.

Feeling (*vedanā*) is until sexual union.
Craving (*tṛṣṇā*) is the state of those who desire enjoyments and sexual union.
Grasping (*upādāna*) is the state of those who run around in search of pleasures.

Existence (*bhava*) is the state of performing actions that have a future result.
Conjunction is the birth (*jāti*).
Old age and death (*jarāmaraṇa*) is the state until sensation (*vedanā*).

This teaching of dependent arising is according to states (*avasthā*).
The members are called by the name of the factor which is most important to it.
It is indicated in order to reverse the delusion regarding the
Past, the future, and the interval between past and future.

Three are afflictions, two are karmic action.
Seven are the phenomenal basis and result as well.
In two sections (*kāṇḍa*), cause and effect are abbreviated,
For they can be inferred from the teaching of the middle [i.e., the present existence].

Here, arising is the cause,
Whereas the arisen is the effect.
Among the twelve links
Five are cause and seven are result.

The aspects of dependent arising are
The projector, the projected,

Materializer, the materialized, and the defects.
They consist respectively of
Three, four, three, one, and one link.

Pervasive suffering, suffering of change,
And suffering of pain consist respectively of
Five, two, and five links.
In the three realms they occur with twelve, eleven, and ten
Links respectively.

Spontaneous birth is through eleven links;
Birth from wombs and eggs are from twelve links;
Birth from heat and moisture may be from any link as is
appropriate.
The modes of birth should be applied to the five realms of
transmigration.

Two links (ignorance and conditioning)
Are from three links (existence, birth, old age and death).
From the two arise the other seven.
And from those seven, the three that again produce two arise.
In this manner, the wheel of existence goes round and round.

The nature and aspects of saṃsāra occur
With a host of limitless problems
For whatever, in whichever place, in whatever way, for however
long, in whichever manner.

Gather up and cast away.
Enter into the Buddha's teaching.
Like a great elephant in a house of mud,
Conquer the Lord of Death's battalions.

Whoever with great circumspection
Practices this discipline of the dharma,
Having abandoned the cycle of rebirth,
Will make an end to suffering.

In nirvāṇa there is the cessation
Of that from which one passes into nirvāṇa,
In nirvāṇa there is the cessation
Of that from which one passes into nirvāṇa,
the one who (attains nirvāṇa), the means, the time,
the place, the purpose, the manner, and so on up
to its nature, aspect, goal divisions, activities,
and qualities.

Tīrthikas are of two kinds;
Emanations and those who are independent.
The latter are through birth or by training.

Those by birth have excluded categories of beings and are attached to mistaken craving.
Those through training reside in concentration or speculative philosophy.
Those in concentration through supersensory powers conceptualize views into sixty-two.

Eternalism is of four kinds
And there are four other kinds of eternalism.
There are four kinds of nonabandonments; four endlessnesses; and two kinds of causelessness.
These eighteen views are conceptualized in terms of the extreme of the beginning.

There are sixteen views which assert that designations exist.
There are eight views that refute designations.
Likewise, there are eight views which uphold "neither-existence-nor-nonexistence."
There are seven nihilistic [views] and five [views] that speak of attaining liberation in this life.
These are forty-four views which conceptualize in terms of the extreme of the end.

Speculative logicians such as the Sāṃkhya and so forth
Establish tenets through reasons.
The Sāṃkhya assert three attributes (*guṇas*),
Goodness (*sattva*), passion (*rajas*), and darkness (*tamas*).

The attributes of goodness,
Which manifests sometimes,
Are held to be joy, satisfaction, bliss,
Happiness, peacefulness, and intellect.

The signs of passion are held to be
Sorrow, distress, grief,
Attachment, and impatience
Because they appear.

Delusion, ignorance, negligence,
Sleep, and distraction,
Which also appear sometimes,
These are the attributes of darkness.

The primal nature which is the nature of the three attributes
Is not visible.
That which is visible
Is exceedingly insignificant, like a magical illusion.

From the primal nature issues the great principle.
From that arises the threefold ego (*ahaṃkāra*).
From that arises the eleven sense capacities and the five subtle elements,
And from the five subtle elements,

The five gross elements, comprise twenty-four that
Are the primal nature and manifestation.
They are not conscious.
The person who knows all these is conscious.

One who knows the twenty-five principles (*tattvas*),
Whether that one has matted hair, a shaven head, or a tuft,
Wherever that person may dwell,
That one becomes liberated without doubt.

The Vaiśeṣikas assert six real things (*arthas*),
Nine substances and twenty-four qualities.
The six real things are: substance (*dravya*), quality (*guṇa*), action (*karma*),
Generality (*sāmānya*), uniqueness (*viśeṣa*), and inherence (*samavāya*).

Action is of five kinds.
Generality, uniqueness, and inherence are all twofold.
The knowledge of the six real things is supreme.
It surpasses all the Vedas.

Digambara Jains assert nine real things:
Life (*jīva*), contamination (*āsrava*), vow (*saṃvara*), youthfulness (*nirjarā*),
Death (*ajīva*), bondage (*bandha*), sin (*pāpa*), merit (*puṇya*), and liberation (*mokṣa*).
Whoever sees these nine becomes pure.

The Nyāyaiyikas assert sixteen real things:
The means of valid knowledge, the object of valid knowledge, doubt,
Purpose, example, tenet, members of a syllogism, confutation, ascertainment,

Discussion, wrangling, cavil, fallacy,
Quibble, analogue, and point of defeat.
One attains liberation through these sixteen.

The Mīmāṃsakas assert four real things:
Earth, water, fire, and air.
They are unconditioned and permanent.
They remain without being produced or destroyed.

There is not action and result.
Likewise, the extremes of the beginning
And the end do not exist.
Therefore, those who examine in this way
Will be liberated by merely seeing.

Those who accept Viṣṇu as the creator claim
Among the Ādityas I am Viṣṇu and
Among luminaries, the sun.
Among the wind gods I am Marīci and
Among stars and constellations, the moon.

Among the Vedas I am the Sāma Veda.
Among the gods I am Indra.
Among the sense faculties I am the mind.
And among the elements I am the earth.

Among the Rudras I am Śaṅkara,
Among Yakṣas and Rakṣas, the Lord of Wealth (Kubera).
Among the Vasus I am fire, among mountains I am Meru,
In the alphabet I am "ā."

The ten incarnations of Viṣṇu are Matsya (Fish), Kūrma (Tortoise), Varāha (Pig),
Narasiṃha (Man-Lion), Vāmana (Dwarf), Paraśurāma, Rāma, Kṛṣṇa, Buddha, and Kalkī.
One who always contemplates the qualities of Viṣṇu will obtain bliss.

Those who accept Śiva as the Lord
Assert that Śiva is the creator
Of this entire world.
He has eight qualities as follows:

Subtlety, lightness, omnipresence,
Pleasures at will, greatness, lordship, subjugation,
And residing wherever he wishes.

With his hands, feet, eyes,
Faces and bodies,
He creates numerous beings and destroys them.
Therefore, he is called "Subtlety" (*aṇimā*).

Enjoying himself residing in space,
Wind, earth, water, and fire,
While contracting and expanding
He is therefore called "Lightness" (*laghimā*).

Venerated in the three realms
Worshipped by animate
And inanimate alike
Therefore, he is called "Greatness" (*mahimā*).

He rules over all beings,
Animate and inanimate,
Doing whatever he desires.
Therefore, he is called "Lordship" (*iśitva*).

Relying upon his self and independent,
Not fearing anyone,
Ruler over all,
Therefore, he is called "Subduer" (*vaśitva*).

Because it pervades everywhere,
In heaven and lower realms of rebirth,
The quality is called "Omnipresence" (*vyāpti*).

Because he arises within a twinkling of an eye
Wherever the three qualities
Of goodness, motility, and darkness exist,
Therefore, he is called "Pleasure at Will" (*prakāmya*).

Whatever he himself might desire,
Whether it be liberation or a divine body,
Since he attains everything according to his desire,
Therefore, he is called "Abiding Wherever He Desires" (*kāmāvaśāyita*).

He who is subtle, solitary, and continues to exist,
Who creates and destroys everything

Who is a god, worthy of veneration, a giver of boons,
A Lord, the creator of all qualities,
He has attained tranquility.

This master does not have knowledge
Of either his own happiness or suffering.
Through the force of Īśvara,
One goes to heavenly rebirths or to hell.

Some say that if Īśvara who,
Like a potter, gives shape to the world, does not exist
Then there would be no Mount Meru, no earth, no ocean,
The beautifully arranged Sun and Moon, the two eyes of the world,
Would not exist. But as all things do exist, therefore Īśvara must have created this world.

Those who wish to attain the happy bliss of peace
Should always meditate on Īśvara as follows:
He is subtle, inconceivable, the creator, omniscient, wise,
The maker of everything, obtained through the practice of yoga,
The meditative object of those who meditate.
And his body is the moon, sun, earth, water, fire, wind, directions, and space.

The Kālavādins maintain that all real things
Are dependent upon and arise from time.
One whose uncle was Govinda and whose father was Dhanañjaya was killed,
Even though he was fearless and full of rage.
Time is difficult to surpass.

Time brings fruition to the material elements.
Time destroys all sentient beings.
Time is awake when others are sleeping.
Time is difficult to surpass.

Whose fort is three-storied, whose moat is the sea,
Whose armies are demons, whose wealth is Kubera,
And whose philosophy was promulgated by Śukrācārya—
That one, Rāvaṇa, perished through the force of time.

Those who assert inherent existence,
Entities are inherently established.
The redness of fire, the altruism of a holy person,
And the lovelessness of an unkindly person—
These three are inherently established.

Who has made the sharpness of thorns?
Who has made the marks on animals and birds?
The sweetness in sugarcane and the bitterness in lemon—
All of these are intrinsically established.

The heat of the sun and the coolness of the moon,
The attachment of ordinary persons and
The nonattachment of sages,
The satisfaction in happiness and
The torture in suffering—
These six are inherently established.

Those who assert causelessness
Explain that things are produced
Without depending upon any causes.

Who makes the manifold diversity
Of the filaments of lotuses and the sun and so forth?
Who has created the variegation
Of the peacock's tail and so forth?

Just as the rain, wind, and so forth,
Have no cause because they are adventitious,
So, too, is suffering and so forth without a cause.

Discouraged by its vastness and profundity,
Ignorant persons, due to their confusion,
Today deride the Mahāyāna and thus become
The foe of themselves and others.[368]

Regression even from moral conduct is preferable,
But regression from the right view is never preferable.
Heaven is attained by means of moral conduct;
One reaches the highest level by means of the right view.[369]

When there is not good rebirth for someone who,
Obscured by the force of ignorance,
Creates obstacles to seeing suchness,
Why speak of liberation?[370]

After seeing that the tīrthikas—
Who are the seeds of misfortune—are many,
Who wouldn't have compassion for the
People who long for the dharma?[371]

Therefore, those who seek liberation
Should perceive the realm of reality!

The Song with a Vision for the Realm of Reality composed by great master Dīpaṃkaraśrījñāna is completed. Translated by the very same Indian abbot and the Tibetan translator, the monk Tsultrim Gyalwa.

CHAPTER 7

Lamp for the Summary of Conduct

Lamp for the Summary of Conduct *is a brief text of twenty-one stanzas that outline daily practices according to the Mahāyāna way of the perfections. While Atiśa and his entourage stayed in Nepal on the way to West Tibet, they resided for a month with a Nepalese sthavira monk who was deaf. The monk requested a teaching on the perfections but he did not wish to follow the way of mantras. In the teaching Atiśa emphasized that both, mantras along with the perfections, lead to awakening, but then focused on the Perfection Path of the bodhisattva.*

In the Indian language: *Caryāsaṃgrahapradīpa*[372]
In the Tibetan language: *Spyod pa bsdus pa'i sgron me*

Homage to Avalokiteśvara!

I bow down to that supreme holy person,
Whose light rays of speech
Opens the lotuses of the hearts
Of all the deluded like me without exception.[373]

As the gurus and the buddhas have said
That awakening is achieved in dependence
Upon the Secret Mantra Vehicle and the perfections
I will write about just that.

I will not describe the Secret Mantra Vehicle here.
I will explain a little bit about
The pure activities of bodhisattvas
Who practice the system of the perfections.

Generating the awakening mind is a preliminary
To taking the bodhisattva vow.
Then one views all the sūtra collections without exception,
And studies the extent of the technical digests (*śāstras*).

When one protects purely, without diminishing,
The vows just as they have been explained
With one's body, speech, and mind,
Then one's conduct will be pure.

One should understand the portions of food,
Bind the doors of the faculties.
In the early and latter portions of the night,
One should exert themselves in yoga and not sleep.

Fear should arise
With even the slighest fault.
Divide the night into three parts and
Rise from sleep in the last part.

Cleanse your face and hands,
Or if you are not able to wash, it is suitable;
Then, while sitting on a comfortable seat,
One should recollect the true nature of things.

If one is not able due to being distracted
By phenomenal marks,

Then rise up and examine all appearances
As entities that are like illusions.
Moreover, the daily virtuous practice between sessions of
meditation,
Should be to complete the Sevenfold Worship.
Offer extensive aspirational prayers,
Or alternatively, cultivate the previous meditation.

Then, during mealtimes, say:
"This essenceless body should seek out
The highest essence."
Set the ship-like mind on the body,
Do not eat for the sake of becoming fat
Or eat due to the craving for taste.

Divide your food into four parts:
First, offer pure food to the gods,
Then give away extensive oblations
To the dharma protectors.
After your own food and drink,
Offer the remains to all the harmful spirits.

Between sessions of meditation,
One should speak enriching and wonderous conversation.
Then, one should arise and walk about a little
Circumambulating an object of worship,
Mutter mantras, read books, or alternatively,
Draw images of the Sugata.

One should circumambulate for
As long as one is not distracted.
Then, offer extensive aspirational prayers.

In brief, perform the tenfold practices[374] explained
By the Protector Maitreya;
Do not be distracted in mind and
Recollect that things are like illusions.

If it exists, offer it to the Saṃgha.
Otherwise, offer a feast for ordinary people.
Giving to those unprotected
Increases the yogi's accumulation of merit.

When the day's activities are complete,
And in the early evening, first,
One should establish cognition, free from elaboration,
In the unconditioned nature of reality.

When midnight comes,
With the perception of illuminating light (*ālokasaṃjñā*)
One should lie down in the lion pose,
And have virtuous sleep.

In general, when the mind is firm in meditative equipoise,
One should primarily refrain from virtuous actions and speech.
Alternatively, if meditative equipoise is not clear,
Then one should do as much virtuous actions and speech
As one is able, being in conformity with the world.

If the world is not in accord with one's thoughts,
Then say, "This is not my dharma."
Let go of your previous good intentions
And inquire about the local worldly practices.

I composed this teaching having been urged
By my friend in the land of Nepal.
If you do not aspire to the way of Secret Mantra Vehicle
O Sthavira, then practice accordingly.

The Lamp for the Summary of Conduct *composed by the Ācārya Śrī Dīpaṃkārajñāna is completed. The Indian preceptor himself and the translator monk Tsultrim Gyalwa translated and edited the text.*

CHAPTER 8

Special Instructions on Unique Mindfulness

Atiśa composed this brief work at the request of his Tibetan translator-disciple Naktso Lotsāwa Tsultrim Gyalwa. The text succinctly outlines the practices of wisdom and means for a bodhisattva who has not yet received a consecration for Secret Mantra practice. Atiśa concludes by citing verses to illustrate that while buddhas are bereft of any mental element, they benefit all sentient beings.

In the Indian language: *Ekasmṛtyupadeśa*
In the Tibetan language: *Dran pa gcig pa'i man ngag*

I pay homage to the Blessed Lord of the World!

After having respectfully bowed to the Omniscient One,
and having paid tribute to Ārya Nāgārjuna and Avadhūtipa,
I will write here the instructions for simultaneous entry/
simultaneous intuitive understanding.

Now, from when a bodhisattva has produced the first generation of the mind for awakening, and holding it close until obtaining the great consecration, there are two activities: the activity of wisdom and the activity of means.

Wisdom consists in the knowledge that all things are, from the beginning, unproduced, and from the very first are the realm of reality itself. The activity of this wisdom is for the beginner, for as long as not obtaining a consecration, to continuously, day and night, meditate on suchness.

Means consists in the awakening mind that does not relinquish sentient beings. The practice of means is to devote all mental, verbal, or physical acts, directly or indirectly, to all sentient beings. It is practiced in two phases: a phase where sentient beings are an object of observation, then a phase without any object of observation. Furthermore, there are the stages of the unskillful with diseased vision, and of the skillful purified of diseased vision.

At the moment when the realm of reality manifests itself, from here on wisdom is no longer acquired and pristine awareness abides becoming the realm itself. The activity of wisdom ceases because of arriving at the goal through practice. The activity of means becomes objectiveless, naturally, spontaneously without effort and striving.

Beginner bodhisattvas, since they still have the notion of a self in individuals, conceive of "sentient beings" and generate compassion for their suffering. Then, through practice they will discover that "sentient being" is only an imputed name for ephemeral entities that have not existed from the very first.

Otherwise, thinking that there is nothing else apart from the dependently arising aggregates, elements, and sensory spheres, or thinking that these things are only one's own mind, there is nothing else other than this, one generates compassion for those sufferings.

When at the level of a buddha there is no objective support, as the *Inquiry of Suvikrāntavikrāmi* states:[375]

> The gnosis of a buddha, a blessed one, sees nothing.
> Why? Because there is no object of gnosis.

Well then, does gnosis exist at this juncture or not? Ārya Nāgārjuna denies that it does, as he states:

> The mind has not been seen, and will not be seen, by all buddhas.
> What will one see of something that has the nature of having no nature.[376]

Thus, this is in accordance with the transmitted oral instructions. Therefore, buddhas do not have any other activity except for accomplishing the purposes of others, and, in this way, the purposes of others are the principal result that is the desired purpose of their practice. The Ārya Nāgārjuna has stated:

> The excellence of the purpose of others is accepted as the foremost
> result of awakening. Other than buddhahood itself and so forth,
> these other benefits are asserted as the result of this goal [i.e., awakening].

May these special instructions to penetrate reality reside in your mind.

As requested by Tsultrim Gyalwa, here is an abbreviated teaching. For the extensive teaching one should look at Nāgārjuna's instructions and the Mahāyāna sūtras. The instructions of simultaneous intuitive understanding were composed by Paṇḍita Dīpaṃkaraśrījñāna. They have been translated by the paṇḍita himself and by Tsultrim Gyalwa.

CHAPTER 9

Bodhisattva's Jewel Garland

Bodhisattva's Jewel Garland *is among Atiśa's most important works on essential practice. Atiśa prescribes a program of bodhisattva conduct in twenty-seven verses. The text is regarded by Atiśa's followers as a significant text on mind training and is the root text for both the Father Teachings and Son Teachings in the* Book of Kadam.[377]

In the Indian language: *Bodhisattvamaṇyāvalī*
In the Tibetan language: *Byang chub sems dpa'i nor bu'i phreng ba*

Homage to great compassion!

Homage to the deities of faith!

Homage to the spiritual teachers!

Abandon all hesitation,
Earnestly practice with sincerity.
Avoid lethargy, dullness, and laziness,
And always strive with energetic diligence.

With mindfulness, introspection, and conscientiousness
Always guard the doors of the senses.

Three times in the day, three times at night,
Repeatedly, examine your mental continuum.

Proclaim your own faults,
But do not seek out faults in others.
Make known the good qualities of others,
But conceal your own qualities.

Abandon gain and respect,
Always eliminate arrogance and fame.
Cultivate love and compassion,
And make firm the awakening mind.

Abandon the ten nonvirtuous deeds,
And always be firm in faith.
Have few desires, be content,
And have gratitude for the kindness of others.

Destroy anger and pride,
And have a humble attitude.
Abandon wrong livelihood,
And live by means according to the dharma.

Abandon material things,
And adorn yourself with the wealth of noble beings.
These are the riches of faith, moral conduct,
Modesty, shame,

Study, generosity,
And wisdom—these are the seven treasures.
These forms of wealth

Are seven treasures that are never exhausted.
Do not tell this to nonhuman persons.

Avoid noisy gatherings
And stay in solitude.
Avoid meaningless words,
Refrain from meaningless chatter,
And always control your speech.
When you see a spiritual teacher or preceptor,
Offer to serve them with respect.

One should recognize as a teacher
Those with extraordinary powers,
Persons with the eye of dharma,
And beginners on the path.

When you see any sentient being,
Recognize them as your parents, children, or relatives.
Avoid misleading friends and
Rely on spiritual friends.

You should abandon places of anger and displeasure,
And go to wherever it is pleasant.
You should abandon that which causes attachment
And reside without being attached to anything at all.

With attachment one does not attain a happy realm of rebirth,
And it kills even the life force of liberation.
Where you see virtuous qualities,
You should always strive to be there.

Whatever you intially set out to establish,
That very thing should be achieved first;
In this way, all will be properly done;
Otherwise, neither will be achieved.

Always detach from taking joy in sinful deeds.
When thoughts become inflated,
At that time deflate your pride,
And recollect your spiritual teacher's personal instructions.

Whenever your thoughts become discouraged,
Encourage yourself and raise up your thoughts.
You should recollect the *Perfection of Wisdom Sūtras* and
Always meditate on emptiness.

When objects of attachment and hatred appear,
See them as illusions or emanations.
When you hear unpleasant words,
Perceive them as echoes.
When your body suffers harm,
You should perceive it as the result of your past actions.

Through residing in the hermitage and wilderness,
Like the carcass of a wild animal,
One should conceal oneself and
Live in a state of nonattachment.

Always have faith in the meditational deity,
And whenever laziness or apathy occurs,
Then have contempt for yourself
And recollect the essence of ascetic practice.

Whenever you see another person,
Speak calmly and be straightforward.
Avoid frowns and angry glares,
And always have a smiling face.

Whenever you see others,
Enjoy in giving without stinginess.
Always eliminate jealousy
In order to protect another's mind.

Avoid all conflicts
And always have patience.
Neither flatter nor be a fickle friend,
But always be steady and reliable.

Avoid disparaging others and
Reside with a respectful attitude.
When giving advice to others,
Do so with compassion and benevolence.

Do not criticize the dharma.
Pursue whatever practice inspires you.
Through the doorway of the ten forms of dharma practice,
Strive day and night.

Examine your speech while among the multitude;
Examine your mind while in solitude.
Whatever virtues are collected in the three times of past, present,
and future,
Dedicate them all to great, unsurpassable awakening.

Bestow your merit to all sentient beings.
You should always offer the great prayer of aspiration
Comprised of seven limbs.
Having done so,

The collections of wisdom and merit will be accomplished,
And the two obscurations will be eliminated.
As you make meaningful the obtained human life,
unsurpassable awakening will be attained.

The Bodhisattva's Jewel Garland *composed by the Indian preceptor Dīpaṃkāraśrījñāna is completed. The Indian preceptor himself and the translator-monk Tsultrim Gyalwa translated, edited, and finalized the text.*

CHAPTER 10

Middle Way Special Instructions for Cultivating All the Qualities in the Scriptures

Atiśa followed the Madhyamaka tradition of Nāgārjuna and Candrakīrti. The following work is a written account of a special teaching that Atiśa gave on Madhyamaka while in Tibet. The special instructions succinctly prescibe the practice of meditation for a Mādhyąmika. The work is similar in content to Atiśa's Special Instructions on the Middle Way (Madhyamakopadeśa) *and its commentaries.*[378]

The Middle Way Special Instruction Collated from the Scriptures[379]

Homage to the Spiritual Teacher!

This is the Middle Way special instructions, the abbreviated meaning of, and meditation upon, all the qualities of the scriptures by the great master Śrīdīpaṃkarajñāna.

First, all things within saṃsāra and nirvāṇa should be ascertained through study and contemplation to be conventionally real as an illusion that is an infallible cause and effect of dependent arising which is empty. Ultimately all things are ascertained as unelaborated emptiness like the center of space.

The time of meditation is put into practice according to three stages: preparation, the main part, and conclusion.

First, engage in the practice of concentration while sitting on a comfortable seat and make requests to the gods and spiritual teachers; settle the body and mind and recite to yourself:

> "Throughout my existence in saṃsāra, from beginningless time until this day, I have wandered in realms from the Peak of Existence to the Avīci Hell undertaking endless rebirths and deaths. There is no place where I have not taken birth. There is no friend I have not met. There is no food that I have not eaten. There is no suffering that I have not experienced. Now, if I do not overturn this cyclic existence, it will be necessary to eternally wander."
>
> The cause of saṃsāra is conceptual thought and the seed of existence is consciousness.
>
> All conceptual thought arises from apprehending things as real.[380]
>
> Moreover, all assertions, from tīrthikas up through Buddhist Mādhyamikas who establish through reasoning, are imputations by thought. It is taught that, "There is no means of finding peace for those outside the system of the Ācārya Nāgārjuna."[381]

The sūtras, as well, condense the bodhisattva path into two: method and wisdom. If one is without method, one falls into being a śrāvaka, and if one is without wisdom, one wanders in cyclic existence. Therefore, one must be endowed with both method and wisdom.

Moreover, at the beginning, it is very important to meditate on method, and the primary method is the awakening mind. It is said that,

> "Without the awakening mind, victorious ones will not occur in this world."[382]
>
> Initially, go for refuge three times and meditate on love, compassion, and the awakening mind.
>
> Think, "All sentient beings have been my mother and there are sentient beings who are lost."
>
> Since kindheartedness protects from harm and is beneficial, meditate on loving-kindness thinking, "May all of them have happiness!" Meditate on compassion thinking, "May all of them be free from suffering!" Meditate with a mind which aspires, "I will attain buddhahood for their sake!"

As a method to accumulate merit and purify obstructions for their benefit, this meditation which cultivates the Middle Way is a meditation of method for the above.

Cultivating wisdom is to meditate through analysis with reasoning on objects of knowledge. Since it is said that, "There are two kinds of entities, material and nonmaterial," Lord Atiśa taught that it is convenient to meditate on only the reasoning of being free from one and the many.[383]

Material form, everything that one can see, depends on subtle atoms when differentiated by wisdom. Moreover, when going through the directional parts, the emptiness of subtle atoms is indictated. When understanding the suchness of material form, one will understand the extent of all things.

The nonmaterial is the mind. Within the mind, the past has disappeared. The future has not yet come to exist, and the present is not established. A sūtra states that the past has the characteristic of being extinguished. The future is not attained. The mind of the present is difficult to examine. Even analysis cannot be found. Wisdom does not find a foothold among the aggregates. Form is not established. Color is not established. There is no identifiable essence. Things are baseless.

"Kāśyapa, the mind has not been seen, is not seen, and will not be seen by the Buddha."[384]

In this way, one posits the condition of not finding when seeing the mind with the mind. As it is said,

> When thoroughly examining the mind, it cannot be found, since anything at all is not established, the subjective mind is not established either.

As a sūtra states,

> Just as when rubbing two sticks together, fire arises, and then the very fire is incinerated, likewise, although insight is produced from the faculties, that very insight which is produced is incinerated.[385]

Just as when fuel is exhausted, fire no longer arises, when both the object to be analyzed and the mind that analyzes remain in the condition of peace, suchness itself emerges.

> When the object to be investigated has been investigated, there exists no objective support for the investigating mind. Because there does not exist an objective support, the mind does arise, and that is called nirvāṇa.[386]

Therefore, by eliminating elaborations, nonconceptuality naturally arises. For the meaning of this, if conceptions arise at the time of engaging in vivid clarity in the condition of nonconceptuality, the conceptions will pass away and depart.

Having meditated, the special instructions are to meditate in longer sessions as much as one is able. Having attained stability, one purifies through restraint. On account of this, if laxity and excitement occur, eliminate the cause of these. Naturally focus. If one becomes excited, relax. In the time after arising from meditative stabilization, all things within saṃsāra and nirvāṇa should be understood to be empty of intrinsic existence like an illusion, and one should eliminate the most subtle nonvirtue. There is great accomplishment due to subtle virtue. Meditative equipoise and the experience after it, at first, should be cultivated separately.

Having practiced meditation, they need to be unified in practice similar to the legs of a person or the wings of a bird. In this way, by training in the experience of the audible yet empty, the unity of awareness and emptiness, those of good fortune will perceive reality in this life. Even if not perceiving this, one will definitely perceive this in future lifetimes as explained in Āryadeva's *Four Hundred Verses*.[387] The *King of Samādhi Sūtra* states,[388]

> When one understands the basic nature of things,
> then after a long time one will become the chief of bipeds.

This completes the uncommon special instructions of Lord Atiśa.

CHAPTER 11

Lamp for the Path to Awakening

Atiśa's Lamp for the Path to Awakening *is his most well-known work. The text contains sixty-eight verses outlining the integration of three forms of discipline, including the vows of the prātimokṣa, bodhisattva precepts, and the precepts of the Secret Mantra Vehicle. Mahāyāna and Vajrayāna practices and cultivations are also discussed. Written in response to questions from King Jangchup Ö in West Tibet around 1042, Atiśa's* Lamp *became "one of the most influential of Indian texts received by Tibetans" and was "the model for mainstream Tibetan monastic Buddhists for the next nine hundred years."*[389]

In the Indian language: *Bodhipathapradīpaṃ*
In the Tibetan language: *Byang chub lam gyi sgron ma*

Homage to the youthful bodhisattva Mañjuśrī!

I pay homage with great reverence to all the victorious ones of the three times, to their teachings, and communities. At the request of the good disciple Jangchup Ö, I shall illuminate a *Lamp for the Path to Awakening.*

Persons should be understood as falling into three spiritual types: inferior, middling, and supreme. The characteristics of each are clear and should be differentiated.

The inferior person seeks only the pleasures of saṃsāra by whatever means possible and pursues his own benefit.

The middling individual cares about his own peace, turning away from the pleasures of existence and reversing unwholesome deeds.

The supreme individual, because of personal suffering, seeks the complete extinction of others' suffering.

For those excellent living beings who desire supreme awakening, I shall explain the correct methods as taught by the teachers.

In front of paintings, images, and so forth of the perfect Buddha, reliquaries and a scripture of the excellent teaching, one should offer flowers and incense—whatever one is able.

With the seven part offering mentioned in the *Royal Scripture Concerning the Resolve toward Noble Conduct*, and with the thought never to turn back until one attains final awakening;

With strong confidence in the three jewels, placing the right kneecap on the ground, and hands pressed together, one first recites taking refuge three times.

Then, beginning with a loving attitude toward all living creatures, one considers all beings suffering through birth in the three lower realms—that is, the realms of animals, hungry ghosts, and hell denizens—death, and rebirth.

Then, due to the desire to liberate these beings from the suffering of pain, from suffering and the causes of suffering, one should immutably develop the resolve to attain awakening.

The good qualities of developing the aspiration for awakening are fully explained by Maitreya in the *Gaṇḍavyūha Sūtra.*

Reading scriptures or listening to teachers, one understands the infinite benefits of the perfect thought of awakening. Repeatedly generate it to make it steadfast.

The *Inquiry of Vīradatta Scripture* fully explains the merit of this thought. Here, in summary, I shall cite just three verses:

If the merit of the awakening mind possessed physical form, it would completely fill all of space, and exceed even that.

Now if a person were to fill with jewels as many buddhafields equal to the grains of sand in the Ganges and offer these jewels to the Protector of the World,

This would be surpassed by the offering of joining one's hands and inclining one's mind toward awakening. This offering is limitless.

Having cultivated the aspiration for awakening, one should increase it through intense effort. The instruction should be kept properly as it was explained, so that it may be remembered in this and also in other lifetimes.

Without the vow of the thought of entering into awakening, the perfect aspiration will not grow. One who wishes for the awakening mind to grow should take hold of it with definite effort.

Only those who maintain any of the seven kinds of prātimokṣa vows are fit for the vows of a bodhisattva.

The Tathāgata spoke of seven kinds of prātimokṣa vows. The best of these is celibacy, the vows of a fully ordained monk.

One should take the vow of the bodhisattva discipline from a good teacher according to the ritual found in the chapter of discipline in the *Bodhisattva Stages*.

Understand that a good teacher is one skilled in the ritual of the vow, observes the vow, and has the patience and compassion to bestow the vow.

If, however, you try but cannot find a teacher, then I shall explain another ritual for taking the vow.

I shall clearly write how, as explained in the *Ornament of Mañjuśrī's Buddhafield Sūtra*, Mañjuśrī, formerly the king Ambarāja, developed the thought of awakening:

"In the visualized presence of the protectors, I generate the thought to gain full awakening. I invite all beings as my guests and may I liberate them from saṃsāra.

"From this moment onward until the attainment of pure awakening, I shall not harbor ill will, anger, avarice, or envy.

"I shall undertake pure conduct, give up transgressions and desire. With joy in the vow of discipline, I will train to follow the buddhas.

"I shall not be eager to attain awakening in the quickest way, but shall stay until the very end, for the sake of a single sentient being.

"I shall purify unlimited inconceivable fields and remain in the ten directions for those who call my name.

"I shall purify all my physical and vocal activities. My mental activities, as well, I shall purify, and I will do nothing that is unwholesome."

When those observing the vow of the active engagement of the awakening mind have trained well in the three forms of discipline, their respect for these three forms of discipline flourishes, which causes the purification of body, speech, and mind.

Thus, through effort in the vow made by bodhisattvas for pure, full awakening, the accumulations which bring complete awakening will be thoroughly accomplished.

All the buddhas say that the development of supersensory knowledge is the cause for the completion of the two accumulations, whose nature is merit and pristine awareness.

Just as a bird with undeveloped wings cannot ascend into the sky, those without supersensory perceptions cannot work for the benefit of sentient beings.

The merit gained in a single day by one with supersensory perception cannot be gained even in a hundred lifetimes by one without such supersensory perception.

Those who wish to swiftly complete the accumulations for complete awakening will accomplish supersensory perception through effort, not through laziness.

Supersensory perception will not occur
Without the attainment of quiescence.
Therefore make repeated efforts
To accomplish quiescence.

If the conditions for quiescence diminish
Concentration will not be achieved
Even if one strenuously meditates
For thousands of years.

Therefore, maintaining well the conditions
Described from the "Collection for Concentration Chapter,"
One should focus the mind on any one
Suitable object of focus that is virtuous.

If a yogin achieves quiescence
The supersensory perceptions will also be achieved.
If one lacks the practice of the perfection of wisdom,
The obstructions will not be eliminated.

Therefore, to eliminate all obstructions
Of the afflictions and of the knowable without exception
The yogin should always cultivate
The perfection of wisdom with skillful means.

Wisdom devoid of skillful means
And skillful means, too, devoid of wisdom
Are what is called bondage.
So, do not abandon either one.

In order to eliminate doubts
Concerning what is called wisdom and what is skillful means,

I will clarify the distinctions between
Skillful means and wisdom.

The victorious ones have described as skillful means
All virtuous practices such as
The perfection of giving and so forth
Excluding the perfection of wisdom.

Whoever, through the force of familiarity
With skillful means, cultivates wisdom,
Will quickly attain awakening,
Not by only meditating on selflessness.

Wisdom is fully explained
As the cognition of the emptiness of intrinsic existence
Which realizes the aggregates, elements, and sensory spheres as
unproduced.

It is not reasonable that something existent can be produced
Nor something nonexistent, which is like a sky flower.
Both of these two faulty assertions are absurd and
Both of the two will not occur either.

An entity is not produced from itself,
Nor from another, also not from both,
Nor does it arise without a cause.
Therefore, it does not intrinsically exist by way of its own nature.

Furthermore, when all things are examined
As to their unity or plurality
They are not perceived to exist by way of their own nature
And are ascertained as lacking intrinsic existence.

The reasonings of the *Seventy Stanzas* and
The *Fundamental Treatise of the Middle Way* and so forth
Explain that the nature of entities
Is established as emptiness.

As there are a great number of passages
I therefore have not elaborated upon them here,
But have explained merely the tenets that have been established
For the purpose of meditation.

Accordingly, whatever meditation
On selflessness that does not observe
Any intrinsic natures in things
Is, here, meditation on wisdom.

Just as wisdom does not perceive
An intrinsic nature in anything,
Wisdom itself should be analyzed with reasoning,
That should be cultivated nonconceptually.

This existence, arisen from conceptualization,
Has conceptualization as its nature.
Therefore, the elimination all conceptualization without
exception
Is the highest nirvāṇa.

In this way, the Blessed One has said,
"Conceptualization is the great ignorance;
It immerses us in the ocean of saṃsāra,
Abiding in nonconceptual concentration,
Nonconceptualization is lucidly clear like the sky."

Also, the Avikalpapraveśa-dhāraṇī states:
"When sons of the Victorious One contemplate
This excellent teaching nonconceptually,
They will transcend conceptuality, so difficult to overcome,
And gradually attain the state of nonconceptualization."

Having ascertained through scripture
And reasoning that all things are
Unproduced and lacking intrinsic existence,
One should meditate without conceptualization.

Having thus meditated on suchness, and
Having gradually attained the stages of "heat" and so forth,
The "very joyful" and other stages are attained.
Then the awakened state of buddhahood is not distant.

If one wishes to create with ease
The collections for awakening
Through activities of pacification,
Increase and so forth, gained by the power of mantra,

And also through the force of the eight
And other great attainments like the "Good Vase";
If you wish to practice secret mantras,
As explained in the action and performance tantras,

Then, to receive the ācārya consecration,
One must please an excellent spiritual teacher
Through service, precious gifts, and so forth,
And follow his instructions.

Having obtained the complete ācārya consecration
By a spiritual teacher who is pleased,
One becomes purified of all transgressions
And fortunate to accomplish the siddhis.

A celibate (*brahmacārin*) should not take
The secret and wisdom consecrations
Because the *Paramādibuddha Tantra*
Strongly prohibits them.

If a celibate ascetic
Takes either consecration,
The ascetic vows are broken
Through doing forbidden behavior.

The fault of defeat
Will occur for that ascetic
And since he is certain to fall to a lower realm of rebirth
There is no possibility of achievement.

One who has received the consecration of ācārya
May hear and explain all the tantras
And perform *homa* rituals and so forth.
There is no fault provided he has awareness of reality.

I, the Elder Dīpaṃkaraśrī, having seen
This explanation of dharma from the sūtras and so forth,
Have made this concise explanation of the path to awakening
At the request of Jangchup Ö.

This concludes the Lamp for the Path to Awakening *by the great master Dīpaṃkaraśrījñāna. It was translated, revised, and finalized by the eminent Indian abbot himself and the great reviser, translator, and ordained monk Gewa Lodrö. The teaching was composed in the Temple of Tholing in Shang Shung.*

CHAPTER 12

Stages of the Path to Awakening, Selections

Atiśa's Stages of the Path to Awakening *is one of his most important works that is virtually unknown to traditional and modern scholarship. The selections that follow appear for the first time in modern scholarship. The work was kept secret among Atiśa's early Kadampa followers and transmitted among Kagyu and Sakya scholars until the thirteenth century. Atiśa's* Stages *consists of prescriptive teachings indicating stages of cultivation to reach buddhahood. The text outlines his instructions for his close and advanced disciples who were laypeople and monks. The stages of the path to awakening are based on the capacities, or inclinations, of three types of person: small (4–75), middling (76–108), and supreme (109–181). The practices of the small and middling individuals that are not explained in the* Lamp *(chapter 11) are described in detail in the* Stages.[390]

In the Indian language: *Bodhipathakrama*
In the Tibetan language: *Byang chub lam gyi rim pa*

Homage to all buddhas and bodhisattvas!

[1] I pay homage to the supreme refuge, the spiritual master, and the three jewels. [2] I will explain the realizations on the stages of the path to awakening.

[3] In this regard, there are three types of individuals: those of small, middling, and supreme capacities. The individual of small capacity does not practice for this life and seeks blissful heavenly rebirth in the future. The middling individual does not seek to rest in the round of rebirth and always practices to achieve liberation. The supreme individual does not seek out their own purpose and has the awareness that wishes to attain buddhahood for the sake of others. One should understand each of the three individuals to possess four qualities: (1) practices, (2) meditation objects, (3) a reversal of tendencies, and (4) a result.

Small Capacity Stages

[4] An individual of small capacity takes refuge, observes one-day precepts, has pure conduct, and protects the vows. One meditates on fortunate rebirth, impermanence, positive and negative actions, and cause and effect. For this life, one reverses the tendency to cling to permanence, abandons transgressions, and in order to eliminate evil states of rebirth, practices virtue to achieve leisure and fortune.

[5] By being frightened by death and lower states of rebirth, with confidence in cause and effect, with faith in refuge, one seeks happiness.

[6] One takes the pledges through the ritual of the ācārya. [7] One makes the promise and takes refuge voluntarily, not relying on another. One should understand the distinctions between outsiders (non-Buddhists) and insiders (Buddhists). One then goes for refuge and places trust by cognizing the good qualities of insiders.

[8] Do not relinquish refuge for the sake of life and reward. Abandon both external non-Buddhists and mundane gods. Abandon

other deities by the means for all that is difficult to do. Be dedicated to the Buddha, do not pay homage to others. Abandon harm to sentient beings wherever they are. Refrain from joining with non-Buddhists. Mindful of virtuous qualities, repeatedly go for refuge. Offer to the three jewels the first portion of whatever food to eat. Offer to the great king offerings for the auspicious occasions (the four periodic offerings). Pay homage to the Buddha of the transmigrators in all directions!

[9] Engage in the morning for the eight great qualities and be a support for all the vows. Past sins that have been done are like the female servant of Śravasti. Guard against harming others, which brings happiness like finding a treasure. Eliminate bad conditions, fulfill all needs and wishes, complete the accumulation of merit, attain nirvāṇa and buddhahood.

[10] Abandon killing, taking what is not given, sexual misconduct, false speech, drinking beer, dance and so forth, sitting on high seats, and eating food at the inappropriate time. Protect the eight branches and attain the higher realms and liberation.

[11] A few of the perpetual laws of good conduct of the Mahāsāṃghikas: First, abandon the taking of life and taking what is not given. The Mahāsāṃghikas have four root downfalls for the sake of abandoning lies, eliminating desire for sexual enjoyment, maintaining celibacy, and eliminating sexual misconduct.

[12] Extensively increase the merit of oneself and others. Daily in world systems, however as much as the particles of dust, make offerings. With generosity, give leftovers to deities. For a layperson the supreme offering is cooked food. The common folk offer oil lamps. The supreme offering of a layperson is to mentally offer butter lamps as large as Mount Meru.

[13] The three lower realms, long-lived gods, the realm of neither perception nor nonperception, belonging to a primitive border tribe, impure faculties, wrong view, not making the aspiration to be born at the time of a buddha—these conditions, due to the lack of good fortune, are explained by the Victorious One as the "abodes of bad rebirth." When one abandons the eight places, it is called the "supreme of leisure."

[14] The presence of the Buddha and his teaching of dharma, his teaching remaining, its subsequent practice, and having kindness to practice are the five riches from others. Having attained a human body, with pure faculties, faith in the right place, turning back from the extremes of action, and birth in a central land are the five personal endowments.

[15] Among the immeasurable sentient beings of the three realms, very few obtain the precious opportunity of human life.

[16] Among the sentient beings in the six realms of cyclic existence, virtuous action as a cause for leisure and fortune is rare.

[17] Just as if the neck of a turtle would enter into the hole of wood floating on the great ocean is the analogy which indicates the extreme difficulty of leisure and fortune.[391]

[18] In this way, unknowing, confused beings having gained this jewel-like human body, free and well favored, with the perceptions of this life in meaningless distractions, from an agitated mind with many afflictions of attachment and hatred perform actions of multiple unvirtuous transgressions and senseless downfalls in bad conditions. One deceives oneself, making great harm to oneself. As

great suffering comes down, one must have compassion for oneself. Even when seeing, hearing, and knowing, still one causes evil, like a crazy person when falling into bad conditions. Although suffering foolishly, once more wrongdoing increases.

[19] In this way, when desiring to achieve happiness and eliminate suffering, do not return empty-handed from the island of jewels. Take up the precious jewel of virtuous holy dharma like obtaining the jewel which fulfills all needs and wishes. With effort to abandon distractions and afflictions, like an accomplished master crossing a river, cross the river of suffering with the supreme support of the human boat. Protect oneself with merely food and clothing and make use of virtue. Abandon laziness and practice vigorously.

[20] Although being healthy, in harmony, and with property, since aging, decline, and the Lord of Death deprive one of life, therefore, do not have confidence due to impermanence. Do not achieve for this lifetime, aim for the hereafter. If one has attained mastery over wealth, when one does not achieve one's own purpose and falls into lower realms of rebirth under another power, at that time what benefit to oneself will wealth be?

[21] The conditioned, impermanent, transient world undergoes creation and destruction. Years, months, days, and nights are constantly changing. Even grass, trees, and leaves wax and wane. Momentary time, impermanent, like a torrent of water over a steep cliff, things constantly change without pause.

[22] Although many previous sentient beings born of a body have died, one says, "This I have not seen, nor have I heard." Again one thinks, "This will not occur, even now there is no death," stating

that it does not exist, but death is certain. Seeing, hearing, and mindful of death in the past, think about all the burial grounds and overturn the fixation on permanence.

[23] All sentient beings' bodies and conditions without exception quickly and definitely disintegrate because they are conditioned. Do not turn one's mind even to good times, or future means of livelihood, do not achieve for this life, think about the hereafter.

[24] Time does not pause for even two moments. Days, months, and years diminish in life. Since whatsoever increase does not come from elsewhere, and as death is definite, eliminate the perception that fixates on permanence.

[25] Some who are possessed by ghosts cause mischief. Some die due to enemies, spirits, fire, water, or prosperity. Some without food and clothing die of cold and hunger. Some die on account of food that is poisoned. Some die by diseases of wind, bile, and so forth. As all is through conditions, one is not able to have confidence, one does not know the time of death. Therefore, eliminate distraction and contemplate impermanence.

[26] Since life in Jambudvīpa is not certain, some elderly at the point of death die in good conditions. Some die in the prime of life and some in the womb. Therefore, one is not able to rely on youth and wealth.

[27] The body of a sentient being is like a fragile reed. There is not established at all even a hair of an essence. Unable to withstand only a little of adverse conditions, like a feather, like dew on grass, the body quickly dies.

[28] There is not a method to overturn the certainty of death, like a lamp running out of oil in the darkness of night. In respect to that, oneself with courage cannot turn back death, the strength and great power of Viṣṇu, tigers, lions, snakes, and so forth, cannot subdue death. Even the power and capability of oneself is unable to overturn death. Death is without escape like someone who has swallowed poison.

[29] Protective deities, extraordinary spells, even skill in the method of dependent arising cannot overturn death. The wealthy, with their wealth, cannot turn back death. Therefore, there is not another way of overturning the Lord of Death.

[30] Friends, relatives, and others, lords of the land and [31] even rulers cannot overturn the Lord of Death. One should contemplate, taking up the path, "Where does one go? Where does one disappear?"

[32] Even knowing while not meditating is like explaining something to protect it. Therefore, attachment to children, relatives, wealth, fame, riches, and honor are enemies that arise. Foolishly fixated on permanence, one commits sinful actions distracted by perception and afflictions for this life. The fixation on permanence, which is like renovating leisure when achieving for this life, is extremely foolish. Having renounced all enemies and friends, wealth and fame, oneself alone will carry the burden of sin upon dying. At that time, without possibility of protection, one's experience of suffering, concern, and regret for previous sin is without benefit. Therefore, contemplate impermanence, cast away perception of this life, and achieve happiness for the future. Possessing leisure and fortune benefits oneself for only a length of time.

[33] For this reason, one should eliminate and identify all sin which is contradictory to bringing forth the fundamental nature.

[34] Sentient beings under the influence of attachment, hatred, and delusion take life with force and cunningly take the wealth of others. A householder protects oneself. With desire one engages in wrongful sexual intercourse. The ways of men have a false pettiness toward spiritual teachers. Actually blind to subtle realities, they speak divisively and falsely and answer with abuse to good qualities. Idle talk that is opposite of truth and correct speech destroys the substance of oneself, others, and both oneself and others. Giving gifts and seeking friends go in the opposite direction. Correct and worldly truths are wrongly perceived. These and so forth are the nature of unvirtuous actions. Whatever individuals who would do as such, the effect that individually arises is suffering. The necessity to negate that which brings forth gives rise to keeping a promise.

---

[51] In this way, the sufferings of the three lower realms of rebirth are uncontrollable,[392] last for a long time, and are meaninglessly experienced. When one contemplates this, there is great fearful purpose to have virtuous actions. One should achieve virtue with distinctive effort, suffering through difficulties. The actions which have become afflictions, wrongdoings, and obscurations should be eliminated with great effort.

[52] One attains sinful rebirth or high heavenly states through concordant causes: killing causes untimely death by the conditions of a short life span. Through taking what is not given, wealth will become small. Through committing adultery one will not find companions. Due to lying one will be deceived by others. If one speaks divisively, one will be bereft of friends. Due to harsh speech oneself

will be blamed. Due to idle talk one's words will not be disciplined. Due to covetousness expectations are destroyed. Through harmfulness enemies, harm, and terror will arise. Due to wrong view one will have a view that clings to a Self.

[53] Action resembling its cause is previously accustomed wrongdoing where one does whatever has been done with a desire to engage in an action with enthusiasm. Therefore, one should eliminate nonvirtue and cultivate virtue. When one becomes accustomed, anything can become easy. Because all things arise from conditions, things occur through bad or good causally concordant conditions.

[54] The general dominant result of negative actions is one is born in a bad region. Killing degenerates the essence of the life force. Stealing results in drought, rain, frost, and hail that destroys the harvest. With adultery one stinks and is not concerned with hot or cold. Telling lies leads to bad food and not achieving contemplation. Divisive speech leads to painful entry to hot and arid land. Wounding speech leads to thorny deep ravines and abysses. Useless speech leads to bad times where the essence of the crops does not ripen. Covetousness leads to scarce crops with poor results. Harmfulness leads to wild crops being cooked by enemy hunters. Wrong view leads to crops not ripening and disappearing. Therefore, one should eliminate subtle nonvirtue.

[55] In this way, the sufferings of the lower realms, hell and so forth, do not exist from without but are like a reflection or echo. Afflictions and wrongdoing are self-manifestations of the mind. Therefore, if one does not desire the sufferings of hell and so forth, one should protect the mind from afflictions and nonvirtue. When the mind eliminates afflictions and wrongdoing, the sufferings of the round

of rebirth, hell and so forth, stop, like the leather soles of boots covering the ground.[393]

[56] In this way, for destroying the enemy of the afflictions, one should produce the power of mental counteragents. Eliminate nonvirtue and achieve virtue. The mere nondoing of nonvirtuous actions is called nonanalytical cessation. Having eliminated negative actions, when relying on the counteragent, there is virtue.

[57] Virtue is preserving life and giving material things to sentient beings, chastity, speaking truthfully, reconciling, speaking softly, being intent on what is beneficial, eliminating attachment, cultivating love, and upholding correct views.

[58] By practicing the ten virtues and characters, one gains the excellent result of the happiness of gods and men. When conjoined with emptiness and compassion, one attains awakening. By preserving life one will be free from disease and have a long life. Due to giving material things, one obtains great wealth. Through pure conduct one will gain good friends. Through speaking truthfully one will not be deceived by another, and through reconciling one has many relatives and friends. Through soft words one's own words are pleasantly heard. Through speaking with intent on what is beneficial, one will be respected. When abandoning attachment the mind achieves contemplation. Cultivating love frees one from enemies, harm, and fear. Through correct view one realizes the good view free from extremes.

---

[60] Make effort in virtuous actions with a wish to engage in its increase, for virtue previously familiarized has the effect of the compatibility of cause.

[61] Preserving life, medicine, and food produces health. Giving material things leads to a good harvest of crops. Pure conduct levels out hot and cold temperatures and cleans an area. Speaking truthfully achieves goodness and contemplation. Reconciling leads to pleasurable conditions without getting angry. Speaking softly leads to rebirth in areas without deep ravines or abysses. Purposeful speech leads to crops ripening on time. When one eliminates attachment, there is the bounty of good crops. Cultivating love, one will have crops free from harmful enemies. With correct view one has ripened crops from natural sources.

[62] Therefore, one should make effort with diligence for virtuous actions. For that reason, practicing for merely food and clothing leads to actions mixed with wrongdoing, exhaustion, and difficulty in cold and hunger. When one is patient for meat broth, where is there achieving the happiness of oneself and others, the higher realms and liberation, and the highest awakening? Knowledge and nonmeditation are like the recitation of a parrot. It is not to care about the great harm of suffering. Do not establish the three doors of body, speech, and mind in the ordinary. Make effort for virtue.

[63] The blazing fires of hell have a scorching iron foundation and one is pricked with blazing weapons by the unkind guardians of hell. One is boiled in the fire of the hot springs of a doorless iron house. Razors and so forth are spread out on the ground. The hot and cold of hell have so much suffering. Furthermore, enemies, evil spirits, and maleficent beings, however much wrongdoing has been done, hatred, harmfulness, killing, striking are the result.

[64] Hungry ghosts suffer and are struck with thinking of hunger and thirst, meeting with frost and hail. Some are bereft of material things due to poverty, some do not have food and clothing, some

are hungry and thirsty at the time of death—the varied forms of previous karma are the result of desire, avarice, and stealing.

[65] Animals mutually eat one another due to stupidity and dullness, deaf, mute, and blind disease, insanity, and so forth, and this is the result of the previous karma of ignorance. Therefore, the afflictions, even a single instant, should not be produced, and if produced, should be eliminated.

[66] The conditions of the happiness of the higher rebirth of gods and men, the wishfulfilling gem, and so forth, the food of the gods, ambrosia, and so forth, having crops, a well-built house, servants, and possessing a lineage with good qualities and prosperity are the manifest result of meritorious karma. Therefore, accomplish even the most subtle virtuous actions.

[67] That and so forth, all appearances of happiness and suffering are not established outside, are not externally caused. Oneself causes virtuous and evil deeds. Those are the resultant maturation of such and such actions. All of whatever appears is like a reflection that is the very embodiment of that which is from within. Therefore, mind does not really exist, external appearances do not really exist, one's own karma does not really exist, whatever is experienced does not really exist. If you wish to achieve happiness, eliminate unfavorable conditions, as it is not achieved otherwise because whatever seeds of one's own momentary mind arise as a result of simultaneous increase. Through understanding the seed and sprout together with the mental continuum, make effort for actions to achieve unmistaken elimination of mental defilements.

———

[69] Nonvirtue discarded and virtue finished are like the small

happiness of an animal. Virtue discarded and suffering finished are to experience a little bit of the suffering of gods and humans. The casting and completion of virtue are the happiness of higher states of rebirth, and the casting and completion of nonvirtue are the suffering of the lower realms of rebirth.

[70] When it is an obstruction, not wrongdoing, latent afflictions all manifest. When it is wrongdoing, not an obstruction, by virtue of the thought the intention is nonvirtue. Actions which are both wrongdoing and obstructions are created from nonvirtue taken up by afflictions. Actions which are neither wrongdoing nor obstructions are indeterminate and may become virtuous.

[71] A single counteragent comes along for a single good or evil deed. Likewise, a single action is augmented by the strength of a deed. It is not definite to experience unaccumulated deeds.

---

[73] All dharmas are the mind, the mind itself is free from all extremes. The multiple various causes and effects of virtue and wrongdoing are unceasing, definitely liberated from the extreme of nihilism. Since whatever appears of the cause and effect of the round of rebirth and nirvāṇa is the nature of one's own mind, it is not at all established, and it is definitely liberated from the extreme of permanence. Emptiness indivisible with cause and effect is the nature of one's own mind, free from the proliferations of extemes, the Great Middle Way.

[74] The eight worldly perceptions of this lifetime, laziness, future plans, wrongdoing, and afflictions are signs that the path of meditation reverses and eliminates. One should possess the signs of progress on the path, not merely words.

[75] Eliminate evil states which are bad and so forth. With confidence in cause and effect, through practicing virtuous actions, states such as Brahma, Indra, a universal monarch, Brahmins, ruling class, upper-class householders, are experienced.

Middling Capacity Stages

[76] Applied to the middling path in addition to the former stages is protecting the thoroughly complete novice vows for the middling and the more powerful full vows of a monk. The faults of the round of rebirth are the cause to cultivate the path of liberation. Reverse the tendencies for the round of rebirth—misknowledge, self-grasping, wrongdoing. Accomplish any bit of nirvāṇa, peace, happiness, and others' welfare.

[77] Possessing the five major laws, one is a complete layperson, and having the signs of a renunciate, one is a novice monk. The supreme monk guards against the five kinds of downfalls. Holding pledges of discipline is the basis that is the support for creating all good qualities.

[78] Without discipline, one is unable to eliminate evil states, and when it is difficult to obtain even the path to higher realms, what need is there to aspire to liberation or omniscience? Just as the blind do not see phenomena, likewise, without moral discipline one does not see the dharma. Just as one without legs is unable to enter a path, likewise, one without moral discipline will not be liberated. Therefore, discipline attains arhatship and the unmatched attainment of omniscience. Struck by the fire of desire in the household life, there is nonvirtuous karma due to too much attachment and aversion for the sake of sons, wife, wealth, enemies, and friends.

Due to the monstrous sense faculties creating a great amount of wrongdoing, one falls into the lower realms with undesirable, scarce abundance and various discordant conditions like poverty and so forth.

[79] Some through the delusion of not hearing the scriptures grasp on to the Lower Vehicle discipline of a monk. Deluded for cause and effect, bereft of correct view, the afflictions are like independent desirable qualities. Pretending for the Great Vehicle and so forth, they fall along the path. Monastic moral disciple in the path of all vehicles is taught by the Victorious One from all sūtras and tantras. Why? Moral discipline is the support which increases merit. The virtue accumulated for a hundred years by a householder is merely one day for one who is a monk. One who resides in the teaching of the Buddha, the former has an infinitesimal portion of merit. With a mind not discouraged to enter into awakening for the sake of all the sentient beings of the billionfold universe, one gives away son and wife for a full eon. More than that, when someone generates the awakening mind while casting away a single familiarization with a mind of renunciation, that is especially the superior merit. The possessions of a precious householder and so forth are offered up to as many buddhas as the sands of the Ganges River, for one who is a monk for a single day and night who thinks of impermanence, suffering, and selflessness is supreme. Why? The arhat buddhas of the three times have arisen from possessing the moral discipline of monastic vows. Released from household affairs, bereft of the distractions that lead astray, free from the attachment of son and wife, unattached to wealth, one attains the great wealth most pleasing of all: performing virtue unafflicted with distraction. One has the practice of virtue in solitude without attachment. One attains the higher realms, liberation, and omniscience.

[80] The sentient beings of the three realms, due to self-grasping through delusion, due to ignorance that grasps as real inner and outer objects, experience multiple sufferings of the round of rebirth. Although the body and mind are repeatedly tormented, the fully developed afflictions cause one to commit wrongdoing due to the desire which engages in the cause of suffering. People have attachment and aversion to enemies and friends, are distracted wasting their time with many activities that increase the afflictions, and they commit much wrongdoing. By being very busy with agriculture and business, the body and mind finish life with distractions. All activities are pointless, a cause of suffering. Having discarded friends, enemies, and wealth, with the burden of wrongdoing, oneself—deluded—falls into lower states from the burden. Deluded in regards to cause and effect, one does not understand how to abandon suffering. Therefore, now, having the freedom to achieve one's happiness, make effort for virtuous karma. In this cyclic existence, with uncertainty, the elevated fall to the low, the low become elevated. Presented with much happiness and suffering, they pass away and transmigrate. A friend becomes an enemy, an enemy becomes a friend. With the transference of birth and death, one is not sure. Although parents encounter a child, it is possible for the child to regard the parents as an enemy. A previous enemy may again become a friend. Due to multiple transferences back and forth between being a friend or an enemy, in this way, to whom should one be attached and to whom should one hate? Therefore, regard all beings equally and abandon attachment and hate.

[81] This life, through delusion, through apprehending things as real, due to the view of permanence, in order to achieve this aim, one is attached to the five objects of desire, continously relying on intention and extreme attachment. As sense desires lack satisfaction, like drinking salty water, sentient beings by these five desires reach

ruin like how the deer by sound, the jackal by smell, the fish by taste, and the elephant by touch are destroyed. The wicked and so forth produce all suffering. Beautiful form and nice clothes should be relied on like a rainbow in the sky, the various multitude of enemies are like an echo, and smell and taste are like salty water and a dream. Tanglible objects are like scratching an itch. Practicing the meditation upon impermanence and emptiness is heroic. On account of the five objects of desire, multiple wrongdoing is created. At the time of death, virtue is not created. When desires, friends, and material things are left behind, the great burden of wrongdoing, delusion, is carried by oneself. Driven by the wind of uncontrollable karma, one engages in the cause again to experience vile suffering. Now, at this time, one has self-control. Eliminate wrongdoing!

---

[85] Likewise, the immeasurable sufferings of aging: The binding imperfections of shape, complexion, as well as skin diminish. The radiance of the skin and bodily strength degenerate. One is unable to work due to fatigue from a little labor. One's bodily temperature degenerates, and one is subject to infection. One's degenerated faculties are unable to experience objects. There is the blundered ugliness of everything. Others have sickness and one's own son is also hot. No one listens to your speech, and people debate in your face. Others have apprehension to see you. Your taste also becomes salty. Powerless to accumulate wealth by oneself, you do not listen to advice from others. Again, there is unpleasing, abusive speech. If you think "We," it is only I, oneself, and it will be like this. Pondering and gloomy, there is not anything to say or praise.

[86] When one becomes sick, a fierce thorn strikes the body, the mind is overcome with fierce suffering. The mind, gathered within, does not engage objects. Food stinks, the complexion of

the body deteriorates. There is much bodily pain for bleeding and moxibustion and so forth. It is not good to be hungry. One must eat rough medicine. As delicious food is harmful, one is powerless to eat. Even with maintaining good bedclothes, one is without happiness. Even when given pleasing food, it stinks. Gentle spoken words are unpleasant to the ear. A great loss of food and wealth occurs and goes to demons and so forth. With the fear of death, the tormented mind suffers. Day and night suffering arises and nurses cannot arrive.

[87] Although surrounded by friends at the time of death, one goes alone like a hair pulled from butter. At that time, there is not the ability to cling to life. Some cry out and guard the desire for wealth. Some call out and die suffering without friends. Some die with hatred by killing. Some have the suffering of seperation from friends and some fasten the mind by attachment to wealth and friends. Some die from excessive thinking about not completing good actions to do such and such. This life ceases and the bestowal of the Lord of Death appears. Some are struck with intense pain and fear and terror arise. Some suffer from gloominess without a method for relief. Alas! Friends, what can I do? Uttering and struck with fierce suffering, one is unable to see anyone who is able to protect them. In accordance with delusion, one will involuntarily die.

[88] In this way, the four streams of birth, aging, sickness, and death are faults of cyclic existence. Think again and again on just this. One should liberate from the streams of suffering, eliminate wrongdoing, and achieve virtue.

[89] The suffering which occurs predominantly against one's will: Someone who has aged must be the servant of another. One has uncontrollable sickness and fatigue is exploited by others, and for

a while is without benefit to others. One needs clothing for aged legs and arms. Given to some are cooling astringents, wool, or iron. Due to the burden of a long path, the putrid fatigued body settles down. Tormented with heat and thirsty with age, one experiences suffering. Some, aged, experiencing the hot and cold of inner thirst beg for soup and the wealth of others. Some kill in battle and so forth for their desires. Some break the law to steal the wealth of others. Foolish to not refrain from wrongdoing, some are hunters. Some, for trading activity, wander for a long time. The thieves of fatigue gather together, and there is much suffering and sickness. These are the immeasurable sufferings of misfortune.

[90] Even if one has wealth, robbers will carry it away and enemies will plunder and destroy it with fire and water. While keeping watch at night, one suffers from sleeplessness. One suffers from heat and cold for the sake of wealth. While fatigued and exhausted, one is powerless to help others. Doing too many activities causes broken bones. Due to the many distractions for this life, through committing many evil deeds, one falls to lower realms of rebirth.

[91] Pride, appeasement, and fear when meeting with enemies, destroying land and killing, entering into imprisonment, accepting injury, extracting the eye, plundering, and so forth—these are the sufferings that torment the body and mind due to hatred.

[92] In the great suffering of separation from kind and beloved friends, their criticisms are remembered as good qualities. One remembers that aspect necessary for oneself. One is fastened by being coerced with compassion due to attachment. Distressed with suffering, the mind tormented—these are the sufferings which are caused while reciting pleasing words.

[93] In dependence upon the five aggregates of clinging, one creates much wrongdoing and nonvirtue that produces the suffering of future aggregates which is called the suffering of conditioned karmic action.

[94] The suffering due to happiness becoming impermanent is like becoming sick when healthy or the wealthy becoming poor. Even though supreme, one becomes inferior. Impermanent happiness becomes suffering.

[95] The aggregates of clinging are suffering, disease arises suddenly, enemies are encountered, one becomes separated from friends. One suffering after another occurs through the conditions of various discordant factors, such as diminishing wealth and so forth. The suffering of gods and asuras are fighting and battles, separation, disintegration, intoxication with desire and no time for virtue, the sufferings of rebirth and falling and so forth; these fierce sufferings arise through one's own supersensory knowledge.

[96] In this way, one should contemplate to stick in the mind the many faults of cyclic existence, stating, "All of the harm while wandering purposelessly in cyclic existence is unbearable when coming down on my mental continuum." Having repeatedly considered the certainty of this, that which is created by all the suffering of cyclic existence, the perception of this life, the eight worldly concerns, and so forth, the many activities created by the afflictions, what should one do in this life about the cause of purposeless suffering? Especially eliminating all the activities of this life, the human body is for the sake of achieving permanent liberation. A fortunate one should make effort in virtuous actions.

[97] The suchness of the mind, through ignorance and delusion, views a Self taking up the cause and effect of grasping inner and external things. With strong attachment to desire, excessive clinging, and aspiration for the future, then anger and hatred will be produced. Then, subtle and gross afflictions will thoroughly expand. The great amount of karma—the various nonvirtue produced by that—accumulates, and one does not create virtue being attached to wrongdoing. All the sufferings of existence without exception will arise. Enduring and not resenting that nonvirtue and the afflictions is senseless confusion that creates great harm to oneself. For a little of this life, one should destroy the enemy, the afflictions, who harms you. When taking up the battle diligently without concern for wealth and life, the enemy who creates the great harm of hells and so forth is suitable for destruction, not looking toward body, life, and wealth. Therefore, marshal the various counteragent forces and destroy the great enemy, the afflictions, who create everlasting suffering.

[98] Among the twelve roots of existence—ignorance, formations, consciousness, name and form, sense bases, contact, feeling, craving, grasping, becoming, birth, and aging and death—the first (ignorance), the eighth (craving), and the ninth (grasping) are afflictions. The second (formations) and tenth (becoming) are the segments for karma. The seven remaining (consciousness and so forth) are the segments for suffering. With the existence of the three afflictions, karma will occur. When the two kinds of karmic action exist, the seven which are suffering arise. The three afflictions arise from the seven segments, thus the cycle of existence continually cycles like an uninterrupted waterwheel. Again and again, one is connected while not ejecting. The arising of conditions liberates from the extremes of permanence and annihilation

and a small cause leads to a great effect, like a nyagrodha tree. An effect occurs that is congruent with the cause. Without a creator, temporary collections give rise to collections of effects that cease when their capacities are exhausted.

[99] The wise are to be followed in order to overturn the stream of karma. If one makes effort with discursive thought to produce wisdom, ignorance up through aging and death comes to cessation. With the permanent end to the suffering of saṃsāra, one attains nirvāṇa. Therefore, one should make effort in study, reflection, and meditation. To meditate with little study is like climbing a rock when you have no arms. One falls into the chasm again, not reaching the top. Study without meditation is like dying of thirst in an ocean. Not eradicating the afflictions and transgressions, one falls into lower states of rebirth. Therefore, first study, then contemplate, and finally meditate in due order. One should strive with effort in unmistakenly having all three factors because of the unmistaken result that occurs for one on the path of liberation.

[100] The unclean material body is like the residue of a swollen corpse of the cremation grounds and a skeleton, as there is no entity which is clean and permanent. Therefore, eliminate attachment to the external and internal body.

[101] The conceptual mind is momentary and is distinguished throughout the three times as emptiness. By understanding that one's own mind is impermanent and emptiness, cognitions of mistaken entities that are apprehended as permanent are brought to cessation.

[102] Feelings of joy are suffering due to being impermanent. Other feelings, as well, have the nature of suffering. The intelligent

should eliminate mistaken attachment to things that are conceived as pleasurable.

[103] That called "dharma" refers to all entities such as internal and external forms and so forth, and since they are selfless, the five external elements do not have a Self. The body and mind also do not have a Self. Since a Self is not established, that which pertains to a Self does not exist. That which apprehends a Self and something as a Self is a mistaken awareness. When one eliminates self-grasping, unpleasant suffering ceases.

[104] With continuous undistracted meditative stablization in quiescence on the meaning of selflessness, one attains the result of arhat, having actualized cessation.

[105] Through residing in quiescence, all feelings cease. Residing on the single session path of application, enjoyments such as food and so forth are not necessary, and one brings to cessation without exception subtle and coarse conceptual thoughts. For as long as conditions do not arise even for an eon, one engages in the meditative stabilization of cessation. One will rise up due to the conditions of clamor, of noise, and so forth.

[106] Special insight destroys all afflictions without exception. Liberated from the seeds and its aspects, one attains the state of arhat. Gradually, when entirely free from suffering, it is the liberation from the factor of the result of arhat. Immediately upon eliminating the afflictions, one is liberated from both sufferings without remainder.

[107] One should reverse tendencies from all of saṃsāra with its six classes of beings. One should reverse ignorance, self-grasping, tendencies due to afflictions, sense pleasures, and transgressions. They are like sorceress spirits on a demonic island.

[108] Entirely eliminate the sufferings of the threefold existence and reach the attainments of stream-enterer up through the state of arhat.[394] When one has attained happiness passing from saṃsāra, one is able to benefit others through emanations and so forth.

Supreme Capacity Stages

[109] Above the paths of the small and middling individuals are the practices of the supreme individual who aspires and engages to produce the awakening mind and apprehend the instruction that leads to the ultimate. One integrates means and wisdom in meditation. One reverses the tendencies for one's own benefit and the explicit holding of extremes. Eliminating obstructions, one completes the benefit of others through attaining omniscience.

[110] When one has virtue that is without hatred, nonviolent, and free from doubts, likes, and dislikes, [111] with limitless and extensive objects and aims wholly filling the extent of space, the results are immeasureable.

[112] Having seen the suffering of the threefold world along with its causes, knowledge of the meaning of the inevitable relation between karma and its results, with objectless, free-from-extremes insight, one should meditate on the four immeasurables, loving-kindness, and so forth. Wishing migrating beings to have happiness, to be free from suffering, and to not be separated from happiness, all equally, are the four immeasurables. Sentient beings have created kindness for oneself many times as one's father and mother in previous lifetimes. Therefore, one should make all migrating beings equally happy, free from suffering, and not separated from happiness.

[113] With omniscient wisdom, the four immeasurables, compassion, various unobstructed activities of the three bodies of a buddha,

one protects beings from all the suffering of the three realms. One produces the aspiration which wishes to attain buddhahood due to seeing, hearing, and contemplating. If the merit of the awakening mind were to take material form, it could not be contained in the realm of space, it is perfect merit which exhausts transgressions. Attaining buddhahood establishes all wishes. For the sake of completing merit, make prostrations and offerings, confess transgressions, rejoice, exhort, and offer aspirational prayers. With faithful motivaton, take refuge for oneself, and motivated with compassion, take refuge for others' welfare. Become a vessel for the common vows and path. Be a vessel and support for Mahāyāna vows and paths. One should train and practice for one's own aim and train in the path for the purpose of others. For as long as one lives traversing the path, take refuge until attaining unsurpassable awakening. The letters of a supreme emanation are a śrāvaka, and the peaceful dharma body is a bodhisattva.

[114] One should perceive the teacher as a buddha. Offer one's own body without attachment. Supplicate the teacher to remove hindrances toward the teacher. The ritual for committing to be without hindrances is to promise three times to liberate the unliberated and so on.

[115] I, having a body composed of effects, will now today become a son in the lineage of buddhas. One should then proclaim the major and minor precepts.

[116] Eliminate belligerent thoughts to sentient beings, and pass beyond resentment.
Do not avoid regret in deceiving the praiseworthy with perverted views.
Do not dwell in points of doubt, do not avoid confessing.

Do not overlook having doubt or proclaiming offensive words
for the awakening mind.
Do not overlook having regret for dishonesty toward others due
to desire.
Moreover, eliminate empty-handed aspirations.

[117] The antidote to these is to meditate with thoughts of love and to not speak false words for the sake of body and life. Generate the mind which establishes virtue in the Great Vehicle for migrating beings. Respectfully praise whoever produces the awakening mind. Honestly, without deceit, you should contemplate the welfare of others.

[118] Contemplate the extensive benefits of the awakening mind. The awakening mind is like a wish-fulfilling jewel which gives rise to the strong desire for oneself and all others to finally be free from any suffering and to have happiness. It is worshipping the highest spiritual principle and the supreme benefit to sentient beings.

[119] One should eliminate temporary and ultimate suffering, carrying the burden of holding in mind sentient beings' suffering along with its causes, and accomplish their happiness. Therefore, contemplate exchanging oneself and others as equals. With the four immeasurables and the four ways of gathering disciples,[395] do as much as possible to fufill the welfare of others and dedicate that to awakening. You should strive with effort for whatever activities of the three doors of body, speech, and mind to be virtuous actions produced with the supreme awakening mind for whatever activities one does.

[120] You should achieve with effort the six perfections and so forth, with actions of purity in object and intent. You should increase the resolve and arouse the application of the awakening mind.

[121] If root infractions should emerge, with the counteragent and regret, confess within a third of a day and restore the former condition. If it goes beyond that, take the vow again. Confess misdeeds imagining the Three Precious Ones in your presence. When confessing three times a day, three times a night, one is undefiled. Undeteriorated, having exhausted wrongdoing, one has immeasurable merit and gains the conditions of happiness ending with buddhahood.

[122] Take whichever suitable of the seven types of prātimokṣa vows as a basis for the bodhisattva vows. Stabilize the wish for awakening and study the scriptures. With the capacity to have faith and protect the scriptures, [123] a skillful capable one who keeps the vows while having compassion should aspire with effort to have a Great Vehicle mental continuum.

[124] Practicing dharma with virtue is the moral conduct of the vow, and benefitting sentient beings is the three vows of moral conduct. The vows are promised through ritual, and one should guard them, keeping them uncorrupted.

[125] The root downfalls of a bodhisattva are as follows: (1) honor and gain, praising oneself, deprecating others; (2) causing suffering to the unprotected; (3) not giving dharma and wealth; (4) not listening to apologies with anger; (5) giving up the Great Vehicle and appearing to teach the excellent dharma; (6) stealing the property of the Three Jewels; (7) completely abandoning the sacred dharma; (8) causing harm to the life and so forth of a monk; (9) deliberately committing the five heinous acts; (10) holding wrong views and ignorance for cause and effect, and so forth; (11) destroying cities and kingdoms; (12) proclaiming emptiness while not training in the Great Vehicle; (13) turning away from engaging in highest

awakening; (14) abandoning the prātimokṣa vows while practicing the Great Vehicle; (15) engaging in and not eliminating desire and so forth through training; (16) speaking falsely, saying, "I know the profound"; (17) persecuting a monk while donating to the three jewels; (18) giving up quiescence and appropriating wealth; and (19) forsaking the awakening mind are the root downfalls.

[126] The faulty actions of bodhisattvas are as follows: (1) passing over day and night not offering to the three jewels; (2) following desires; (3) voluntarily accepting riches and honor; (4) not having respect for elders with conceit and so forth; (5) speaking joyfully and not offering a reply to questions; (6) not accepting an invitation for a feast and not accepting gold, wealth, and so forth; (7) not giving to those seeking the holy dharma; (8) forsaking those with offensive qualities and so forth; (9) not training for the sake of arising faith; (10) not protecting the mind; (11) not obtaining wealth for the benefit of others; (12) not committing a nonvirtuous action for others' welfare with compassion; (13) earning a living through wrong livelihood; (14) wasting time on frivolous actions and distracting others and so forth; (15) not having joy for liberation; (16) not being fearful of afflictions and so forth; (17) not living up to precepts that might decrease one's reputation; (18) not correcting a mind which is capable but endowed with afflictions; (19) replying to exposing one's faults by striking with abuse; (20) neglecting those who are angry with you; (21) refusing to accept the apologies of others; (22) keeping in one's mental continuum the arousal of anger within oneself; (23) gathering disciples out of desire for material gain and respect; (24) wasting time and not countering laziness; (25) relying on frivolous talk; (26) not seeking mental concentration while having pride and so forth; (27) not abandoning obstacles such as desires and aspirations, and so forth; (28) viewing the enjoyment of concentration as a virtuous quality;

(29) abandoning the doctrines of the Śrāvaka Vehicle and being of the Great Vehicle while making effort in the Śrāvaka Vehicle; (30) making effort in outsider practices while not making effort in Buddhist practices, and making effort in outsider practices for their own sake; (31) abandoning the great extensive vehicle; (32) praising oneself and belittling others with a turbulent mind; (33) not attending dharma ceremonies or increasing the teachings; (34) disparaging the dharma preacher and not relying on his words; (35) not assisting those who need help; (36) avoiding the duties of caring for the sick; (37) not working to alleviate those who suffer; (38) not teaching to those who are careless; (39) not repaying the kindness of others; (40) not consoling the distress of others; (41) not giving to those who desire food and resources; (42) not caring for one's companions with dharma and material resources; (43) not acting in accordance with others' wishes; (44) not praising those who have good qualities; (45) not preventing harmful acts permitted by circumstance; (46) not wishing to act and so forth while having miraculous powers.

---

[128] With a desire to produce the ultimate mind for supreme awakening, offer one's body or possessions to view the guru as the dharma body. Offer whatever one can afford and take highest refuge. Serve with motivation for the sake of being established in buddhahood. In one million worlds while traversing cycle existence, the object of observation is the guru, who is the great Vajradhara. The path to train in is actually one's own mind free from extremes. It is activity carried out as a vessel of that path. In this way, one should practice the procedure of going for refuge in the supreme.

[129] Aggregates, elements, sensory spheres, subjects and objects, are primordially unborn, sameness, with the awakening mind.

Generating the awakening mind in the condition of being free from extremes is practicing to view the guru as the Buddha, the dharma body.

[130] As one's own mind, primordially, is free from elaborations in the three times, there is nothing anywhere to meditate upon. One should be established within the effortless, naturally perfected state. Later on, do not interrupt the session in the middle of the day.

[131] Although realizing concepts as empty, one should achieve virtue and abandon wrongdoing. Even though realizing the equality of self and others, one should benefit others. Although abiding in the condition of equanimity, keep to secluded places. Even though realizing nonduality, abandon deprecating things. Although being without hope or fear, abandon wrongdoing and achieve virtue. Although attaining the result, the three bodies, keep in accord with others. At all times and occasions, eliminate wrong view. As the activity of a beginner bodhisattva is not actually able to achieve great benefit for others, through contemplation, abandon one's own concerns and achieve others' welfare. What is the use of generating the awakening mind if one does not achieve others' welfare? With activity of body, speech, and mind setting to achieve others' happiness and welfare, one should desire to free beings from suffering and to have happiness. In this way, when equalizing oneself and others, one should accomplish as much as one can the welfare of others. Furthermore, with as much resources as possible through body, speech, and mind, at first one should practice giving small portions of giving, even a mere mouthful of food, to animals and so forth. Then, later, one can give even one's own body for the welfare of others without difficulty. When cultivating love, compassion, and the awakening mind, do not cause harm to others such as ene-

mies, evil spirits, and animals. Be free from the fear of fire, water, precipices, and so forth. One should have faith in oneself whatever is perceived. If you have hateful or harmful thoughts, then turn away from them. Whatever is within you is how the external world appears. Because of that, you should furthermore understand all external and internal things this way. Ascertain experiences to be nothing but karma and conditions. Quickly purify with certainty any collected defilements.

[132] The chief principal of happiness is benefitting others, and benefitting and respecting others achieves happiness. The situation of greatly benefitting others brings happiness to oneself as well. And, in the end, the benefitting of others leads to complete buddhahood. Acting for one's own benefit is to become a slave or dog. It makes one stupid, ugly, and disdained by others. In the end, one experiences unbearable sufferings of the hells and so forth. In the past, one has immeasurable sufferings in the six realms of saṃsāra. All of that is misfortune and calamity created by seeking one's own benefit.

[133] Therefore, abandon one's own benefit and achieve the welfare of others, doing as much as one is able and always keeping them in mind like one's own son, and through that, one will complete the accumulations of merit and attain extensive happiness. Therefore, always train in the awakening mind. Since the faulty nature of sentient beings is like fire, one should not proclaim others' faults, one should refrain from belligerence, and hearing or seeing the faults of others should be kept secret. Listen and speak about others' good qualities because it is the cause of producing happiness for oneself and others. One should make happy the minds of others with whatever actions are suitable.

[134] Parents, children, relatives, health, wealth, possessions, pleasure, comfort, enemies, disease, hunger and thirst, cold and hunger, all the various sufferings are discordant due to conditions. Since they are not at all real entities, for example, like a lifeless dream, the delusion which produces joy and sadness, although like a cool beverage when thirsty, they are unquenchable. Likewise, the hungry are not satisfied with food. With respect to this, hunger and thirst do not really exist and food and drink do not really exist. Likewise, all the various joys and sufferings are not actually real, like a dream. Therefore, as they are not real, one should abandon attachment or aversion to appearances. As the impermanent is false since it is deceptive, impermanent entities should not be entrusted to awareness. Things that are not real like an illusion should not be apprehended as real; they are a mere illusion. If one knows they are false, the suffering of attachment and aversion is cleared away. Therefore, all the joys and sufferings are mere mistaken appearances that are not actually established.

[135] When grasping and imagining joy and suffering for nothing whatsoever, then suffering arises again and flourishes. In this way, even while one understands, suffering is not cleared away, and even while one hears many dharma teachings, when afflictions are not cleared away, one is devoid of practice and proclaiming with mere words like a chattering, starving person.

[136] When one with special instructions takes up practice, gradually the suffering of grasping things as real comes to cessation. Therefore, when one always meditates on things to be like an illusion, discordant suffering experiences cease. In this way, practice what is pointed out by the example of a dream. Look at appearances as not being real things.

[145] All things of saṃsāra and nirvāṇa are one's own mind, for example, like a mirror, reflection, or echo. All is unmixed, the union of all transcends limited views. The essence of one's own mind is luminous and naturally empty. The unified characteristic is liberated from the extremes of elaborations. Whatever happiness or suffering that appears is one's own mind. There is not another dharma not cognized from the mind. When it is construed as another established elaboration, it is mistaken.

[146] It is from the beginning, innately pure, unconditioned, free from extremes, sameness, without acceptance or rejection of views. In this way, the mind itself is established as the way of things; mind-as-such is pure like the sky. Whether the victorious ones of the three times teach it or not, whether sentient beings realize it or not, from the beginning perfect gnosis is the dharmakāya, unfabricated, not taken up; from the beginning it is the awakening mind. From the beginning it is stainless and pure; the afflictions and sufferings of cyclic existence are not at all established.

[147] Mind itself, from the beginning, innately established, cannot be realized by the many who deliberately seek out signs of it. Meditating without a view and free of activity, the result, not to be sought elsewhere, is established from the beginning. [148] Whether through the condition of the spiritual teacher's teaching or not, whether a yogi meditates or not, [149] whether wise ones realize or not, the unconditioned mind-as-such is free from causal conditions. It is not permanent, and is free from the extremes of nihilism; it is without arising, cessation, sameness, difference, coming, or going. Pacified of these eight extremes of elaboration, it has the characteristic of the self-arisen awakening mind.

[150] Since saṃsāra is not established as other than mind, the sufferings of the lower realms and so forth are not eliminated. Since buddhahood is not established as other than mind, the equalizing of saṃsāra and nirvāṇa and happiness and suffering is one's own mind.

[151] All without exception who have a view of the perishable aggregates, who grasp extremes, who view things as real, who think themselves supreme, do not see one's own mind. Not seeing anything at all is established as the nature of the mind itself. From the beginning, free from elaborations, the nature of the mind is unestablished, without shape and color, free from signs. Without a mind for the sense faculties, there is not an object. There is not a mind other than that; it is emptiness. The empty mind does not have heavenly or lower rebirth; as it is selfless, it is free from suffering. The individual who apprehends the sense of "I" takes up a mistake; due to the fact that a self does not exist, one is suitable to abandon self-grasping. The nonmind is emptiness. The Buddha does not see, has not seen, will not see the mind. Because a Buddha, who has eyes without dust, is without a mind, even if badly agitated the mind is not born nor does it die. Likewise, even by the fire at the end of an eon, mind itself, emptiness, is not burned. Because one's own mind from the beginning is emptiness, seeing, searching, training, meditating is not empty. Naturally, from the beginning, there is emptiness; there is not an object at all to be cultivated. There is not a meditator, free from all views and practices, everything is unestablished, one's own mind is empty and everywhere, uncultivated, undisturbed, this is the nature of emptiness.

[152] When in a manner without establishing or taking things up, then subtle and coarse conceptual mental facets (*caitta*) are ascertained as empty. While flowing down like water, appearing from itself to itself, appearances that lack intrinsic essence are directly

identified as subtle or coarse flickers of thought. They spontaneously subside by themselves, vanishing into the fundamental nature of existence.

[153] After that, the body and all appearances without exception should be imagined as emptiness. Mental facets, appearances like external objects, are not truly existent and should be perceived like reflections, echoes, dreams, apparent objects, mirages, hairs in one's vision, or like clouds in the sky, self-arising, and dissolving. In this way, all appearances and conceptual thoughts are eradicated by the mind in emptiness, which lets go of the mind of self-grasping. One should apply oneself to the counteragents for all negative conditions.

[154] Sufferings of the factions of wrathful guardians of hell and the lower realms of rebirth, such as the pretas and so forth, all sufferings, although emerging as an enemy to oneself, all those do not taint the mind. Likewise, the mind in emptiness is not tainted by the afflictions, conceptions, sufferings, and discordant obscurations. Just as water or fire at the end of an eon does not taint the sky, likewise the mind is insubstantial, free from the sufferings of birth and death. Therefore, one's own mind from the beginning is emptiness. Practice to definitely realize that it is. One who is not established in the natural disposition of emptiness should train in undistracted mindfulness.

[155] With the weapon of wisdom which realizes emptiness, one should eradicate the enemies of Self and Self-grasping due to ignorance and eradicate apprehending due to the delusion of a Self and what pertains to a Self. Moreover, with the total abandonment of conceptual thought purifying by application of the fourth time of great equality, that will be established by correct mindfulness.

Moreover, do not be separated from the weapon of emptiness, and eradicate all subtle and coarse conceptual thought.

[156] When not cutting off discordant factors while even realizing emptiness, because one is without the power and blessing of the spiritual teacher, emptiness that is the mere intellectual understanding of words is not effective for one's mental continuum. All negative conditions become suitable concordant conditions with the friend of the path of awakening. When practiced, it produces all good qualities.

[157] When one realizes the meaning of emptiness, transgressions are consumed and great merit is completed, discordant conditions do not subdue the mind, all the sufferings of cyclic existence, hells, and so forth, are destroyed. Effortlessly abide in the meaning of unity; if emptiness did not exist, unity would be chasing mere words. When there exists the realization of emptiness, all external things are realized to be like reflections—inner and external, causes and effects, the multiple dependent arisings, the totality of things that appear. Cut the elaborations of the mind! Mere words are utterly mundane when speaking about emptiness. When one is liberated from all of cyclic existence without exception, omniscient buddhahood will be realized.

[158] The union of the basis, the path, and the result is self-arisen, emptiness, the realm of reality, pure, unconditioned, naturally free from elaborations, with nothing at all established, as in empty space. The signs of entities are not established in that. It is the coemergent way of things, the essence, the factor of clarity, without object, without conceptual thought, inherent translucent radiance, unceasing, appearing like the sun in a cloudless sky, the union of the unelaborated character of coemergence, self-illuminating,

the unceasing appearance of lucidity and awareness, indivisibile appearance and emptiness, like a conch shell and the whiteness of a conch shell. There is not anything at all not indivisible from one's own mind. Nonconceptual awareness is without a grasping subject and graspable object, while the unceasing agitated mind is like the wind. The appearance factor of indivisble coemergence is own-form, like five lights without objects, the pure light of crystal. Saṃsāra and nirvāṇa appear as two from conceptual and nonconceptual thought.

[159] The mind itself, pure from the beginning, is the realm of reality; it pervades whatever entities that appear even if they do not directly appear due to delusion; it is all-pervading like sesame oil in sesames. The apprehending subject and apprehended object of karma and appearance are like an illusion. Appearances, reflections, deluded appearances, emanations, nonconceptual appearances, and mirages are like space. All that appears is one's own mind. The nature of all that appears is empty, and all various appearances without exception are nondually unified with one's own mind. Cause and effect are indivisibly empty like waves. Whatever appears is not other than the mind, like the variety of golden things that do not change from their golden form. The formations of virtuous and nonvirtuous mental facets are variegated activities like reflections, the pure dharmakāya free from passing stains, inseparable from manifest self-cognizant wakefulness, pure like the sky free from clouds. Just as the bodies, buddhafields, along with mansions, are appearances of pure gnosis—not other—one's own mind is an appearance of merit.

[160] Cognize the realm of reality with gnosis, like space. The body, fields, and so forth, all appear pure as indivisible appearance and emptiness; the self-arising two collections do not come from another. They do not externally appear. The unstained powers,

fearlessness, buddha qualities, the minor and major marks and other qualities, the streaming rain of sacred dharma from the clouds of omniscient mercy, recollecting the cause of the obstinate three realms, the fully ripened harvest of the three bodies—these are the ripened activities of virtuous qualities.

[161] Continuously practicing the view free from extremes, the beginner individual meaning of unity is practiced inseparably based on intellectual understanding. One should establish in practice the nature of virtue, nonvirtue, cause, effect, subtle, and coarse in terms of the subtle emptiness of intrinsic nature. Even all that is practiced does not pass beyond emptiness. Therefore, because it is free from the elaboration of extremes, the various conditions which occur are undeceiving cause and effect; one's own mind is liberated from the extreme of nihilism. Since nonconceptual mere appearance is empty, it is free from the extreme of permanence. One's own mind is liberated from the extremes of permanence and nihilism. Indivisible cause/effect and emptiness are the meaning of view. It is an error of yogic vision when one falls to limited views. Therefore, do not fall into an established philosophical position. The inseparable clear mind is pervaded with emptiness, the nature for all dharmas, like sesame pervaded by sesame oil. What is the use of apprehending emptiness with the mind? Emptiness and the mind are inseparable like the wings of a bird.

[162] A yogi should not abandon cause and effect even when realizing all things as empty because the mere appearance from virtue and sin arises from various results. For the happiness of oneself and others, the cause and effect of virtue and sin should be subtly taken up like an illusion. Because one's own empty mind is the inseparability of cause and effect, the meaning of dependent arising is free from limitations. When entities and nonentities are apprehended as

permanent, it is a downfall that misunderstands the vision in yoga. Therefore, one should practice the indivisibility of emptiness and positive/negative actions. Although realizing emptiness, since it is possible to fall to nihilism, like two legs walking on the path, do not cast away cause and effect. With the weapon of wisdom that realizes things as empty yet discerns unmistakable cause and effect, eliminate unfavorable conditions.

[163] The yoga which engages emptiness as cause and effect is devoid of seeking out the undifferentiated. One's own mind free from extremes like space is the meaning of the Great Middle Way. One should, in this way, practice constantly and not get established in the immediate intellectual understanding of the nature. When nonvirtuous karma is mixed with emptiness, the generated force of the nonvirtue quickly ripens a great result. When virtuous karma is mixed with emptiness, the generated force of virtue quickly ripens a supremely good result. Therefore, although realizing sameness, vigorously generate and achieve in practice the most subtle in regards to virtue and sin. An emptiness where virtue and sin do not exist falls to nihilism. Therefore, practice cause/effect and emptiness as inseparable. Do not be established in the intellectual understanding of mere words, purify the mental continuum, and put into practice the vision of unmistaken coalescence.

[164] Even if realizing one's own mind as emptiness becomes stable, without the supreme method of the awakening mind and compassion, the path of omniscience will not be found. Although having love, compassion, and the awakening mind, if one does not comprehend things with emptiness, one will not be liberated from the place of saṃsāra for a long time. When one unifies the supreme method of compassion with emptiness and puts into practice the very great path that is correct and unmistaken, the excellent results

of extraordinary rebirth as gods and humans and the supreme result of buddhahood will be attained. This is the great path of all buddhas. If means is separate from wisdom, like someone with broken legs that tries to walk down a path, one will not be able to proceed. Therefore, means and wisdom are inseparable. Intelligent individuals should put them into practice. Furthermore, when one engages in all activities, generating love, compassion, and the awakening mind, all activities should be attained with emptiness. The virtue of integrating emptiness, compassion, and the awakening mind should be dedicated to supreme awakening. In this way, one puts in practice the union of means and wisdom.

---

[181] May sentient beings without exception achieve supreme awakening due to whatever roots of virtue that have arisen from writing this text.

The Stages of the Path to Awakening *composed by Śrī Dīpaṃkārajñāna (for the sake of Dromtönpa) is concluded.*

CHAPTER 13

Tārā, the Savioress, Selections

Atiśa had dreams, visions, and predictions from Tārā throughout his life. His charismatic devotion to the goddess was the impetus for the faithful worship of Tārā in Tibetan Buddhist culture. Atiśa's lineage tradition of Tārā is the most distinguished among the five teaching traditions of Tārā in Tibet.[396] *The entire ritual edifice of worshipping Tārā in Tibet is built upon Atiśa's major works on the goddess.*[397] *The following selections demonstrate his devotion and ritual meditations for approaching the great Buddhist goddess Tārā.*

Praise to Tārā as the Three Jewels

Homage to you, Tārā, the Buddha,
Who eliminates wrong views, ignorance, lethargy,
The supreme wisdom pervading all objects of knowledge,
She who has attained complete perfect excellence.

Homage to you, Tārā, the noble dharma.
Great bliss, peaceful, nirvāṇa,
The ten-letter supreme noble dharma
The method of the ten perfections,[398]

Homage to you, Tārā, the spiritual community,
The secret body, speech, and mind

Of all the sugatas of the three times
Aggregation of wisdom ḍākiṇīs.

A Means of Achieving White Tārā[399]

Homage to the venerable Tārā!

First the practitioner of mantra should cleanse his or her face and so forth and then, in a clean place of meditation which is pleasant, one should sprinkle sweet perfume.[400] Sitting cross-legged on a clean, comfortable seat, bless an offering cake for all harmful spirits and recite the following mantra up to ten times:

OṂ ĀḤ VIGHNĀNTAKṚT HŪṂ PHAṬ[401]

This should expel all the hindrances residing in the ten directions.

Then, visualize at one's own heart radiating white light-rays, like the autumn moon, which indicate that all things have the unproduced nature of the realm of reality, and which strongly radiate, illuminating one's own body. Transforming the rays, visualize an essential drop (*bindu*) of white light, like pure crystal, which gradually expands into the form of a moon disk. On top of this, visualize the syllable TĀṂ radiating a mass of white light-rays like a jeweled lamp. Then, one should visualize that the TĀṂ syllable illuminates all world realms with masses of extremely white light-rays and invokes and invites the goddess Tārā and so forth, the buddhas, bodhisattvas, and spiritual teachers to the area of space directly in front of you. In addition to this, one should make offerings which are of a mental nature. The following is the ritual sequence for the offerings:

Recite the mantra OṂ VAJRA-PUṢPE HŪṂ![402] and make the offering with masses of offerings of flowers that arise from the syllable TĀṂ.

Then, recite the mantra OṂ VAJRA-DHŪPE HŪṂ![403] and make the offering with masses of offerings of incense from the very same TĀṂ syllable.

After that, recite the mantra OṂ VAJRA-DĪPE HŪṂ![404] and make the offering with jeweled lamps emanated from the very same TĀṂ syllable.

Then, recite the mantra OṂ VAJRA-GANDHE HŪṂ![405] and make the offering by sending out real offering clouds that come from the very same TĀṂ syllable.

Next, recite the mantra OṂ VAJRA-NAIVEDYĀ HŪṂ![406] and make the offering by sending out from the very same TĀṂ syllable various offering clouds of divine food offerings having excellent taste placed in various vessels of precious stones.

Then, recite the mantra OṂ SARVA-VIŚIṢṬA-PŪJA-MEGHA-PRASARA-SAMUDRA ĀḤ HŪṂ![407] and make the offering with parasols, banners, bells, pennants, canopies, and so forth, of the seven precious jewels and the seven royal treasures of a universal monarch from the very same TĀṂ syllable.

Having performed the offering in this way, in front of those spiritual beings, one should confess one's transgressions, rejoice in merit, invoke them to teach dharma, request them to stay until the end of saṃsāra, dedicate the merit, and go for refuge in the three jewels.

Next, having meditated on the four abodes of Brahma—that is, loving-kindness, compassion, sympathetic joy, and equanimity—one should make firm the awakening mind.

Then, recite three times the following mantra:

OṂ SVABHĀVAŚUDDHĀḤ SARVADHARMĀḤ SVABHĀVAŚUDDHO 'HAṂ[408]

One should perceive all migrating beings as the nature of emptiness, like dreams, illusions, and mirages.

Then, visualize the syllable A transforming into a moon disk upon which the white syllable TĀṂ is visualized as a collection of white light-rays. This transforms into a blue utpala flower at the center of which is visualized on top of a moon disk the white syllable TĀṂ.

From this, white light-rays radiate in the ten directions, and having purified all sentient beings, the light-rays themselves transform into the form of the goddess Tārā and dissolve into the utpala flower and syllable TĀṂ.

In the center of a white lotus,
On top of a seat in the form of a moon,
Sitting in a cross-legged vajra pose,
Granting boons and holding an utpala,
Resting the back upon a moon of color like the autumn moon,
Complete with all the ornaments having the body of a sixteen-year-old,
As the mother of the perfect buddhas and their sons, I fulfill all wishes.

Through transforming the white TĀṂ on top of the moon-disk at the heart of this noble Tārā,

Visualize a wheel of white light-rays,
Its eight spokes are
Surrounded by eight syllables

While at the hub are OṂ and TĀ
With the name of that to be practiced at the center.
Devoted and firm for six months
Visualize with a one-pointed mind
This ten-syllable mantra
Recite with the mind until you are tired.
First place the syllable OṂ,
Then after that connect TĀRE,
After that TUTTĀRE and TURE,
SVĀHĀ at the end fashions all deeds.

From the wheel at the heart, white light radiates invoking and exhorting the naturally established wisdom being (*jñānasattva*), which is like the pledge being (*samayasattva*), visualizing her in the space in front of you. Correctly make offerings as before.

Then, one should bind with the pledge hand gesture (*samayamudrā*) and join the palms with a hollow inside, join the forefingers to the backs of the middle fingers, and bend the thumbs inside: this is the hand gesture of the utpala (*utpalamudrā*).

In the center of that, visualize a white TĀṂ syllable radiating with golden light-rays from that, which encircle the wisdom being.

Then, inviting with the four syllables JAḤ HŪṂ BAṂ HOḤ, the entity of the pledge being is summoned, bound, and gratified, and then, with the pride of being the deity, recite,

OṂ DHARMADHĀTU-JÑĀNA-VAJRA-SVABHĀVĀTMAKO 'HAM[409]

After that, emanating light-rays from the wheel along with the syllables, visualize the five tathāgatas arriving in the space in front of you and purposefully cast this verse of empowerment:

Just as the Bodhivajra
Requested the most supreme to the buddhas,
Now I request the vajra of space
For the sake of my protection.

Then, visualize that Locanā, Māmakī, Pāṇḍaravāsinī, and Tārā emanate from the bodies of the tathāgatas, holding in their hands precious vases of the nectar of wisdom that consecrate, reciting the following verse:

The empowerment of the great Vajra,
Worshipped by the three realms
Will be bestowed by all the buddhas
Who emerge from the places of the three secrets.

As soon as the consecration is completed, visualize on her crown jewel the tathāgata Amitābha, his body white in color, with one face and two arms, in the hand gesture of concentration.

For the blessings of body, speech, and mind, fully arrange at her crown a white OṂ resting on a moon disk; at her throat a red ĀḤ resting on a moon disk; and at her heart a dark blue HŪṂ resting on a moon disk.

Clearly visualize white light-rays radiating from the ten letters purifying all migrating beings so that they achieve buddhahood and are then drawn back and absorbed into the wheel and syllables while muttering the mantra.

Having visualized and muttered until you are tired, if you wish to rise up, in order to restore any faults in the ritual, recite the mantra known as "the hundred-syllables," the heart of Vajrasattva. Then make proper offerings to the wisdom being, dedicate the merits, and ask her to leave.

The verse of requesting the wisdom being to leave is:

OṂ!
You accomplish all the aims of sentient beings;
Grant me favorable siddhis!
Having departed to your buddhaland,
I request that you come again.
MUḤ!

The mantra which is recited is: OṂ TĀRE TUTTĀRE TURE SVĀHĀ

In this regard, the mantra of the one-hundred syllable heart of Vajrasattva is:

> OṂ VAJRASATTVA SAMAYAM ANUPĀLAYA, VAJRASATTVA TENOPATIṢṬHA, DṚḌHO ME BHAVA, SUTOṢYO ME BHAVA, SUPOṢYO ME BHAVA, ANURAKTO ME BHAVA, SARVASIDDHIM ME PRAYACCHA, SARVAKARMASU CA ME CITTAṂ ŚREYAḤ KURU HŪṂ, HA HA HA HA HOḤ BHAGAVAN SARVATATHĀGATAVAJRA MĀ ME MUÑCA, VAJRĪBHĀVA MAHĀSAMAYASATTVA ĀḤ[410]

Through these merits, may all migrating beings
Become like Venerable Tārā!
May I, as well, having achieved this concentration
Become a buddha for the benefit of migrating beings!

A Means of Achieving the Venerable Tārā *composed by the great Ācārya Śrī Dīpaṃkarajñāna is complete. The Indian master Dīpaṃkaraśrījñāna and the Tibetan translator-monk Gewa Lodrö translated, revised, and finalized the text.*

Protection from the Eight Fears[411]

Tārā is famous for protecting against eight great fears. The eight fears have an outer aspect, such as elephants and lions, as well as an inner aspect that correlate with mental afflictions. The eight great fears in their outer and inner aspects are: (1) water/drowning, (2) robbers/false views, (3) lions/pride, (4) snakes/jealousy, (5) fire/anger, (6) flesh-eating demons/doubt, (7) imprisonment/greed, and (8) elephants/ignorance.

Homage to the bhagavatī Tārā!

A master of yoga enters a residence for meditation and, sitting on a comfortable seat, promises, "With great compassion I will raise up all migrating beings." Then one should meditate on the goddess Tārā.

This should be practiced according to the following stages. At the yogin's own heart, visualize the syllable TĀṂ on top of a moon disk arising from the syllable A. Hook-like light-rays emanate outward from this, and you should clearly see in the space in front of you one's own spiritual teacher as well as the perfectly complete buddhas.

Pay homage to them, confess your transgressions, go for refuge in the three jewels, dedicate your roots of virtuous qualities, offer your body, and make aspirational prayers.

Then, meditate on emptiness by contemplating, "Ultimately, I, the deity, and so forth, are without intrinsic nature and are unproduced from the very beginning," and in order to make it firmly established say,

OṂ ŚŪNYATĀ-JÑĀNA-VAJRA-SVABHĀVĀTMAKO 'HAM[412]

Next, in the center of an eight-petalled lotus arising from the syllable PAṂ, one's own mind, by the power of previous aspirational prayers, produces the goddess Tārā from the syllable TĀṂ.

She is green in color, with one face and two arms. Her right hand rests in the hand gesture of giving boons and her left hand holds an utpala flower. She has Amoghasiddhi as a head ornament and sits in the half cross-legged position.

Meditate on this until tired. When tired one should engage in recitation. The mantra garland, OṂ TĀRE TUTTĀRE TURE SVĀHĀ, emerges from your heart and enters your mouth. Gradually arising from one's own heart, one should visualize the mantra as white in color gently rotating and recite it.

When you are tired even of reciting, make offerings and offering-cakes, and make aspirational prayers. You should reside in all activities with the pride of the goddess. You should enter emptiness when going to sleep. When waking up, instantly arise with the pride of the goddess.

Protection from the Eight Fears, *composed by the great master Ācārya Śrī Dīpaṃkarajñāna is completed.*

The Abridged Clear Realization of Noble Tārā

In the Indian language: *Ārya tārā abhisamaya piṇḍārtha*
In the Tibetan language: *'Phags ma sgrol ma'i mngon par rtogs pa bsdus pa*

Homage to the venerable Tārā!

One who wishes to visualize the Venerable Lady in an abridged manner of clear realization should first go for refuge to the Three

Jewels three times. Then generate the altruistic awakening mind for the sake of sentient beings. Next visualize a green syllable TĀṂ on top of a moon disk that has arisen from the syllable A at one's heart, which, having purified obstacles and hindrances, takes the form of the Venerable Lady.

Sitting on a lotus and moon seat
The color of green, with one face and two arms
Her right hand in the hand gesture of giving boons, her left hand
holding at her heart the root of an utpala flower
Her right and left legs in the cross-legged pose
Adorned with all the ornaments.

Through radiating light-rays from the seed at her heart, the wisdom being is invited. Through making reverence and offerings and so forth, the four syllables JAḤ HŪṂ BAṂ HOḤ summon, draw in, make enter, and bind the wisdom being. Then, at her crown is the letter OṂ, at her throat is the letter ĀḤ, at the heart is the letter HŪṂ. Single-pointedly visualize those syllables.

Then, if you become tired, at the final phase of residing, the letter TĀṂ on a moon disk at one's heart should be visualized, and recite OṂ TĀRE TUTTĀRE TURE SVĀHĀ. Clearly focus the mind on the ten letters skillfully, slowly reciting to eliminate the faults of distraction. Also recite many times the following dhāraṇī:

NAMAH ĀRYĀVALOKITEŚVARĀYA, BODHISATVAYA, MAHĀSATVAYA, MAHĀKARUṆIKĀYA, TADYATHĀ, OṂ TĀRE TUTTĀRE TURE, SARVADUṢṬĀṂ, PRADUṢṬĀṂ MAMA KṚTE JAṂBHAYA JAṂBHAYA, STAMBHAYA STAMBHAYA, MOHAYO MOHAYA, BANDHAYA BANDHAYA HŪṂ HŪṂ HŪṂ, PHAṬ PHAṬ PHAṬ, SARVADUṢṬASTAMBHANITĀRE SVĀHĀ.

Dedicate for the purpose of all sentient beings at the time of application.

If you wish to utter a praise of the Venerable Lady Tārā, go for refuge, generate the altruistic awakening mind, and at your heart visualize a moon disk from the syllable A, and on top of that a green syllable TĀṂ. Then, having purified obstacles and hindrances with the light-rays from the syllables, one is the Venerable Lady Tārā with a green-colored body sitting on a white lotus and moon-disk seat, her hand gestures are in the positions as mentioned before. One then invites the Venerable Lady Tārā radiating light-rays from the seed at the heart center, enacts the seven pure actions [of confession, rejoicing, arousing absolute bodhicitta, refuge, arousing the aspiring awakening mind, arousing the engaging awakening mind, and dedicating the merit], enters into the self-identifying gesture of granting refuge, and contemplates engaging with the wishes of all sentient beings without exception. When saying "I pay homage," each time make a prostration mentally. Recite many times praises with a one-pointed mind on the body in front of you. Then recite as much as one is able to the Venerable Lady.

When seeking protection from the Venerable Lady, recite one hundred thousand root mantras according to the method discussed earlier. Through the yoga of residing in the concentration of the Venerable Lady Tārā, having established the name which is to be achieved in the center of the mantra explained earlier, recite for as long as you wish. Then, perceive that light-rays arise from the seed syllable and pervade all the bodies to be achieved. Perceive that the bodies become satisfied due to the light-rays and become unharmable by dangers. This is the protection of pacification.

Then for banishing: with the mantra possessed of the former mental concentration, at one's own heart, radiate green light-rays from the syllable TĀṂ, striking the body to be practiced upon.

Visualize the opponent as naked, trembling with loose hair, unprotected, stiff with fright, ignorant, suppressed, and bound. When you become tired from this, recite the formerly discussed mantras. Having performed this practice in four meditation sessions, one will bind opponents and so forth.

Likewise, through mental concentration while going on the path, having abandoned bonds, when going while mindful of the mantras, thieves, tigers, bears, grizzly bears, snakes, forest deer, and creatures in the water will be unable to subdue you. You will be free from any great fears and liberated again from any bonds.

The Abridgement of the Clear Realization Method of Reciting the Noble Tārā *composed by Śrī Dipaṃkarajñāna is completed.*

CHAPTER 14

Essential Condensed Summary of the Special Instructions on Coemergent Union

The Essential Condensed Summary of the Special Instructions on Coemergent Union[413] *(hereafter* Coemergent Union*) is a brief compilation on Atiśa's oral instructions on coemergent union (*lhan cig skyes byor*), or coemergent yoga, to his disciple Gönpawa. Atiśa's* Coemergent Union *instructs that the coemergent mind is the dharma body and that any appearances that arise are derived from the dharma body. The text initially clarifies that the mind in its coemergent essence, nature, and character is free from limitations and is naturally clear when in a state of nonconceptuality. The text outlines a set of four yogas that gradually appear in the practice of this meditation and are found in later literature on Mahāmudrā.* Coemergent Union *then outlines how the practice of meditating on the clear light allows one to recognize the natural clear light at the time of death. The meeting of the natural clear light and the clear light of meditation is stated to be the attainment of Mahāmudrā.*

Lord Atiśa's Great Seal Bestowed upon Gönpawa

Namo Devaguru! The teacher previously stated: what is called coemergent union is an extremely profound special instruction that Atiśa bestowed upon Gönpawa, to the effect that the coemergent mind itself is the dharma body and coemergent appearance is the light of the dharma body, and they abide like the moon and the light of the moon, or like sandalwood and the fragrance of sandalwood. Moreover, at the time of practice, the special instruction of the guru is about the essence, nature, and character of the mind.

In this regard, the essence of the mind is free from production, perdurance, and cessation. For example, when summer clouds disappear, or when winter snowstorms do not emerge, or when one sees the pure sky of autumn, then an indescribable vivid clarity comes at once. Likewise, the concepts of one's own mind, which have previously ceased, will not be produced in the future, do not abide at all in between, and are said to be vivid, limpid clarity without intrinsic nature. The nature of the mind appears in various aspects: its nature is empty of production, cessation, or abiding. The character of mind is that it cognizes and variously appears as happiness and suffering, white and red, and joy and sadness. Accordingly, the essence, nature, and character do not exist as three separate things. The coemergent mind is itself unfabricated, while it is elaborated according to its mode of its appearance. Further, the basis is unfabricated, the path is unwavering and unceasing, and the result is beyond hope and fear.

At the time of practice: Seated on a pleasant seat with a cross-legged posture and the other six of the seven qualities of Vairocana,[414] meditate on the four immeasurables[415] for all sentient beings. Then, all things that appear and exist in saṃsāra and nirvāṇa are one's own mind. Eradicate the misunderstanding that the mind truly begins, remains, or comes to an end, recognizing it as unfabricated, unceasing, unthinking, and unestablished. Do not examine previous thoughts afterward; do not greet later thoughts beforehand; in the present, do not observe anything at all. As clarity is vividly established in the state of nonconceptuality, settle into it in a relaxed and composed manner. When random thoughts arise, those passing thoughts are from the outset self-originated, coemergent mind itself. For as long as thoughts abide, they abide as the coemergent mind itself, and although in the end they dissolve, they dissolve into the coemergent itself and vividly release into the state of dharma body. For example, passing clouds that arise in the pure sky at first arise from the sky, abide for a while in the sky itself, and dissipate in the end, dissolving into the sky itself.[416]

When you understand thus that nothing surpasses the coemergent, and meditate, then four aspects of yoga will successively appear. When, within the clear essence of mind, the vivid clarity of the lack of intrinsic nature does not diverge, this is called the yoga of one-pointedness. At the time that yoga arises in the mental continuum and a worldly appearance is slightly apprehended as true, at times you think that a good meditation has occurred, and at times, when cognition is bereft of the moisture of *dharmatā*, you think you are stable, but thoughts undergo multiple ups and downs.

When you have apprehended the special instructions, have repeatedly and unwaveringly entered equipoise, and expanded the nature of cognition that has entered into meditation, then nonconceptuality is bereft of all extremes of proliferation, such as existence and nonexistence, permanence and annihilation, coming and going, and so forth. That realization of everything as the dharma body is called the yoga bereft of proliferations. At the time this is generated in the continuum, all previous phenomena that have passed, conventional fabrications, are cut off.

When that experience arises in one's mental continuum, then all past phenomena turn into emptiness and conventional proliferations are severed. Like an impoverished person finding a treasure, through cultivating this, all appearances of the worlds of inanimate and sentient beings are understood as one's own mind, and the nature of one's own mind is understood to be unproduced—that is the yoga of multiplicity as having one taste.

When that arises in the mental continuum, then, through the realization that appearances that variously appear as the concepts of graspable object and grasping subject are the mind itself, coemergent as the dharma body, purified thoughts return to their own abode. When you meditate in this way, then your own cognition is liberated from meditator and meditation object, and as equipoise and postmeditation do not exist, objects and their subjects are cognized as nondual—that is called the yoga of nonmeditation.

When that arises in the mental continuum, then, through the realization of one's own mind as dharma body, the fires of the mental afflictions disappear and are pacified. It is taught that all virtuous qualities are naturally produced. Furthermore, the radiant essence of mind is without concepts, and its inherent nature is free from production, cessation, and abiding. Characteristics, saṃsāra, nirvāṇa, and so forth appear as mere concepts, and at that time one one-pointedly realizes the mere essence.

In this way, through sequential meditation on the four yogas, one's own unarisen mind is realized as dharma body, but when pains, aches, suffering, and so forth come about, they envelop the ordinary bodily configuration. It is like the example of the king of beasts, who completes the three powers in the womb of his mother but is still enveloped by the mother's body; or a garuḍa who spreads his wings within an egg but is still enveloped in the egg.[417] Likewise, one's inner mind may be realized as dharma body, but because one is not free from the bodily configuration produced though previous karma, it is not contradictory for happiness, suffering, and so forth, to arise.

Thus, through practice, at the time of death, earth dissolves into water, water dissolves into fire, fire dissolves into wind, wind dissolves into consciousness, and when both wind and the mind enter into the central channel, they naturally ascend to the place where gnosis is coemergent with reality (*dharmatā*).[418] In this way, a person who is already familiar with this through the power of meditation recognizes it upon encountering it, and when the natural clear light and the clear light of meditation meet, one gains the accomplishment of the Great Seal.

Then, having taken up a deity's body unified from within the state of empty clear light, anyone trained in this who manifests such a body produces benefit for sentient beings and further helps others through taking up an illusion-like mental body consisting of uncontaminated karma.[419] If one does not meditate in this way, the natural clear light will not be recognized. Even if it is recognized, one will, by virtue of natural grasping at entities and signs, be terrified and afraid of that clear light and will assume a body that is comprised of grasping and craving, the causes of saṃsāra. When, through karma and so forth, one thusly circles uninterruptedly in the circle of cyclic existence, one must take on immeasurable suffering. Thus, having obtained from the discourse of a holy spiritual teacher the antidote to cyclic existence, this special instruction on coemergent union, one should meditate unwaveringly on it. In order to enhance realization, in the times between meditation sessions, undertake immeasurable efforts to offer maṇḍalas and so forth, make requests to the spiritual teacher and the three jewels, make tsa tsas, circumambulate, prostrate, recite mantras, distribute gifts, and so forth. Through practicing in this way, you will produce a result in a month or a year. Furthermore, it is taught that in all situations postmeditative awareness should cognize things as illusion-like.

This Essential Condensed Summary of the Special Instructions on Coemergent Union *was written down by the Śākya monk Kumara. The lineage was transmitted successively from Vajradhara, Tilopā, Nāropa, Ḍombi Heruka, Lord Atiśa, Gönpawa, Geshé Tönpa, Sharwapa, and Tapkhawa. Later, came the great master Jamnyak, the spiritual teacher Drakgyalwa, then myself.*

Notes

1. Atīśa, *Byaṅ Chub Lam Gyi Rim Pa: Writings of Lord Atīśa on the Theory and Practice of the Graduated Path.* Leh: Thupten Tsering, 1973.
2. Miyazaki 2007a, 2007b.
3. As noted in Eimer 1982, 47n1, and in Sopa et al. 2001, 24n2, the form Atiśa is derived from the Sanskrit *atiśaya*, "eminent, superior" (*phul* (*du*) *byung* (*ba*)), rather than the Sanskrit *ati* + *īśa*, "the great Lord," which is not permitted by the rules of Sanskrit grammar. Tibetans often refer to Atiśa as *jo bo*, "Lord." Note, as well, that early biographies depict the teacher Serlingpa as referring to Dīpaṃkaraśrījñāna as "*adhi sha*" (≈ Adhīśa) (Chim Namkha Drak 2012a, 97.7, 107.10, 161.21, 162.17, 164.9, 173.1). However, in Naktso's biography (2014, 399.2, 399.5), his name is already attested as Atiśa. See Apple 2019a.
4. Bautze-Picron 2016, 165.
5. On "entirely devoted to the Buddha" (*paramasaugataḥ*) see Sanderson 2009, 87.
6. See Blumenthal (2004) on the life and thought of Śāntarakṣita.
7. Eimer (1977, 1979, 1982, 2003).
8. *Rnam thar rgyas pa.*
9. *Rnam thar yongs grags.*
10. Chattopadhyaya (1967, 445–502) lists 117 works, Mochizuki (2016) lists 109 works, Negi (1992, 123–29) lists 120 works, and the *A ti sha gsung 'bum* lists 109 works.
11. Quote from Drukpa Künlé (born in 1455) with slight modification (Divalerio 2015, 65).
12. Phun tshogs tshe brtan 2011, 14.
13. On the location of Sahor see Torricelli 2018, 128–30.
14. Eimer 2010, 306. See van der Kuijp 2013 on Sahor (Za hor) and its place in Indian and Tibetan history.

15. bsTan 'dzin blo gros 2012, 1.
16. See Apple 2019a on Jitāri or Jetāri (*dgra las rnam rgyal*).
17. Tucci 1956, 250–52.
18. Dromtönpa Gyalwai Jungné 2014, 4–6; Jinpa 2006, 41.
19. Cf. Dromtönpa Gyalwai Jungné 2012a, 230.16–18, Decleer 1997b, 171.
20. bsTan 'dzin blo gros 2012, 1.
21. Chattopadhyaya (1967, 73) identifies the mountain as Kālaśilā on the side of Isigili near Rajgir.
22. *ye shes gsang ba'i rdo rje*.
23. On the awareness observance (*rig pa brtul zhugs kyis spyod pa*) see Jamgön Kongtrul Lodrö Tayé 1998, 506.
24. Phun tshogs tshe brtan 2011, 10–11.
25. The dialogue is from Pawo Tsuklak Trengwa 2006, 33625–28. Cf. *Extensive Biography*, 279.6, Eimer 1979, 125.
26. On this type of esoteric Buddhist conduct see Stearns (2001) and DiValerio (2015).
27. *Extensive Biography* 280, Eimer 1979, 127; *Universally Known Biography* 2012, 51.
28. Path of preparation (*prayogamārga*).
29. *dpal mar me mdzad ye shes*. *Extensive Biography* 280–81, Eimer 1979, 129; *Universally Known Biography* 2012, 51–52.
30. bsTan 'dzin blo gros 2012, 2; Eimer 1979, 130, 153. The seven texts of the Sarvāstivādin Abhidharma are: *Discourses on Saṅgīti* (*Saṅgītiparyāya*), *Aggregation of Factors* (*Dharmaskandha*), *Treatise on Designations* (*Prajñaptiśāstra*), *Collection on the Elements* (*Dhātukāya*), *Collection on Discursive Consciousness* (*Vijñānakāya*), *Exposition* (*Prakaraṇapāda*), and *Foundations of Knowledge* (*Jñānaprasthāna*).
31. See Sopa et al. (2001) on Atiśa's teacher Dharmarakṣita. Ordination lineages (*nikāya*) are generally groups of monks or nuns differentiated based on Vinaya rules. See Buswell and Lopez 2013, s.v. *nikāya*.
32. *hetuvidyā*.
33. Dharmakīrti's seven works of valid knowledge (*pramāṇa*) are the *Commentary on Valid Knowledge* (*Pramāṇavārttika*), *Ascertainment of Epistemology* (*Pramāṇaviniścaya*), *Drop of Reasoning* (*Nyāyabindu*), *Drop of Logical Reasons* (*Hetubindu*), and *Logic of Argumentation* (*Vādanyāya*), *Analysis of Relations* (*Sambandhaparīkṣā*) and *Proof of Other Minds* (*Saṃtānāntarasiddhi*) (Tillemans 2017).

34. The five fields of knowledge (*rig gnas lnga, pañcavidyāsthāna*) include (1) linguistic science (*śabda*), (2) medical sciene (*cikitsā*), (3) science of fine arts and crafts (*śilapakarmasthāna*), (4) logical science (*hetu*), and "inner" science (*adhyātma*).
35. Phun tshogs tshe brtan 2011, 15. Note that the oldest sources discuss this episode and the following narrative episodes *after* Atiśa returns from Sumatra.
36. *Universally Known Biography* 2012, 92.
37. On Dharmakīrtiśrī as royal advisor (*rājaguru*) see Schoterman 2016.
38. Skilling 1997, 187–88.
39. See Decleer 1996b and Jinpa 2006 for details of the journey.
40. *Extensive Biography* 283.3–7, Eimer 1979, 134; Phun tshogs tshe brtan 2011, 17; *Universally Known Biography* 2012, 80.7.
41. *Abhisamayālaṃkāra*. See Apple 2018a for an overview of the *Ornament for Clear Realization* and its content.
42. Skilling 1997, 188.
43. *Śikṣāsamuccaya* and *Bodhicāryavatāra*, respectively.
44. *Extensive Biography* 281.20, Eimer 1979, 132.
45. See Apple 2019a on Atiśa's Mādhyamika.
46. *Durbodhālokā*.
47. *Abhisamayālaṃkāravivṛti*.
48. *Āryācalasādhana-nāma* (*'phags pa mi g.yo ba'i sgrub thabs*, P. 3883, *rgyud 'drel,* tu, 103a4–33b3), *Krodhagaṇapatisādhana* (*tshogs kyi bdag po khro bo'i sgrub thabs*, P. 4994, *rgyud 'drel,* 'u, 104b6–106a3).
49. For activities in the Vajrāsana area, Eimer 1979, vol.1, 196–205, 137–69; then Vikramaśīla Monastery, Eimer 1979, vol 1, pp. 205–13.
50. *Universally Known Biography* 2012, 95.18–20. Phun tshogs tshe brtan 2011, 27.
51. *Universally Known Biography* 2012, 97.11–20. Phun tshogs tshe brtan 2011, 29.
52. Pawo Tsuklak Trengwa 2006, 339.19–23.
53. Phun tshogs tshe brtan 2011, 25–26.
54. *trisaṃvara, sdom pa gsum.*
55. *byang sdom.*
56. *sngags sdom.*
57. *Extensive Biography* 300; Eimer 1979, 186.

58. Phun tshogs tshe brtan 2011, 26. See Sopa et al. (2004, 26–32) for an overview on Atiśa's practice of upholding the three types of vows.
59. As crown jewel (*gtsug gi nor bu*), see Eimer 2003, lines 58–70; Eimer 1979, 183; *Extensive Biography* (299.9–13); *Universally Known Biography* (2012, 103.15–20).
60. "Eminent, superior" (*atiśaya*, *phul* {*du*} *byung* {*ba*}), Eimer 1977, 18–22.
61. Chattopadhyaya (1967, 129–42) discusses the later Tibetan sources which describe Atiśa's position as a director of monks in a monastery (*dge skyos*, *upadhivārika*) or disciplinarian (*chos khrims pa*). See Jansen 2016 for these positions in modern Tibetan Buddhist monasteries.
62. *Universally Known Biography* 2012, 104.3–6.
63. On Maitrīpa's works and philosophy see Mathes 2015.
64. *Extensive Biography* 302, Eimer 1979, 195–96; *Universally Known Biography* 2012, 104.7–105.6 On this episode in Atiśa's life see Tatz (1988) and Shizuka (2015).
65. *Extensive Biography* 292, Eimer 1979, 159; *Universally Known Biography* 2012, 98.7–99.8. Phun tshogs tshe brtan 2011, 31. Vogel 1997, 21.
66. Kapstein 2006, 96.
67. Cook 2018.
68. *stod 'dul.*
69. See Karmay 1998, 6, on the decree (*bka' bcad*) called *bKa' shog chen mo* (? = *sNgags log sun byin*).
70. *mtho lding gser gyi lha khang.*
71. See Karmay 1998, Kapstein 2006, 93, Van der Kuijp 2015.
72. Tshe ring rgyal po, Gu ge 2006, 471.
73. Phun tshogs tshe brtan 2011, 36.
74. *Universally Known Biography* 2012, 109–10. Phun tshogs tshe brtan 2011, 36–37.
75. Karmay 1998, 10–15.
76. *Universally Known Biography* 2012, 109–10. Phun tshogs tshe brtan 2011, 36–37.
77. *Universally Known Biography* 2012, 111–12. Phun tshogs tshe brtan 2011, 43–45.
78. This paragraph is drawn from Decleer (1997b) with slight modification. See Decleer (1997b) for the whole episode which is based on *The Itinerary*.
79. *Extensive Biography* 312–13, Eimer 1979, 223–24; *Universally Known Biog-*

raphy 2012, 116. Lang Darma (*glang dar ma*, d. 842) was the last Tibetan emperor of the Yarlung dynasty who purportedly persecuted Buddhism.

80. *Extensive Biography* 313, Eimer 1979, 225–26; *Universally Known Biography* 2012, 116.
81. *Extensive Biography* 314, Eimer 1979, 227; *Universally Known Biography* 2012, 117.
82. *Extensive Biography* 314, Eimer 1979, 228–29; *Universally Known Biography* 2012, 118.
83. Eimer 2003, 42–43.
84. On the life and teachings of Nāropa see Guether 1963.
85. *Extensive Biography* 315, Eimer 1979, 231; *Universally Known Biography* 2012, 119.
86. *Extensive Biography* 317, Eimer 1979, 238–39; *Universally Known Biography* 2012, 121.17–22.10.
87. *Extensive Biography* 318, Eimer 1979, 240; *Universally Known Biography* 2012, 123.5–11.
88. *Extensive Biography* 319, Eimer 1979, 241; *Universally Known Biography* 2012, 123.14–20.
89. *rlung gshog bya*.
90. *The Itinerary (of Atiśa's Travels)* 244.5–45.19. See Decleer 1997b, 4–6 for details of this episode. I have adapted Decleer's translation in portions of the text. As Dan Martin (2013, 171, note 26) points out, Atiśa's tasting of tea occurs six hundred years before the first tasting of tea in England.
91. The following is based on *Extensive Biography* and *Universally Known Biography*. See Decleer 1998 for the *The Itinerary (of Atiśa's Travels)* account of this episode.
92. Translation cited from Vitali 2004, 14, note 18.
93. *Extensive Biography* 320; Eimer 1979, 247; *Universally Known Biography* 2012, 125.10–20.
94. On Atiśa's *Vimalaratnalekha* (*Dri ma med pa rin po che'i spring yig*, Tôh. no. 4188), see Basu (1928) and Nance (2015). .
95. *Extensive Biography* 320; Eimer 1979, 247.
96. On the activities of Atiśa in Nepal see Decleer (1996b) and Locke (1985, 411).
97. *The Itinerary (of Atiśa's Travels)* 252.15–55; Phun tshogs tshe brtan 2011, 57.
98. *chu gtor gyi lugs*.

99. *Extensive Biography* 321–22; Eimer 1979, 250–51.
100. *byang chub gling*.
101. Phun tshogs tshe brtan 2011, 63; *Universally Known Biography* 2012, 128.
102. *las rgyu 'bras*.
103. *yi dam gyi lha*.
104. *Extensive Biography* 322, Eimer 1979, 253; *Universally Known Biography* 2012, 128–29.
105. *Extensive Biography* 323–25, Eimer 1979, 255–58; *Universally Known Biography* 2012, 129–31. See Apple 2019a, 35–49 for a complete analysis of this episode.
106. *skyed rim*, *utpattikrama*, and *rdzogs rim*, *niṣpannakrama*, respectively.
107. Quoted from Rinchen Zangpo's biography (Snellgrove and Skorupski, 1980, vol. 2, 109.20–22).
108. The three natures in Yogācāra works are the imagined (*parikalpita*), the dependent (*paratantra*), and the perfected (*pariniṣpanna*).
109. Three Continuums (*rgyud gsum*) are usually associated with the Hevajra Tantra and the Sakya school in Tibetan Buddhism. Stearns (2001, 184, note 163) provides a brief discription: "The 'three continuums' (*rgyud gsum*) are the cause continuum of the universal ground (*kun gzhi rgyu rgyud*), the method continuum of the body (*lus thabs rgyud*), and the result continuum of Mahāmudrā (*phyag rgya chen po 'bras bu rgyud*).
110. In Mahāyāna forms of Buddhism the three bodies of a Buddha (*trikāya*) are a fundamental doctrine. They consist of the dharma body (*dharmakāya*), enjoyment body (*saṃbhogakāya*), and emanation body (*nirmāṇakāya*) (Buswell and Lopez 2013, 923). The five wisdoms (*pañcajñāna*) are facets of perfect awakening and consist of (1) the wisdom of the Realm of Reality (*dharmadhātujñāna*), (2) the mirrorlike wisdom (*ādarśajñāna*), (3) the wisdom of equality (*samatājñāna*), (4) the wisdom of specific knowledge (*pratyavekṣaṇajñāna*), and (5) the wisdom of accomplishing what was to be done (*kṛtyānuṣṭhānajñāna*) (Buswell and Lopez 2013, 614).
111. *Universally Known Biography* 2012, 133.11–34.16.
112. *Sarvasamayasaṃgraha*.
113. *Universally Known Biography* 2012, 132–35. Phun tshogs tshe brtan 2011. See also Snellgrove and Skorupski 1980, 96 for a different version of the dialogue.
114. See, for example, colophons to Tôh. catalog numbers 369, 501, 1533, 1748, 1893, 3708, 3971, 3791, 3794, 4175, and 4631.

115. Skilling 1997, 188.
116. *Guhyasamājalokeśvarasādhana* (*Dpal gsang ba 'dus pa'i 'jig rten dbang phyug gi sgrub pa'i thabs*). Tôh. 1892. Dergé Tanjur, vol. *pi*, folios 220b6–231b5.
117. O'Brien 2016, 278n9.
118. Phun tshogs tshe brtan 2011, 71.
119. Phun tshogs tshe brtan 2011, 72.
120. *Extensive Biography* p. 328; Eimer 1979, 266; *Universally Known Biography* 2012, 135–36.
121. Dkon mchog rgyal mtshan (1764–1853), *Byang chub lam gyi sgron me'i 'grel ba phul byung dgyes pa'i mchod sprin*, Collected Works, vol. 4, Delhi, 1975, 51–52. See also Fazun 1972.
122. English translation Jinpa 2008, for the full translation of the advice see Jinpa 2008, 563–66. Tibetan in Phun tshogs tshe brtan 2011, 71–73.
123. Phun tshogs tshe brtan 2011, 74.
124. Iuchi 2013, 218–20.
125. Chim Namkha Drak 2012b, fol. 174a–75a.
126. *lha khang dkar po*.
127. Chim Namkha Drak 2012b, fol. 176a6–78a2. See also *Extensive Biography* 336; Eimer 1979, 282; *Universally Known Biography* 2012, 145.4–47.3.
128. Phun tshogs tshe brtan 2011, 76.
129. *Bodhimārgapradīpapañjikā*, *Commentary on the Difficult Points in the Lamp for the Path to Awakening*. See Sherburne 2000 for a translation and Tibetan edition.
130. Phun tshogs tshe brtan 2011, 77.
131. *Universally Known Biography* 2012, 149.
132. Phun tshogs tshe brtan 2011, 82.
133. See Apple 2019a on Setön Drachan Dzin meeting Atiśa.
134. Phun tshogs tshe brtan 2011, 83.
135. Phun tshogs tshe brtan 2011, 77. Gtsang smyon He ru ka 1982, 77–78. Padma dkar po 1973, 445.
136. Pawo Tsuklak Trengwa 2006, 349.15.
137. *mdo khams smad*.
138. Array of the Three Pledges (*Trisamayavyūha*), also known as *King of the Three Pledges* (*Trisamayarāja*), is a Yoga Tantra and is mentioned in Śāntideva's *Compendium of Training* (*Śikṣāsamuccaya*).
139. Pawo Tsuklak Trengwa 2006, 349.22; Phun tshogs tshe brtan 2011, 84.
140. Phun tshogs tshe brtan 2011, 85.

141. *Extensive Biography* 341.3–12; Eimer 1979, 296; *Universally Known Biography* 2012, 154.10–17.

142. *Extensive Biography* 341.12–42.2; Eimer, 1979, 297; *Universally Known Biography* 2012, 154.10–17.

143. *Extensive Biography* 342.15–20; Eimer, 1979, 300.

144. *dkor mdzod dpe dkar gling.*

145. The translated texts were the *Five Stages* (*Pañcakrama*), *Buddha Skull Tantra* (*Buddhakapālatantra*), *Sādhana of Vajrapāṇi Who Wears a Blue Robe* (*Nīlāṃbaradharavajrapāṇisādhana*), *Explanation of the Five Aggregates* (*Pañcaskandhaprakaraṇa*), *Eight Branches of Medical Cures* (*Sman dpyad yan lag brgyad pa*), the *Instructions on the Compendium of Discourses* (*Sūtrasamuccayopadeśa*), the *Bodhisattva's Jewel Garland* (*Bodhisattvamaṇyāvalī*, see chapter 9), the *Brief Instruction on Bodhisattva Practice* (*Bodhisattvacaryāsūtrīkṛtāvavāda*), and the *Supramundane Sevenfold Ritual* (*Lokottarasaptāṅgavidhi*). *Extensive Biography* 2014, 343.11–14; Eimer 1979, 303; *Universally Known Biography* 2012, 157.11–15; Phun tshogs tshe brtan 2011, 87.

146. *Extensive Biography* 2014: 343.22–44.1; *Universally Known Biography* 2012, 157, 15–17; Phun tshogs tshe brtan 2011, 87. The six texts of Madhyamaka reasoning (*dbu ma rigs pa'i tshogs drug*) are: (1) *Fundamental Verses on the Middle Way* (*Mūlamadhyamakakārikā, Dbu ma rtsa ba'i tshig le'ur byas pa*), (2) *Sixty Verses on Reasoning* (*Yuktiṣaṣṭikā, Rigs pa drug cu pa*), (3) *Seventy Verses on Emptiness* (*Śūnyatāsaptatiḥ, Stong pa nyid bdun cu pa*), (4) *Refutation of Objections* (*Vigrahavyāvartāni, Rtsod pa bzlog pa*), (5) *The Finely Woven* (*Vaidalyaprakaraṇa, Zhib mo rnam par 'thag pa*), and (6) *Precious Garland* (*Ratnāvalī, Rin chen phreng ba*). Sometimes *Establishing [the Validity of] the Conventional* (*Vyavahārasiddhiḥ*) is included in the list rather than the *Precious Garland.*

147. *bram ze chen po'i gdams pa.*

148. *Extensive Biography* 343.15–22; Eimer 1979, 304; *Universally Known Biography* 2012, 157. 15–158.4. See Wedemeyer 2012 on these types of esoteric Buddhist conduct.

149. Eimer 1979, 308; Phun tshogs tshe brtan 2011, 89.

150. Eimer 1979, 319; Phun tshogs tshe brtan 2011, 90. See Kano 2015 for an account of Sanskrit manuscripts and Atiśa in Tibet.

151. Ruegg 1992, 265–66. Note that other Tibetan scholars claimed different

dates for Atiśa's calculation. Modern scholars date Gautama Buddha to approximately 480–400 BCE.

152. *mched grogs.*
153. *Uttaratantra.*
154. *Dharmadharmatāvibhāga.*
155. *Extensive Biography* 346.15–20; Eimer 1979, 311; *Universally Known Biography* 2012, 160–61; Phun tshogs tshe brtan 2011, 91.
156. *Extensive Biography* 346.20–47.3; Eimer 1979, 312; *Universally Known Biography* 2012, 161–62; Phun tshogs tshe brtan 2011, 92.
157. Phun tshogs tshe brtan 2011, 93.
158. *Extensive Biography* 347–49; Eimer 1979, 314–17; *Universally Known Biography* 2012, 162–64; Phun tshogs tshe brtan 2011, 94–95.
159. See Pasang Wangdu (2007) on the Keru Lhakhang in 'On Valley in present-day Nedong County of Lhokha Prefecture, Tibet.
160. A *khal* equals twenty to thirty pounds.
161. *Extensive Biography* 349; Eimer 1979, 318–19; *Universally Known Biography* 2012, 164; Phun tshogs tshe brtan 2011, 94.
162. Phun tshogs tshe brtan 2011, 95.
163. *Extensive Biography* 351.7–13; Eimer 1979, 324; *Universally Known Biography* 2012, 167.
164. *Extensive Biography* 351–52; Eimer 1979, 326–27; Phun tshogs tshe brtan 2011, 96–97.
165. *thugs dam gyi rten.*
166. *Extensive Biography* 353.2–7; Eimer 1979, 331; *Universally Known Biography* 2012, 169.1–8. See Apple 2019a for the content of these teachings and their context.
167. *Extensive Biography* 353.18–54; Eimer 1979, 334; *Universally Known Biography* 2012, 170.
168. Phun tshogs tshe brtan 2011, 99.
169. See English 2002 on the cremation grounds in esoteric Buddhism.
170. *Extensive Biography* 355.19; Eimer 1979, 339; *Universally Known Biography* 2012, 172.
171. *yer pa lha ri snying po'i mgul.*
172. The seven deities are Śākyamuni, Acala, Avalokiteśvara, Tāra, and the Three Baskets (*tripiṭaka, sde snod gsum*). These teachings are known as *Bka' gdams lha chos bdun ldan gyi man ngag.* The sixteen seminal drops are

known as *Thig le bcu drug dbang.* See Jinpa 2008. On the transmission of these teachings see Franz-Karl Ehrhard 2002.

173. *Extensive Biography* 357.4–10; Eimer 1979, 343–44; *Universally Known Biography* 2012, 172.10; Phun tshogs tshe brtan 2011, 102. On the *Book of Kadam* (*bka' gdams glegs bam*) see Jinpa 2008.

174. *Universally Known Biography* 2012, 177–78.

175. *Universally Known Biography* 2012, 178.

176. *Extensive Biography* 361.9–14; Eimer 1979, 356; *Universally Known Biography* 2012, 178–79.

177. These teachings are preserved in the recently published *Gnyis su med pa shes rab kyi pha rol tu phyin pa'i gdams pa don brgyad du bsdus nas rgyas par bshad pa*, 603–700 in *Jo bo rje dpal ldan a ti sha'i gsung 'bum*, volume 2. The eight topics for the *Ornament for Clear Realization* are (1) Total Omniscience, (2) Path Omniscience, (3) Empirical Omniscience, (4) Full Realization of All Aspects, (5) Realization That has Attained the Summit, (6) Progressive Realization, (7) Instantaneous Realization, and (8) the Dharma Body. See Apple 2018a for an overview of the *Ornament for Clear Realization.*

178. "Perfections According to the Method of Kham" (*phar phyin khams lugs ma*), *Extensive Biography* 369.15–21; Eimer 1979, 357. *Universally Known Biography* 2012, 179.

179. *Extensive Biography* 361–62; Eimer 1979, 358; *Universally Known Biography* 2012, 179. Cf. Jinpa 2013, 27.

180. *Universally Known Biography* 2012, 180.15–20.

181. *Extensive Biography* 362–63; Eimer 1979, 360–61; *Universally Known Biography* 2012, 180.19–81.6.

182. The twelve virtues of purity (*sbyangs pa'i yon tan, dhūtaguṇāḥ*) are listed in Asaṅga's *Śrāvakabhūmi* (Sherburne 2000, 146, n. 37) and are (ibid. 572): "(1) to wear robes made from rags, (2) to have only three changes of robes, (3) to use felt for clothing, (4) to eat only food that is begged, (5) to eat at one sitting, (6) to eat only once daily, (7) to live as a forest hermit, (8) to dwell at the foot of a tree, (9) to live in an unsheltered place, (10) to live near a cemetery, (11) to sleep wherever one finds onseself at night, and (12) to sit up while sleeping."

183. *Extensive Biography* 364.22–65.6; Eimer 1979, 366; *Universally Known Biography* 2012, 183.4–11.

184. *Extensive Biography* 365; Eimer 1979, 368–69; *Universally Known Biography* 2012, 183–84.

185. *Extensive Biography* 365.20–66.5; Eimer 1979, 369; *Universally Known Biography* 2012, 184.
186. *Extensive Biography* 366.14–20; Eimer 1979, 371.
187. *Universally Known Biography* 2012, 185.
188. *Extensive Biography* 367.4–13; Eimer 1979, 373; *Universally Known Biography* 2012, 185–86.
189. *Extensive Biography* 367.13–19; Eimer 1979, 374; *Universally Known Biography* 2012, 186.
190. *Spyan ras gzigs dbang phyug zhal gsum phyag drug pa'i sgrub thabs.*
191. *Extensive Biography* 367.19–68.6; Eimer 1979, 375.
192. *Avalokiteśvarasaptadharmaka-pariprcchā.*
193. *Cittopādavidhi* and *Śīlaparivartabhāṣya*, respectively. *Extensive Biography* 368.7–13; Eimer 1979, 376; *Universally Known Biography* 2012, 187.2–9.
194. *Extensive Biography*, 368.13–19; Eimer 1979, 377. *Universally Known Biography* 2012, 187.15–20.
195. *Bodhisattvabhūmi*, *Mahāyānasūtrālaṃkāra*, and *Bodhipathapradīpa*, respectively.
196. *Śikṣāsamuccaya.*
197. *Sūtrasamuccaya.*
198. *Extensive Biography*, 369.13–19; Eimer, 1979, 380. *Universally Known Biography* 2012, 188.
199. *Theg pa rnal 'byor la' jug.*
200. *Extensive Biography* 370.4–9; Eimer 1979, 382.
201. *Dharmadhātudarśanagīti*, *Saṃsāramanoniryāṇīkārasaṃgīti*, *Bde ba drug gi glu*, and *Byang chub sems kyi glu*, respectively.
202. *Caryāgīti*, *Vajragīti*, and *Vajradharmagīti*, respectively.
203. *Extensive Biography* 370.9–15; Eimer 1979, 383; *Universally Known Biography* 2012, 189.6–14.
204. *Extensive Biography* 371.3–7; Eimer 1979, 386; *Universally Known Biography* 2012, 190.1–15.
205. *Extensive Biography* 371.7–15; Eimer 1979, 387. The biography states at this point that the painting "is still in Radreng (or Reting) today," which would be around the year 1150. On the paintings at Radreng see Martin 2001.
206. *Extensive Biography* 371; Eimer 1979, 388; *Universally Known Biography* 2012, 190.15–191.

207. *Extensive Biography* 372, states "In East India, pandits painted the pictures and sent them back to Nyethang, where they are now."
208. Families of the Victorious Ones (*rgyal ba rigs lnga*). *Extensive Biography* 371–72; Eimer 1979, 389; *Universally Known Biography* 2012, 191.12–15.
209. *Extensive Biography* 372; Eimer 1979, 391; *Universally Known Biography* 2012, 192.1–6.
210. Phun tshogs tshe brtan 2011, 115.
211. *Extensive Biography* 372–73; Eimer 1979, 392; *Universally Known Biography* 2012, 192.15–93.5.
212. *Extensive Biography* 372–73; Eimer 1979, 393; *Universally Known Biography* 2012, 193.
213. Phun tshogs tshe brtan 2011, 117.
214. *Extensive Biography* 373–74; Eimer 1979, 394–95; *Universally Known Biography* 2012, 195.
215. *Universally Known Biography* 2012, 195.5–9; Phun tshogs tshe brtan 2011, 117.
216. *Universally Known Biography* 2012, 199.4–11; Phun tshogs tshe brtan 2011, 118; *Extensive Biography* 379.14–19; Eimer 1979, 410 states that Atiśa died at the age of seventy-one.
217. Phun tshogs tshe brtan 2011, 118–19.
218. *Universally Known Biography* 2012, 199.18–200.1.
219. Pleasant Doctrine-Bearing Joyous Place (*kun dga' ra ba yid 'dga' chos 'dzin*) is a special pure land in Tuṣita Heaven. See Apple 2019b.
220. Phun tshogs tshe brtan 2011, 119.
221. *Āryamahāparinirvāṇasūtra*.
222. *Universally Known Biography* 2012, 200.1–4.
223. *Universally Known Biography* 2012, 201; Phun tshogs tshe brtan 2011, 120.
224. *mantranaya*.
225. *Pāramitāyāna*.
226. *guru-paramparā*.
227. *gdams ngag*.
228. *sādhana*, *sgrub thabs*.
229. On Dharmakīrti see Dunne 2004.
230. McCrea and Patil, 2010.
231. See, for example, the *Vṛttamālāstuti of Jñānaśrīmitra with Śākyarakṣita's Vṛttamālā(stuti)vivṛti* edited by Hahn 2016.
232. Isaacson 2013; Apple 2018b.

233. *Antarvyāptisamarthana.*
234. Kajiyama 1999. Note that these titles reflect the Tibetan translator's reconstruction of the Sanskrit as *Sārottamā* and *Śuddhamati*, respectively.
235. See Apple 2018b and Apple 2019a.
236. See Thakur 1975 and Patil 2009.
237. Apple 2018b.
238. Miyazaki 2007a.
239. *Garbhasaṃgraha*, *Hṛdayanikṣepa*, *Caryāsaṃgrahapradīpa*, and *Bodhisattvamaṇyāvalī*, respectively.
240. *Karmavibhaṅga.*
241. See Apple 2019a, 171–268.
242. Sevenfold Supreme Worship (*Saptavidhā-anuttarapūjā*) includes (1) homage (*vandanā*), (2) worship (*pūjanā*), (3) confession of faults (*pāpadeśanā*), (4) rejoicing (*anumodanā*), (5) prayer (*adhyeṣaṇā*), (6) supplication (*yācanā*), and (7) transfer of merit (*pariṇāmanā*). Atiśa discusses these in his *Bodhimārgapradīpapañjikā* (Sherburne 2000, 43, 49–51).
243. Sherburne 2000, 139.
244. Sherburne 2000, 123. As suggested by Miyazaki (2007a, 75), the number may related to the *Vinayasaṃgrahaṇī* (*'Dul ba bsdu ba*) attributed to Asaṅga. See Clarke 2015 for comparison of the approximate number of rules among various Buddhist ordination lineages.
245. *Bodhisattvasaṃvaraviṃśakapañjikā.*
246. Sherburne 2000, 149–88.
247. *Cittotpādasaṃvaravidhikrama.*
248. Translated from Tibetan in Sherburne (2000, 540). Atiśa also recommends this prayer for recitation in his *Instruction on Entering the Path of the Beginner Bodhisattva* (*Bodhisattvādikarmikamargāvatāradeśanā*) (Sherburne 2000, 424).
249. *Samādhisaṃbhāraparivarta.*
250. The six supersensory perceptions (*abhijñā*) are (1) magical powers (*ṛddhividhi*), (2) divine eye (*divyacakṣu*), (3) divine ear (*divyaśrotra*), (4) recollection of previous lifetimes (*pūrvanivāsānusmṛti*), (5) knowledge of others' states of mind (*cetoparyāyābhijñāna*), and (6) knowledge of the extinction of pollutions (*āsravakṣaya*). The first five are mundane based on meditative absorption and the sixth is supramundane attained through special insight.

251. *Bodhimārgapradīpapañjikā* in Dergé Tanjur, vol. 111 (*khi*), folios 241a4–93a4; See also Sherburne, 2000, 208–209.
252. Innate (*lhan gcig skyes pa*) or gradual three wisdoms (*prajñā*) of learning (*śrutamayī*), reflection (*cintāmayī*), and meditation (*bhāvanāmayī*).
253. Meditative equipoise (*samāhita, mnyam bzhag*) and postmeditative experience (*pṛṣṭhalabdhajñāna, rjes las thob*).
254. Chim Namkha Drak 2012a, 133–34. See chapter 2.
255. *dbu ma chen po.*
256. See Apple 2019a, 58–60.
257. *Satyadvayāvatāra*, v. 10 (Ejima 1983, 363): *mngon sum dang ni rjes su dpag / / sangs rgyas pa yis de gnyis gzung / / gnyis pos stong nyid rtogs so zhes / tshul rol mthong ba'i rmongs pa smra //*
258. *hetuvidyā.*
259. *pramāṇa.*
260. Apple 2018c, 2019a.
261. Citation from *Mahāyānapathasādhanavarṇasaṃgraha*, in Dergé Tanjur, vol. 111, folio 301a–b. See Apple 2018c and Sherburne 2000, 452–53.
262. See Apple 2019a for Atiśa's use of the four reasons (*gtan tshigs chen po bzhi*). The four reasons (Sherburne 2000, 230–36) are the reason refuting production according to the tetralemma (*mu bzhi skye 'gog gi gtan tshigs, catuṣkoṭyutpādapratiṣedhahetu*), the diamond-splinters reason (*rdo rje gzegs ma'i gtan tshigs, vajrakaṇahetu*), the reason of being neither one nor many (*ekānekaviyogahetu, gcig du bral gyi gtan tshigs*), and the reason consisting in dependent arising (*pratītyasamutpādahetu, rten 'brel gyi gtan tshigs*).
263. Apple 2019a, 40–42.
264. The two realities (*satyadvaya*) in Sanskrit are *paramārthasatya* (ultimate reality) and *saṃvṛtisatya* (conventional reality).
265. *pratibhāsamātra, snang ba tsam.*
266. *darśanamārga, mthong lam.*
267. *viśuddhalaukikajñāna.*
268. *Madhyamakahṛdaya* and *Tarkajvālā*, respectively.
269. *tathyasaṃvṛtisopānam.*
270. *śūnyatākaruṇāgarbha*. Cf. Wangchuk 2007: 257–58, 258n125.
271. See chapter 4, *Open Basket of Jewels* 2.5.
272. *Daśabhūmikasūtra.*
273. On this point in Atiśa's thought and practice see Apple 2019a.
274. See the remarks by Onians (2002) and English (2002) on the nuances

of Atiśa's understanding of the higher-level consecrations. The nuances suggested by Onians were known by Atiśa's followers and the commentator Dkon mchog rgyal mtshan (1764–1853) shares this understanding regarding the higher-level consecrations.

275. *devatāviśuddhi*.

276. *mahāmudrā*.

277. Action (*kriya*, *bya ba*), Performance (*caryā*, *spyod pa*), Practice (*kalpa*, *rtog pa*), Dual (*ubhaya*, *gnyi ga*), Yoga (*yoga*, *rnal 'byor*), Great Yoga (*mahāyoga, rnal 'byor chen po*), and Highest Yoga (*yoganiruttara*, *rnal 'yor bla na med pa*) are listed in *Extensive Biography* 262–64; Eimer 1979; 64–72 and Sherburne 2000, 283–87. See Dalton 2005, 152–54 on Atiśa's teachings on the classes of tantras.

278. *iṣṭadevatā*.

279. Eimer 2003, 26; Eimer 1979, 77.

280. *gsang ba sngags kyi blo sbyong*.

281. *Pañcakrama*, *Caryāmelāprakapradīpa*, and *Pradīpodyotanaṭīkā*, respectively.

282. See Apple 2019a, 91.

283. Kano 2016.

284. Schaeffer 2005, 61–62.

285. *Vajrāsanavajragīti*. See Apple 2017 on this work.

286. The transmitted oral lineages *(snyan brgyud)* in Tibetan are: (1) *da ki ma'i snyan rgyud*, (2) *lta sgom chen mo*, (3) *thun mong ma yin pa'i skor*, (4) *nor bu phreng ba*, (5) *phag mo*, (6) *bde mchog dpa' bo gcig pa*, (7) *sgrol ma dkar mo*, (8) *lhan cig skyes sbyor*, and (9) *rkyen bzhi*.

287. *rang bzhin gyis 'od gsal ba*.

288. *bsgoms pa'i 'od gsal*.

289. *trisaṃvara*, *sdom gsum*.

290. *Abhisamayavibhaṅga*.

291. *nges don lam gyi rim*. See Apple 2017, 4 for further discussion.

292. The *Byang chub lam gyi rim pa'i dka' ba'i gnas che long* commentary to Atiśa's *Stages* cites the *Saṃvarārṇavatantra* and the *Piled Up Stūpas Tantra* (*mchod rten brtsegs pa'i rgyud*) as sources for viewing the guru as the Buddha. See also English 2002, 28.

293. The full title is *Open Basket of Jewels, Special Instructions on the Middle Way* (*Ratnakaraṇḍodghāṭamadhyamakopadeśa*). See Apple 2019a, 63–113 for a complete annotated translation and analysis of this work.

294. *Piṇḍīkṛtasādhana*, k.3.

295. Atiśa's Tibetan differs from the Tengyur. Cf. *Bodhicittavivaraṇa*, vv. 74–75 (Lindtner 1997b, 56–58).

296. The "four immeasurables" (*catvāry apramānāṇi, tshad med bzhi*), also known as the four "abodes of Brahma" (*brahmavihāra*), the contemplations of immeasurable love (*maitrī*), compassion (*karuṇā*), joy (*muditā*), and equanimity (*upekṣā*). *Mahāvyutpatti*, 1503–507.

297. Aspirations to liberate (*bsgrol ba*) beings, free (*dgrol ba*) them from obstacles, free them from great powerful suffering (*dbugs dbyung ba*), and to free those not passed beyond nirvāṇa (*mya ngan las bzla*).

298. The six antidotes are (1) recitation of sūtras, (2) meditation on emptiness, (3) recitation of mantras, (4) making statues or paintings of buddhas, (5) making offering to buddhas or stūpas, and (6) recitation of the names of buddhas.

299. These comprise the seven-limbed (*saptāṅga, yang lag bdun*) prayer liturgy based on the *Samantabhadracārya-praṇidhāna*: praise (*vandana*), offering (*pūjanā*), confession (*pāpadeśanā*), rejoicing (*modanā*), requesting (*adhyeṣaṇā*) to turn the wheel of dharma, begging [the buddhas not to abandon beings] (*yācanā*), and dedication (*pariṇāmanā*); see Crosby and Skilton 1995, 9–13.

300. *so sor rtog pa'i shes rab*.

301. The five obstacles to be relinquished are laziness, forgetting the instructions, dullness and agitation, nonapplication, and overapplication. There are eight antidotes to these five; see *Madhyāntavibhāga*, IV.4–6ab (Pandeya 1999, 130–31).

302. Eight similies of illusion (*aṣṭamāyopamā, sgyu ma'i dpe brgyad*). The eight are said to be a twinkling star (*skar mar*), optical illusion (*rab rib*), lamp (*mar me*), dream (*rmi lam*), flash of lightning (*glog*), moon in the water (*chu zla*), mirage (*smig rgyu*), and cloud (*sprin*).

303. "Divide into four portions" is explained by Atiśa in his *Lamp for the Summary of Conduct*), see chapter 7, vs 12.

304. Cf. *Bodhicittavivaraṇa* (Lindtner 1997b, 32 (translation 33): "When a bodhisattva, having practiced a course by way of mantras, has thus produced the bodhicitta that in its relative aspect has the nature of aspiration, he must by means of meditational development produce the absolute bodhicitta."

305. *Bodhicittavivaraṇa*, v. 73 (Lindtner 1997b, 56).

306. Cf. *Ratnaguṇasaṃcayagāthā*, 15.3cd (Obermiller 1937, 57).

307. *Guhyasamāja*, 2.3–4 (Matsunaga 1978, 10).
308. *Bodhicittavivaraṇa*, v. 43 (Lindtner 1997b, 46). Buddhas not perceiving the mind goes back to *Kāśyapaparivarta* 98 (Vorobyova-Desyatovskaya 2002, 35).
309. Miyazaki 2007b, 9n13; *Jñānasārasamuccaya* v. 33abc.
310. "Endowed with all excellent features" (*rnam pa thams cad kyi mchog dang ldan pa'i stong pa nyid*, *sarvākāravaropetā śūnyatā*; translation Wangchuk 2007, 210) is an important concept in Tathāgatagarbha and Vajrayāna traditions. This expression is discussed by Ruegg 1981, 84, 97, 98.
311. *Bodhicittavivaraṇa*, k. 2. Atiśa's Tibetan of this verse differs from the version in Lindtner 1997b, 32.
312. Compare Miyazaki 2007b: 10n16; *Sāgaramatiparipṛcchā*, Tôh. 152, vol. *pha*, 58b7–59a1.
313. Compare Miyazaki 2007b, 11n17; *Bodhisattvagocaropāyaviṣayavikurvāṇanirdeśa*, Tôh. 146, vol. *pa*, 87a7–b5.
314. *Bodhisattvabhūmi* (Dutt 1996, 10).
315. This most likely refers to the *Sūtra of the Three Heaps* (*Triskandhakasūtra*, Dergé 384), used for the confession of downfalls and featuring thirty-five buddhas of confession. The "three heaps" or three sections referred to in the title are (1) confession of sin (*pāpadeśanā*), (2) rejoicing at merit (*puṇyānumodanā*), and (3) requesting instruction from a buddha (*buddhādhyeṣaṇā*).
316. *Abhidharmakośa*, 4.32 (Pradhan 1975, 216).
317. The three jewels of (1) ultimate truth are the emptiness or *śūnyatā* of the Buddha, dharma, and saṃgha; the three jewels (2) in front of oneself are the physical representations of the three jewels; and the three jewels (3) of realizations (*mngon par togs pa*) are realizations attained on the path.
318. Miyazaki 2007b, 14n20 notes that this citation is not in the *Karuṇāpuṇḍarīka*. Cf. *Tathāgatajñānamudrāsamādhi*, Tôh. 131, vol. *da*, 240a7–b7.
319. Miyzaki 2007b, 15n21: *Daśadharmakasūtra*, 168a1–7. Cited in the *Śikṣāsamuccayasūtra* (Bendall 1897–1902, 8).
320. *Mahāyānasūtrālaṃkāra*, 4.7 (Lévi 1911, 14).
321. *Bodhisattvabhūmi* (Dutt 1966, 9.12).
322. See Sparham 1987 regarding debates on the relation of awakening mind (*bodhicitta*) to mental factors (*caitta*) such as the wish (*'dun pa*), the desire (*'dod pa*), and the aspiration (*smon pa*).
323. *Abhisamayālaṃkāra*, 1.18ab (Stcherbatsky and Obermiller 1929, 4).

324. Comprare with *Akṣayamatinirdeśa* (Braarvig 1993, 20). Also Sherburne 2000, 77–81.
325. See Apple 2019a, 269–325.
326. Cf. Atiśa's *Bodhisattva's Jewel Garland* (see chapter 9).
327. *Ten Great Blessings of the Vajra Banner* (*Rdo rje rgyal mtshan gyi bsngo ba chen po bcu*) is chapter 30 of the *Buddhāvataṃsakasūtra* (Mochizuki 1999, 79).
328. *Bhadracaryā*.
329. *Bodhicittavivaraṇa*, v. 74–75. Atiśa's Tibetan of these verses differs from the following version in Lindtner 1997b, 56–58.
330. *Bodhisattvasaṃvaraviṃśaka*, k. 18c. Cf. Tatz 1987, 29: "Not to repay a good turn."
331. *Aṣṭasāhasrikāprajñāpāramitā*, (Wogihara 1932, 117–18).
332. These are bodhisattva downfalls listed in the *Bodhisattvasaṃvaraviṃśaka*, Tôh. 4081, vol. *hi*, 166b4–5: (v. 7ab) *gzhan gyis bsags kyang mi nyan par / khros nas gzhan la 'tshog pa dang /* (167a1, v. 13c) *pha rol shad kyis 'chags pa spong /* (13ab) *gshe la lan du gshe la sogs / khros pa rnams ni yal bar 'jog /*. Tatz 1985, 28.
333. The five sins of immediate retribution (*ānantaryakarma*) are killing one's father, mother, or an arhat, drawing the blood of a buddha, and creating a schism in the monastic community. See Silk 2007.
334. *Cittaviśuddhiprakaraṇa*, v. 32 (Patel 1949, 3).
335. Miyazaki 2007b, 21n37; cf. *Catuḥśataka*, 6.11; Sanskrit text is found in the *Subhāṣitasaṃgraha* (Bendall 1903, 385).
336. Cf. *Madhyamakahṛdaya* 3.296cd, 297a, 301ab (Lindtner 2001, 41). For comments on these verses, see Eckel 1992, 27–28, 174–76; and Eckel 2008, 45–46.
337. *Smṛtyupasthānasūtra*.
338. Cf. *Gaganagañjaparipṛcchā*, Tôh. 148, vol. *pa*, 323a7–b1. Cited in the *Śikṣāsamuccaya*, 45.15–16.
339. English translation by Dunne and McClintock 1997, 69, *Ratnāvalī*, 5.82 (Hahn 1982, 160).
340. *The Collected Works of Atiśa* (*Jo bo rje'i gsung 'bum* 601.18) cites from the *'phag pa blo gros mi zad pa'i mdo*.
341. Miyazaki 2007b, 22n42; *Pratibhāṇamatiparipṛcchā*, Tôh. 151, vol. *pa*, 339a3.
342. The Tibetan here differs from the Sanskrit. Cf *Mahāyānasūtrālaṃkāra*, 13.22 (Lévi 1907, 89). See Thurman et al., 2004, 172.
343. *Śrīparamādyamantrakalpakhaṇḍa*, Tôh. 488, vol. *ta*, 173b3–4; Cf. *Adhyardha-*

śatikā, v. 1 (Tomabechi 2009, 23). Also cited in the *Bodhipathapradīpapañjika* (Sherburne 2000, 267).

344. The four means of gathering disciples (*bsdu ba'i dngos po*, *saṃgrahavastu*) are: generosity (*dāna*), kind words (*priyavāditā*), beneficial acts (*arthacaryā*), and sympathy (*samānārthatā*). *Mahāvyutpatti*, 924–28.

345. Also known as the five sciences (*pañcavidyā*): linguistic science (*śabda*), logical science (*hetu*), "inner" science (*adhyātma*), medical science (*cikitsā*), and the science of fine arts and crafts (*śilpakarmasthāna*). *Mahāvyutpatti* 1554–559.

346. Cf. *Kāśyapaparivarta* 4 (Vorobyova-Desyatovskaya 2002, 6).

347. Miyazaki 2007b, 25n48, *Avalokiteśvaraparipṛcchāsaptadharmaka*, Tôh. 150, vol. *pa*, 331a7–b2.

348. Atiśa cites two half-verses in inverse order from the *Bodhicaryāvatāra* (5.26cd, 25cd) making it difficult to determine the subject of the citation. The Sanskrit of the regular order of the half-verses is as follows (Vaidya 1960, 57): 5.25cd, then 5.26.

349. *Śikṣāsamuccaya* 27c–d (Bendall 1902, 356).

350. *Bodhisattvasaṃvaraviṃśaka*, Tôh. 4081, vol. *hi*, 166b7, v. 10c, 167a3, v. 17dc, 166b7, v. 11b. See Tatz 1985, 28–29.

351. *Kāśyapaparivarta*, 3 (Vorobyova-Desyatovskaya 2002, 4–5).

352. Miyazaki 2007b, 28n56, *Sarvapuṇyasamuccayasamādhi*, Tôh. 134, vol. *na*, 101a4–7.

353. I have translated this seemingly out of place sentence at the location where it occurs in the manuscript.

354. Cf *Aṣṭasāhasrikā* (Wogihara 1935, 832).

355. The preceding irregular sequence of citation follows the order given in the Tibetan.

356. *Kuśalamūlasaṃparigraha*.

357. *Bodhicaryāvatāra* 4.9 (Vaidya 1960, 44).

358. Citation not identified.

359. *Mahāyānasūtrālaṃkāra* 3.7 (Lévi 1907, 11).

360. Cf. *Abhisamayālaṃkāra* 4.6, 7abd (Stcherbatsky and Obermiller 1929, 18).

361. *Prasādaprabhāvanāsūtra*.

362. Miyazaki 2007b, 34n66; *Mahāyānaprasādaprabhāvanā*, Tôh. 144, vol. *pa*, 15a6–b3.

363. *Bodhicaryāvatāra* 1.9–10 (Vaidya 1960, 7–8).

364. *Bodhicaryāvatāra* 1.17 (Vaidya 1960, 12–13).

365. *Bodhicaryāvatāra* 1.19 (Vaidya 1960, 13).
366. See Apple 2019a, 117–266 for analysis with commentaries to this work and Atiśa's exegesis of the two realities.
367. I have translated the text based on the critical edition by Blo bzang rdo rje rab gling (1999: 66–213). A partial translation is found in Brunnhölzl (2007b, 77–89).
368. Ratnāvalī 4.79; translation Dunne and McClintock 1997, 69.
369. Catuḥśataka 12.11; translation Lang 1986, 113.
370. Catuḥśataka 12.10; translation Lang 1986, 113.
371. Catuḥśataka 12.18; translation Lang 1986, 117.
372. *Caryāsaṃgrahapradīpa* (*Spyod pa bsdus pa'i sgron ma*). Tôh. 3960 (also, 4466). Dergé Tanjur, vol. *khi*, folios 312b2–313a7. See also Sherburne 2000, 346–51.
373. This is the same initial homage verse as Atiśa's *Special Instructions on the Middle Way*. See Apple 2019a.
374. The tenfold practices are ten kinds of activities in relation to sūtras based on the *Madhyāntavibhāgabhāṣya*: (1) copying (*lekhanā*), (2) worship (*pūjanā*), (3) giving to others (*dāna*), (4) listening (*śravaṇa*), (5) reading (*vācana*), (6) accepting (*ud-grahaṇa*), (7) teaching (*prakāśanā*), (8) chanting (*svādhyāya*), (9) reflecting (*cintanā*), and (10) cultivation (*bhāvanā*). See Apple 2009, 199 note 12.
375. *Suvikrāntavikrāmi-paripṛcchā-prajñā-pāramitā-nirdeśa*, *Rab kyi rtsal gyis rnam by gnon pas zhus pa shes rab kyi pha rol tu phyin pa bstan pa*.
376. *Bodhicittavivaraṇa*, v. 43 (Lindtner 1997b, 46).
377. I have translated the text based on the critical edition by Blo bzang rdo rje rab gling (1999: 1–29). For other translations of this text see Jinpa (2006, 2008).
378. See Apple 2019a, part III, for Atiśa's *Special Instructions on the Middle Way* along with Indian and Tibetan commentaries.
379. *Sde snod kyi chos thams cad sgom pa dbu ma'i man ngag.*
380. *bden par 'dzin pa.*
381. Candrakīrti's *Madhyamakāvatāra,* 6.79ab.
382. *Ratnaguṇasaṃcayagāthā* 5.5c.
383. Among the four reasons taught by Atiśa, this refers to the reason of being neither one nor many (*gcig du bral gyi gtan tshigs*, *ekānekaviyogahetu*).
384. *Kāśyapaparivarta*, 98 (Vorobyova-Desyatovskaya 2002, 35).

385. *Kāśyapaparivarta* (*'Od srung gi le'u*, Tôh. 87, *dkon brtsegs*, vol. *cha*, 133a7–133b1). Staël-Holstein 1977 [1926], 102, 69.
386. *Bodhicaryāvatāra* 9.111, translation Williams 1998, 15.
387. *Catuśataka*.
388. *Samādhirājasūtra*.
389. Davidson 1995, 293. Other translations of the *Lamp* include Das (1893), Davidson (1995), Sonam (1997), and Sherburne (2000, 1–20, 328–45).
390. Section numbers are based on the scribe notations of the manuscript TBRC W1KG506. A complete annotated translation and study of this work along with its accompanying texts are forthcoming.
391. The analogy of the turtle is found at *Bodhicaryāvatāra* 4.20 among numerous traditional Buddhist sources.
392. Sections 35–50 detail the sufferings of the three lower realms of hell-denizens, hungry ghosts, and animals.
393. The analogy of leather covering the ground is found in Śāntideva's *Bodhicaryāvatāra* 5.13.
394. See Apple 2008 on the attainments of stream-enterer to arhat.
395. The four ways of gathering disciples (*catvāri saṃgrahavastūni*, *bsdu ba'i dngos po bzhi*) include generosity, pleasing speech, beneficial conduct, and consistency between words and deeds.
396. Beyer 1973, 418.
397. Beyer 1973, 11.
398. The ten letters are Tārā's root mantra: *oṃ tāre tuttāre ture svāhā*. The ten perfections (Apple 2016b) are (1) generosity (*dāna*), (2) morality (*śīla*), (3) patience (*kṣānti*), (4) vigor (*vīrya*), (5) concentration (*dhyāna*), and (6) wisdom (*prajñā*), (7) skill-in-means (*upāya-kauśalya*), (8) resolution (*praṇidhāna*), (9) strength (*bala*), and (10) knowledge (*jñāna*).
399. See also Willson 1986, 345–50.
400. See comments of Beyer (1973, 460–61) regarding cleansing in this ritual.
401. Oṃ Āḥ Hindrances End! Hūṃ Phaṭ!
402. Oṃ Diamond Flower Goddess Hūṃ!
403. Oṃ Diamond-Incense Goddess Hūṃ!
404. Oṃ Diamond-Lamp Goddess Hūṃ!
405. Oṃ Diamond-Fragrance Goddess Hūṃ!
406. Oṃ Diamond-Food-Offering Goddess Hūṃ!
407. Oṃ Ocean of Clouds of All Distinguished Offerings Hūṃ!

408. Oṃ All existents are pure by nature; I am pure by nature!

409. Oṃ I am identical with the essence of the nondual knowledge of the realm of reality!

410. O Vajrsattva! Guard the pledge! Be present to me as Vajrasattva! Be firm for me! Be very glad for me! Be very abundant for me! Love me deeply! Grant me all siddhis! And in all actions, make my intention... [laughter]...O blessed one, vajra of all tathāgatas! Do not desert me! Grant me the vajra nature, great samaya being!

411. Sanskrit of the title is *Aṣṭabhayatrāṇa*. See Willson (1986, 343–44) for another translation. On the eight fears see Willson (1986, 87–93) and Beyer (1973, 229–36).

412. Oṃ I am identical with the essence of the nondual vajra knowledge of emptiness!

413. *Lhan cig skyes sbyor gyi gdam ngag mdor bsdus snying po*. See Apple 2017 for analysis, translation, and Tibetan transcription of this work.

414. The seven qualities of the sitting position of Vairocana (*rnam snang chos bdun*) are having: (1) the legs crossed, (2) hands on the lap, (3) back straight, (4) shoulders spread, (5) head with chin slightly lowered, (6) tip of the tongue touching the palate of the mouth, and (7) eyes gazing past the tip of the nose.

415. The "four immeasurables" (*catvāry apramāṇi*, *tshad med bzhi*) also known as the four "abodes of Brahma" (*brahmavihāra*), are the contemplations of immeasurable love (*maitrī*), compassion (*karuṇā*), joy (*muditā*), and equanimity (*upekṣā*). *Mahāvyutpatti*, 1503–507.

416. For the image of clouds melting in the sky see Tilopā's *Mahāmudropadeśa*, verse 11 (Tiso and Torricelli 1991: 212).

417. See Jackson 1992 on the image of the lion cub or garuḍa bird in Buddhist discourse.

418. For this dissolution process see Nāgabodhi's *Karmāntavibhaṅga*, D, rgyud, Ngi, fol. 145b–147a.

419. On the *manomayakāya* in Buddhist soteriology and cosmology see Lee 2014.

Table of Tibetan Transliterations

Amé Naljorpa Jangchup Rinchen (a.k.a. Naljorpa, Naljorpa Chenpo)	A mes Rnal 'byor pa Byang chub rin chen
Aro	A ro
Ba	Rba
Balpo Dzong	Bal po rdzong
Bangtön Jangchup Gyaltsen	Bang ston Byang chub rgyal mtshan
Barak	Sba rag
Chakdar Tönpa	Phyag dar ston pa
Chanak	Bya nag
Chasa	Bya sa
Chim Namkha Drak	Mchim Nam kha' grags
Chimphu	'Chims phu
Chingru	'Phying-ru
Chökyi Lodrö	Chos gyi blo gros
Danma	Lda ma
Denma	'Dan ma
Dergé	Sde dge
Dokham	Mdo khams

Dren	'Dren
Drepung	'Bras spungs
Dring	'Bring
Dring Yeshé Yönten	Bring Ye shes yon tan
Dromtönpa	'Brom ston pa
Dromtönpa Gyalwai Jungné	'Brom ston Rgyal ba'i 'byung gnas
Gargewa	Mgar dge ba
Gelukpa	Dge lugs pa
Geshé	Dge bshes
Geshé Garmi Yontan Yungdrung	Geshe Gar mi Yon tan g.yung drung
Geshé Kawa	Dge bshes ska wa
Geshé Naljorpa	Dge bshes Rnal 'byor pa
Geshé Tönpa (=Dromtönpa)	Dge bshes Ston pa
Gewa Lodrö	Dge ba blo gros
Gompa Gyamon	Sgom pa Rgya mon
Gönpawa	Dgon pa ba
Gönpawa Wangchuk Gyaltsen	Dgon pa ba Dbang phyug rgyal mtshan
Gya Lotsāwa	Rgya Lo tsā ba
Gya shing	Rgya zhing
Gya Tsöndrü Sengé	Rgya Brtson 'grus seng ge
Gyal	Rgyal
Gyalrin	Rgyal rin
Gyaphip	Rgya phibs

Jang	Byang
Jangchup Ling	Byang chub gling
Jangchup Ö	Byang chub 'od
Jangtsun Darma Jangchup	Jang btsun dar ma Byang chub
Jowo Chimmo	Jo bo
Jomo	Jo mo mchim mo
Kachu	Kva chu
Kadampa	Bka' gdams pa
Kagyüpa	Bka' rgyud pa
Kawa Shākya Wangchuk	Ka ba Shā kya dbang phyug
Kham	Khams
Khutön Tsöndrü Yungdrung	Khu ston Brtson 'grus g.yung drung
Khyungpo Naljor	Khyung po rnal 'byor
Kyirong	Skyi rong
Lekpai Sherap (a.k.a. Sangphuwa)	Legs pa'i shes rab
Lha Lama Yeshé Ö	Lha bla ma Ye shes 'od
Lhading	Lha sdings
Lhatsunpa	Lha btsun pa
Lumé	Klu mes, Slu mes
Lumé Sherap Tsultrim	Klu mes Shes rab tshul khrims
Mangnang Gomchen	Mang nang sgom chen
Mangyul	Mang yul
Marpa Chökyi Lodrö	Mar pa Chos gyi blo gros
Metsun Yönten Sherap	Sme btsun Yon tan shes rab

Mokchok Rinchen Tsondru	Rmog lcog rin chen brtson 'grus
Naktso Lotsāwa Tsultrim Gyalwa	Nag tsho lo tsā ba tshul khrims rgyal ba
Naljorpa	Rnal 'byor pa
Naljorpa Amé Jangchup	Rnal 'byor pa A mad byang chub
Naljorpa Chenpo Jangchup Rinchen	Rnal 'byor pa chen po Byang chub rin chen
Narthang	Snar thang
Nätan Dadpa Lama	Gnas brtan Dad pa bla ma
Ngari	Mnga' ris
Ngari töd	Mnga' ris stod
Ngok Jangchup Jungné	Rngog Legs pa'i shes rab
Ngok Lekpai Sherap (a.k.a. Sangphuwa)	Rngog Byang chub 'byung gnas
Nonda	Snon mda'
Nyamogur	Nya mo gyur
Nyethang	Snye thang
Nyethang Ö	Snye thang 'od
Phuchungwa	Phu chung ba
Phuchungwa Shönu Gyaltsen	Phu chung ba Gzhon nu rgyal mtshan
Potowa Rinchen Sal	Po to ba Rin chen gsal
Purang	Pu hrang
Radreng	Rag
Rak	Rwa sgreng, Ra sgreng, Ra sgyeng

Ratöd	Ra stod
Ratshigkhang	Ra brtsigs khang
Rinchen Sangpo	Rin chen bzang po
Sai Sangga	Sa'i sang ga
Samyé	Bsam yas
Sangphu (monastery)	Gsang phu
Sangphu Neuthok	Gsang phu Ne'u thog
Sangphuwa (a.k.a. Ngok Lekpai Sherap)	Gsang phu ba
Sedur	Se rdur
Serlingpa	Gser gling pa
Setön Drachan Dzin	Se ston Sgra gcan 'dzin
Setsun Wangchuk Shönu	Se btsun Dbang phyug gzhon nu
Shang Chenpo	Zhang chen po
Shang Nachung Tönpa	Zhang sna chung ston pa
Shang Nanam Dorjé Wangchuk	Zhang sna nam Rdo rje dbang phyug
Shang Shung	Zhang zhung
Shangtsun Ögür Bar	Zhang btsun 'ol rgod 'bar
Shang Wangchuk Gön	Zhang Dbang phyug mgon
Sölnak Tangboché	Sol nag thang po che
Song Nge	Srong nge
Takkar	Stag dkar
Tholing	Mtho lding
Tölung	Stod lung

Trichok	Khri mchog
Tri tri Sakya lodrö	Tri tri Sakya blo gros
Trisong Detsen	Khri srong Ide brtsan
Trulnang	'Phrul snang
Trulnang Tsuglakhang	'Phrul snang gtsug lag khang
Tsang	Gtsang
Tsangpa	Gtsang pa
Tsangpo	Gtsang po
Tsang Taktsal	Gtsang Stag tshal
Tsöndrü Sengé	Brtson 'grus seng ge
Tsongkhapa Losang Drakpa	Tsongkhapa Blo gzang grags pa
Tsultrim Gyalwa	Tshul khrims rgyal ba
Ü	Dbus
Üntrana	'On Khra sna
Urupa	Dbu ru pa
Wölka	'Ol kha
Yarlung	Yar lung
Yorpo	G.yor po
Zhalu	Zha lu
Zhung	Gzhung

Bibliography

Acri, Andrea, ed. 2016. *Esoteric Buddhism in Mediaeval Maritime Asia: Networks of Masters, Texts, Icons*. Singapore: ISEAS–Yusof Ishak Institute.

Apple, James B. 2008. *Stairway to Nirvāṇa: A Study of the Twenty Saṃghas Based on the Works of Tsongkhapa*. Albany: State University of New York Press.

———. 2009. "Contributions to the Development and Classification of *Abhisamayālaṃkāra* Literature in Tibet from the 9th to 14th century." *Journal of the International Association of Tibetan Studies* 5: 1–57. THL #T5689.

———. 2010. "Atiśa's Open Basket of Jewels: A Middle Way Vision in Late Phase Indian Vajrayāna." *Indian International Journal of Buddhist Studies* 11: 117–98.

———. 2013. "An Early Tibetan Commentary on Atiśa's *Satyadvayāvatāra*." *Journal of Indian Philosophy* 41.3: 263–329.

———. 2015a. "A Study and Translation of Atiśa's Madhyamakopadeśa with Indian and Tibetan Commentaries." *Acta Tibetica et Buddhica* 7: 1–82.

———. 2015b. "Candrakīrti and the Lotus Sutra." *Bulletin of the Institute of Oriental Philosophy* 31, no. 1: 97–122.

———. 2016a. "An Early Bka'-gdams-pa Madhyamaka Work Attributed to Atiśa Dīpaṃkaraśrījñāna." *Journal of Indian Philosophy* 44: 619–725.

———. 2016b. "Perfections (Six and Ten) of Bodhisattvas in Buddhist Literature." In *Oxford Encyclopedia of Religion: Buddhism*. http://oxfordre.com/religion/view/10.1093/acrefore/9780199340378.001.0001/acrefore-9780199340378-e-193.

———. 2017. "Atiśa's Teachings on Mahāmudrā." *The Indian International Journal of Buddhist Studies* 18: 1–42.

———. 2018a. "Abhisamayālaṃkāra (Ornament for Clear Realization)." In *Oxford Research Encyclopedia of Religion*. http://oxfordre.com/religion/view/10.1093/acrefore/9780199340378.001.0001/acrefore-9780199340378-e-608.

———. 2018b. "Atiśa and Ratnākaraśānti as Philosophical Opponents with

Attention to *Yuktiṣaṣṭikā*, Verse 34." *Critical Review for Buddhist Studies* 23: 9–38.

——. 2018c. "The Spiritual Exercises of the Middle Way: Reading Atiśa's Madhyamakopadeśa with Hadot." In *Hadot and Buddhist Thought*, edited by Luis Gómez and David Fiordalis, 105–44. Berkeley: Mangalam Research Center.

——. 2019a. *Jewels of the Middle Way: The Madhyamaka Legacy of Atiśa and His Early Tibetan Followers*. Boston: Wisdom Publications.

——. 2019b. "Maitreya's Tuṣita Heaven as a Pure Land in Gelukpa Forms of Tibetan Buddhism." In *Pure Lands in Asian Texts and Contexts: An Anthology (Pure Land Buddhist Studies)*, edited by Georgios T. Halkias and Richard K. Payne. Honolulu: University of Hawai'i Press.

Atiśa Dīpaṃkaraśrījñāna. *A Means of Achieving White Tārā*. *Tārābhaṭṭārikāsādhana*. *Rje btsun sgrol ma'i sgrub thabs*. Dergé Tanjur, vol. *mu*, ff. 315a2–317a4. Tibetan translation by the author and Dge ba'i blo gros.

——. *Bodhisattva's Jewel Garland*. *Bodhisattvamaṇyāvalī*. *Byang chub sems dpa'i nor bu'i phreng ba*. Tôh. no. 3951 (also, no. 4471). Dergé Tanjur, vol. *khi*, ff. 294b7–296a1. Tibetan translation by the author and Tshul khrims rgyal ba.

——. *Entry to the Two Realities*. *Satyadvayāvatāra*. *Bden pa gnyis la 'jug pa*. Tôh. no. 3902 (also, no. 4467). Dergé Tanjur, vol. *a*, ff. 72a2–73a7. Tibetan translation by the author and Rgya Brtson 'grus seng ge.

——. *Essential Condensed Summary of the Special Instructions on Coemergent Union*. *Jo bo rjes dgon pa ba la gnang ba'i phyag chen*. In *Gsung 'bum/ A ti sha*. Vol. 1, 876–78. Pe cin: Krung go'i bod rig pa dpe skrun khang, 2006. TBRC W1GS66286.

——. *Lamp for the Path to Awakening*. *Bodhipathapradīpa*. *Byang chub lam gyi sgron ma*. Tôh. no. 3947. Dergé Tanjur, vol. *khi*, ff. 238a6–241a4. Tibetan translation by the author and Dge ba'i blo gros.

——. *Lamp for the Summary of Conduct*. *Caryāsaṃgrahapradīpa*. *Spyod pa bsdus pa'i sgron ma*. Tôh. no. 3960 (also, no. 4466). Dergé Tanjur, vol. *khi*, ff. 312b2–313a7. Tibetan translation by the author and Tshul khrims rgyal ba.

——. *Middle Way Special Instructions for Cultivating All the Qualities in the Scriptures*. *Sde snod kyi chos thams cad sgom pa dbu ma'i man ngag*. In *Gsung 'bum/ A ti sha*. Vol. 1, 861–63. Pe cin: Krung go'i bod rig pa dpe skrun khang, 2006. TBRC W1GS66286.

——. *Open Basket of Jewels*. *Ratnakaraṇḍodghāṭa-nāma-madhyamakopadeśa*. *Dbu ma'i man ngag rin po che'i za ma tog kha phye ba*. Tôh. no. 3930. Dergé Tanjur, vol. *ki*, ff. 96b1–116b7. Tibetan translation by the author, Rgya Brtson 'grus seng ge, and Tshul khrims rgyal ba.

———. *Protection from the Eight Fears. Aṣṭabhayatrāṇa. 'Phags pa 'jigs pa brgyad las skyob pa.* Dergé Tanjur, vol. *mu*, 322b1–323a1.

———. *Special Instructions on Unique Mindfulness. Ekasmṛtyupadeśa. Dran pa gcig pa'i man ngag.* Tôh. no. 3928 (also, no. 4476). Dergé Tanjur, vol. *ki*, folios 94b4–95b1. Tibetan translation by the author and Tshul khrims rgyal ba.

———. *Stages of the Path to Awakening. Bodhipathakrama. Byang chub lam gyi rim pa.* In *Byang chub lam gyi rim pa*, 21–63.7. Leh, Ladakh: Thupten Tsering, 1973. TBRC W1KG506. Also in *Bka' gdams gsung 'bum phyogs bsgrigs glegs bam go gcig*, 21–202. Dpal brtsegs bod yig dpe rnying zhib 'jug khang, 2015.

———. *The Abridged Clear Realization of Noble Tārā. Sgrol ma'i mngon rtogs bsdus pa.* In *Gsung 'bum/ A ti sha*. Vol. 1, 1014–1015. Pe cin: Krung go'i bod rig pa dpe skrun khang, 2006. TBRC W1GS66286.

———. *The Song with a Vision for the Realm of Reality. Dharmadhātudarśanagīti. Chos kyi dbyings lta ba'i glu.* Tôh. no. 2314 (also, no. 4475). Dergé Tanjur, vol. *zhi*, ff. 254b7–260b5. Tibetan translation by the author and Tshul khrims rgyal ba. See also Blo bzang rdo rje rab gling 1999, 66–214.

Bautze-Picron, Claudine. 2016. "Images of Devotion and Power in South and Southeast Bengal." In *Esoteric Buddhism in Mediaeval Maritime Asia: Networks of Masters, Texts, Icons*, edited by Andrea Acri, 163–90. Singapore: ISEAS–Yusof Ishak Institute.

Beyer, Stephan. 1973. *The Cult of Tārā: Magic and Ritual in Tibet*. Berkeley: University of California Press.

Blo bzang rdo rje rab gling. 1999. *Five Treatises of Ācārya Dīpaṃkaraśrījñāna*. Sarnath, Varanasi: Central Institute of Higher Tibetan Studies.

Blumenthal, James. 2004. *The Ornament of the Middle Way: A Study of the Madhyamaka Thought of Śāntarakṣita*. Ithaca, NY: Snow Lion Publications.

Brunnhölzl, Karl. 2007a. *In Praise of Dharmadhātu: Nāgārjuna and the Third Karmapa, Rangjung Dorje*. Ithaca, NY: Snow Lion Publications.

———. 2007b. *Straight from the Heart: Buddhist Pith Instructions*. Ithaca, NY: Snow Lion Publications.

Buswell, Robert E., and Donald S. Lopez. 2013. *The Princeton Dictionary of Buddhism*. Princeton, NJ: Princeton University Press.

Carlton, Donald. 1979. "Atīsha's View of Avalokiteshvara: A Translation of the *Srī Samāja Lokeshvara Sādhanām*, with Commentary." MA diss., Indiana University.

Chattopadhyaya, Alaka. 1967. *Atiśa and Tibet: Life and Works of Dīpaṃkara Śrījñāna in Relation to the History and Religion of Tibet*. Indian Studies, Past and Present. Calcutta: Motilal Banarsidass.

Chim Namkha Drak (Mchims nam mkha' grags). 2012a. *The Universally Known*. In *Jo bo rin po che rje dpal ldan a ti sha'i rnam thar rgyas pa yongs grags bzhugs so*, 41–217. Ziling: Mtsho sngon mi rigs dpe skrun khang.

———. 2012b. *Spiritual Biography of Geshé Tönpa. Dge bshes ston pa'i rnam thar*. In *Bod kyi lo rgyus rnam thar phyogs bsgrigs*, vol. 2, 351–424. Ziling: Mtsho sngon mi rigs dpe skrun khang.

———. 2014. *Jo bo rin po che rje dpal ldan a ti sha'i rnam thar rgyas pa yongs grags bzhugs so*. In *Jo bo rje dpal ldan a ti sha'i rnam thar phyogs bsgrigs*, 65–205. Lhasa: Bod ljongs mi dmangs dpa skrun khang.

Chowdhury, A.M. "Vikramapura." In *Banglapedia, National Encyclopedia of Bangladesh*. Online ed., accessed April 30, 2018. http://en.banglapedia.org /index.php?title=Vikramapura.

Clarke, Shayne. 2015. "Vinayas." In *Brill's Encyclopaedia of Buddhism*, vol. 1, 60–87. Leiden: Brill.

Cook, Lowell. 2018. "Lha Lama Yeshe O." In *The Treasury of Lives: A Biographical Encyclopedia of Tibet, Inner Asia, and the Himalaya*. http://treasuryoflives.org /biographies/view/Lha-Lama-Yeshe-O/11056.

Dalton, Jacob. 2005. "A Crisis of Doxography: How Tibetans Organized Tantra during the 8th–12th Centuries." *Journal of the International Association of Buddhist Studies* 28, no.1: 115–81.

Das, Sarat Chandra. 1893. "Bodhi Patha Pradīpa by Dīpaṅkara Śrī Jñāna." *Journal of the Buddhist Text Society* 1, pt. 1: 39–48, 57–64; pt. 3: 21–26.

Davidson, Ronald M. 1995. "Atiśa's *A Lamp for the Path to Awakening*." In *Buddhism in Practice*, edited by Donald S. Lopez Jr., 290–301. Princeton, NJ: Princeton University Press.

Decleer, Hubert. 1996a. "Master Atiśa in Nepal: The Tham Bahīl and Five Stūpas' Foundations according to the 'Brom ston Itinerary." *Journal of the Nepal Research Centre* 10: 27–54.

———. 1996b. "Atiśa's Journey to Sumatra." In *Buddhism in Practice*, edited by Donald S. Lopez Jr., 532–40. Princeton, NJ: Princeton University Press.

———. 1997a. "Atisha's Arrival in Nepal." *Buddhist Himalaya: Journal of Nagarjuna Institute of Exact Methods* 8, nos. 1–2: 1–15.

———. 1997b. "Atiśa's Journey to Tibet." In *Religions of Tibet in Practice*, edited by Donald S. Lopez, Jr., 157–77. Princeton, NJ: Princeton University Press.

——. 1998. "Death of the Translator Virya Siṃha." *Buddhist Himalaya: Journal of Nagarjuna Institute of Exact Methods* 9, nos. 1–2: 1–19.

Divalerio, David M. 2015. *The Holy Madmen of Tibet*. Oxford: Oxford University Press.

Dkon mchog rgyal mtshaṇ. 1975. *Byang chub lam gyi sgron me'i 'grel ba phul byung dgyes pa'i mchod sprin*. In *Gsung 'bum*, vol. 4, 51–52. Delhi: Gyaltsen Gelek Namgyal.

Dromtönpa Gyalwai Jungné ('Brom ston pa rgyal ba'i 'byung gnas). 2012a. *The Itinerary (of Atiśa's Travels)*. *'Brom ston pa rgyal ba'i 'byung gnas kyis mdzad pa'i jo bo rje'i rnam thar lam yig chos kyi 'byung gnas*. In *Jo bo rje dpal ldan a ti sha'i rnam thar bka' gdams pha chos*, 218–75.

——. 2012b. *Jo bo rin po che rje dpal ldan a ti sha'i rnam thar rgyas pa yongs grags bzhugs so*. In *Jo bo rje dpal ldan a ti sha'i rnam thar bka' gdams pha chos*, 41–217.

——. 2012c. *Jo bo rje dpal ldan a ti sha'i rnam thar bka' gdams pha chos*. Ziling: Mtsho sngon mi rigs dpe skrun khang.

——. 2014. *Dpal ldan a ti sha'i rnam par thar ba chos kyi 'byung gnas zhes bya ba bzhugs so*. In Dromtönpa Gyalwai Jungné et al., *Jo bo rje dpal ldan a ti sha'i rnam thar phyogs bsgrigs*, 1–64.

Dromtönpa Gyalwai Jungné et al. 2014. *Jo bo rje dpal ldan a ti sha'i rnam thar phyogs bsgrigs*. Lhasa: Bod ljongs mi dmangs dpa skrun khang.

Dunne, John D. 2004. *Foundations of Dharmakīrti's Philosophy*. Boston: Wisdom Publications.

Dunne, John, and Sarah McClintock. 1997. *The Precious Garland: An Epistle to a King*. Boston: Wisdom Publications.

Ehrhard, Franz-Karl. 2002. "The Transmission of the *Thig-le Bcu-drug* and the Bka' Gdams Glegs Bam." In *The Many Canons of Tibetan Buddhism*, edited by Helmut Eimer and David Germano, 29–56. Leiden: Brill.

Eimer, Helmut. 1977. *Berichte über das Leben des Atiśa (Dīpaṃkarásrījñāna): Eine Untersuchung der Quellen*. Wiesbaden: O. Harrassowitz.

——. 1978. *Bodhipathapradīpa: Ein Lehrgedict des Atiśa (Dīpaṃkaraśrījñāna) in der tibetischen Überlieferung*. Asiatische Forschungen 59. Wiesbaden: O. Harrassowitz.

——. 1979. *Rnam thar rgyas pa: Materialien zu einer Biographie des Atiśa (Dīpaṃkaraśrījñāna)*. Vol. 1, *Einführung, Inhaltsverzeichnis, Namensglossar*. Vol. 2, *Textmaterialien*. Wiesbaden: O. Harrassowitz.

——. 1982. "The Development of the Biographical Tradition concerning Atiśa (Dīpaṃkaraśrījñāna)." *Journal of Tibet Society* 2: 41–52.

——. 2003. *Testimonia for the Bstod-pa brgyad-cu-pa: An Early Hymn Praising Dīpaṃkaraśrījñāna (Atiśa)*. Lumbini, Nepal: Lumbini International Research Institute.

——. 2008. "Sources for the *Vita* of 'Brom ston rgyal ba'i 'byung gnas." In *Contributions to Tibetan Buddhist Literature*, edited by Orna Almogi, 377–92. Beiträge zur Zentralasienforschung 14. Halle (Saale), Germany: International Institute for Tibetan and Buddhist Studies.

——. 2010. "Das Loblied auf Atiśa in dreißig Strophen." In *From Turfan to Ajanta: Festschrift for Dieter Schlingloff on the Occasion of His Eightieth Birthday*, edited by Eli Franco and Monika Zin, vols. 1–2, 303–314. Lumbini: Lumbini International Research Institute.

English, Elizabeth. 2002. *Vajrayoginī: A Study of Her Visualizations, Rituals & Forms*. Studies in Indian and Tibetan Buddhism. Boston: Wisdom Publications.

Fazun. 1972. "Bodhipathapradīpa." In *Encyclopedia of Buddhism*, vol. 3, no. 1, 212–17. Ceylon: Government Press.

Gardner, Alexander. 2018. "Rinchen Zangpo," In *Treasury of Lives: A Biographical Encyclopedia of Tibet, Inner Asia, and the Himalaya*. http://treasuryoflives.org/biographies/view/Rinchen-Zangpo/10199.

Gtsang smyon He ru ka. 1982. *The Life of Marpa the Translator: Seeing Accomplishes All*. Boston: Shambhala.

Guenther, Herbert V. 1963. *The Life and Teaching of Nāropa*. London: Oxford University Press.

Hahn, Michael. 2016. *Vṛttamālāstuti of Jñānaśrīmitra with Śākyarakṣita's Vṛttamālā(stuti)vivṛti*. New Delhi: Aditya Prakashan.

Isaacson, Harunaga. 2013. "Yogācāra and Vajrayāna according to Ratnākaraśānti." In *The Foundation for Yoga Practitioners: The Buddhist Yogācāra Bhūmi Treatise and Its Adaptation in India, East Asia, and Tibet*, edited by Ulrich Timme Kragh, 1036–1051. Cambridge: Harvard University Press.

Ja Dulzin Tsöndrü Bar (Bya 'dul 'dzin brtson 'grus 'bar). 2014. *The Extensive Biography*. *Jo bo chen po rje lha cig gi rnam thar ba zhugs so*, In *Jo bo rje dpal ldan a ti sha'i rnam thar phyogs* bsgrigs, 245–392. Lhasa: Bod ljongs mi dmangs dpa skrun khang.

Jackson, David. 1992. "Birds in the Egg and Newborn Lion Cubs:Metaphors for the Potentialities and Limitations of 'All-at-Once' Enlightenment." In *Tibetan Studies: Proceedings of the 5th Seminar of the International Association for*

Tibetan Studies, Narita 1989, edited by Ihara Shoren and Yamaguchi Zuiho, 95–114. Narita: Naritasan Shinshoji.

Jackson, Roger Reid. 2004. *Tantric Treasures: Three Collections of Mystical Verse from Buddhist India*. New York: Oxford University Press.

Jamgön Kongtrul Lodrö Tayé. 1998. *Buddhist Ethics*. Ithaca, NY: Snow Lion Publications.

Jansen, Berthe. 2016. "The Disciplinarian (dge skos/ dge bskos/ chos khrims pa/ zhal ngo) in Tibetan Monasteries: His Role and His Rules." *Revue d'Etudes Tibétaines* 37: 145–61.

Jinpa, Thupten. 2006. *Mind Training: The Great Collection*. Boston: Wisdom Publications.

——. 2008. *The Book of Kadam: The Core Texts*. Boston: Wisdom Publications.

——. 2013. *Wisdom of the Kadam Masters*. Boston: Wisdom Publications.

Kajiyama, Yūichi. 1999. *The Antarvyāptisamarthana of Ratnākaraśānti*. Tokyo: Soka University, The International Research Institute for Advanced Buddhology.

Kano, Kazuo. 2015. "The Transmission of Sanskrit Manuscripts from India to Tibet: The Case of a Manuscript Collection in the Possession of Atiśa Dīpaṃkaraśrījñāna (980–1054)." In *Transfer of Buddhism Across Central Asian Networks (7th to 13th Centuries)*, edited by Carmen Meinert, 82– 117. Leiden: Brill.

Kapstein, Matthew. 2006. *The Tibetans*. Malden, MA: Blackwell Publishing.

Karmay, Samten Gyaltsen. 1998. *The Arrow and the Spindle: Studies in History, Myths, Rituals, and Beliefs in Tibet*. Kathmandu, Nepal: Mandala Book Point.

Lang, Karen. 1986. *Āryadeva's Catuḥśataka: On the Bodhisattva's Cultivation of Merit and Knowledge*. Copenhagen: Akademisk Forlag.

Lee, Sumi. 2014. "The Meaning of 'Mind-made Body' (S. *manomaya-kāya*, C. *yisheng shen* 意生身)in Buddhist Cosmological and Soteriological Systems." *Buddhist Studies Review* 31, no. 1: 65–90.

Locke, John K. 1985. *Buddhist Monasteries of Nepal: A Survey of the Bāhās and Bahīs of the Kathmandu Valley*. Kathmandu, Nepal: Sahayogi Press.

Martin, Dan. 2001. "Painters, Patrons and Paintings of Patrons in Early Tibetan Art." In *Embodying Wisdom. Art, Text and Interpretation in the History of Esoteric Buddhism*, edited by Rob Linrothe and Henrik Sørensen, 139–84. Vol. 6 in SBS Monographs Series. Copenhagen: The Seminar for Buddhist Studies.

——. 2013. "Ritual Indigenisation as a Debated Issue in Tibetan Buddhism (11th to Early 13th Centuries)." In *Challenging Paradigms: Buddhism and Nativism: Framing Identity Discourse in Buddhist Environments*. Leiden: Brill.

Mathes, Klaus-Dieter. 2015. *A Fine Blend of Mahāmudrā and Madhyamaka: Maitrīpa's Collection of Texts on Non-Conceptual Realization (Amanasikāra)*. Wien: Verlag der Österreichischen Akademie der Wissenschaften.

McCrea, Lawrence J., and Parimal G. Patil. 2010. *Buddhist Philosophy of Language in India: Jñānaśrīmitra on Exclusion*. New York: Columbia University Press.

Miyazaki, Izumi. 2007a. "Atiśa (Dīpaṃkaraśrījñāna): His Philosophy, Practice and Its Sources." In *Memoirs of the Research Department of the Toyo Bunko*. No. 65, 61–89. Tokyo: The Tokyo Bunko.

——. 2007b. "Annotated Tibetan Text and Japanese Translation of the Ratnakarandodghaṭa-nāma-madhyamakopadeśa of Atiśa." *Memoirs of the Faculty of Letters, Kyoto University*. No. 46, 1–126. Kyoto: Department of Literature, Kyoto University. https://repository.kulib.kyoto-u.ac.jp/dspace/handle/2433/73130?mode=full.

Mochizuki, Kaie. 2015. "On the Ekasmṛtyupadeśa of Dīpaṃkaraśrījñāna and His View on Nāgārjuna." *Journal of Indian and Buddhist Studies* 63, no. 3: 1307–314.

——. 2016. *Dyīpankarashurījunyāna kenyū*. PhD diss., Rissho University. http://hdl.handle.net/11266/5774.

O'Brien, Kate. 2016. "The Tale of Sudhana and Manoharā on Candi Jago: An Interpretation of a Series of Narrative Bas-reliefs on a 13th-Century East Javanese Monument." In *Esoteric Buddhism in Mediaeval Maritime Asia: Networks of Masters, Texts, Icons*, edited by Andrea Acri, 275–322. Singapore: ISEAS–Yusof Ishak Institute.

Onians, Isabella. 2002. "Tantric Buddhist Apologetics or Antinomianism as a Norm," PhD diss., Oxford University.

Negi, Ramesh Chandra. 1992. *Atīśaviracitā Ekādaśagranthaḥ: Eleven Treatises by Atiśa*. Varanasi: Central Institute of Higher Tibetan Studies.

Padma dkar po. 1973. *Chos 'byung bstan pa'i padma rgyas pa'i nyin byed*. In *Collected Works (gSuṅ-'bum) of Kun-mkhyen Padma-dkar-po*, vol. 2. 1–619. Darjeeling: Kargyud Sungrab Nyamso Khang.

Pawo Tsuklak Trengwa (Dpa' bo gtsug lag phreng ba). 2006. *Dam pa'i chos kyi 'khor lo bsgyur ba rnams kyi byung ba gsal bar byed pa mkhas pa'i dga' ston*. Beijing: Mi rigs dpe skrun khang.

Patil, Parimal G. 2009. *Against a Hindu God: Buddhist Philosophy of Religion in India*. New York: Columbia University Press.

Pha bong kha pa Byams pa bstan 'dzin 'phrin las rgya mtsho, Khri byang Blo bzang-ye-ses-bstan-'dzin-rgya-mtsho, and Michael Richards. 1991. *Liberation in the Palm of Your Hand: A Concise Discourse on the Stages of the Path to Enlightenment*. Boston: Wisdom Publications.

Phun tshogs tshe brtan. 2011. *Mnyam med jo bo rje dpal ldan a ti sha'i rnam par thar pa phyogs bsdus dad pa'i 'jug ngogs*. Beijing: Krung-go'i bod rig pa dpe skrun khang.

Rinchen, Geshe Sonam, and Ruth Sonam. 1997. *Atisha's Lamp for the Path to Enlightenment*. Ithaca, NY: Snow Lion.

Ruegg, David Seyfort. 1992. "Notes on Some Indian and Tibetan Reckonings of the Buddha's Nirvāṇa and the Duration of his Teaching." In *The Dating of the Historical Buddha/Die Datierung des historischen Buddha*, edited by Heinz Bechert, pt. 2, 263–90. Göttingen: Vandenhoeck und Ruprecht.

Sanderson, Alexis. 2009. "The Śaiva Age." In *Genesis and Development of Tantrism*, edited by Shingo Einoo, 41–349. Tokyo: University of Tokyo.

Schaeffer, Kurtis R. 2005. *Dreaming the Great Brahmin: Tibetan Traditions of the Buddhist Poet-Saint Saraha*. New York: Oxford University Press.

Schoterman, Jan A. 2016. "Traces of Indonesian Influences in Tibet." In *Esoteric Buddhism in Mediaeval Maritime Asia: Networks of Masters, Texts, Icons*, edited by Andrea Acri, 113–22. Singapore: ISEAS–Yusof Ishak Institute.

Sherburne, Richard. 1983. *A Lamp for the Path and Commentary of Atīśa*. The Wisdom of Tibet Series 5. London: Allen & Unwin.

———. 2000. *The Complete Works of Atīśa Śrī Dīpaṁkara Jñāna: Jo–Bo–Rje: The Lamp for the Path and Commentary, Together with the Newly Translated Twenty-Five Key Texts (Tibetan and English Texts)*. New Delhi: Aditya Prakashan.

Shizuka, Haruki. 2015. "Expulsion of Maitri-pa from the Monastery and Atiśa's Participation." *Journal of Indian and Buddhist Studies* 63, no. 3:1315–321. Also in *Transfer of Buddhism Across Central Asian Networks (7th to 13th Centuries)*, edited by Carmen Meinert, 82–117. Leiden: Brill.

Skilling, Peter. 1997. "Dharmakīrti's *Durbodhāloka* and the Literature of Śrīvijaya." *Journal of the Siam Society* 85: 187–94.

Sinclair, Iain. 2016. "The Appearance of Tantric Monasticism in Nepal: A History of the Public Image and Fasting Ritual of Newar Buddhism, 980–1380." Unpublished PhD diss., Monash University, Melbourne.

Snellgrove, David L., and Tadeausz Skorupski. 1980. *Cultural Heritage of*

Ladakh, Vol. 2: Zangskar and the Cave Temples of Ladakh. Warminster: Aris and Phillips Ltd.

Sopa, Geshe Lhundup, Michael J. Sweet, Leonard Zwilling, and Dharmarakṣita. 2001. *Peacock in the Poison Grove: Two Buddhist Texts on Training the Mind: The Wheel Weapon (Mtshon Cha 'Khor Lo) and the Poison–Destroying Peacock (Rma Bya Dug 'Joms) Attributed to Dharmarakṣita*. Boston: Wisdom Publications.

Sopa, Geshe Lhundub, David Patt, Dalai Lama, and Beth Newman. 2004. *Steps on the Path to Enlightenment: A Commentary on Tsongkhapa's Lamrim Chenmo, Volume 1: The Foundation Practices*. Boston: Wisdom Publications.

Sparham, Gareth. 1987. "Background Material for the First of the Seventy Topics in Maitreyanātha's Abhisamayālaṃkāra." *Journal of the International Association of Buddhist Studies* 10, no. 2: 139–58.

Stearns, Cyrus. 2001. *Luminous Lives: The Story of the Early Masters of the Lam 'bras tradition in Tibet*. Boston: Wisdom Publications.

Tatz, Mark. 1987. "The Life of the Siddha-Philosopher Maitrīgupta." *Journal of the American Oriental Society* 107, no. 4: 695–711.

——. 1988. "Maitrī-pa and Atisa." In *Proceedings of the 4th International Seminar on Tibetan Studies*, edited by Helga Uebach and Jampa Losang Panglung, 473–81. Studia Tibetica, Band 2. Munich: Kommission Zentralasiatische Studien, Bayerische Akademie der Wissenschaften.

Thakur, Anantalal, ed. 1975. *Ratnakīrtinibandhāvaliḥ: Buddhist Nyāya Works of Ratnakīrti*. Vol. 3. Patna: K. P. Jayaswal Research Institute.

Tillemans, Tom. 2017. "Dharmakīrti." In *The Stanford Encyclopedia of Philosophy*, edited by Edward N. Zalta, Spring 2017, online ed. https://plato.stanford.edu/archives/spr2017/entries/dharmakiirti/.

Tiso, Francis, and Fabrizio Torricelli. 1991. "The Tibetan Text of Tilopa's "Mahāmudropadeśa." *East and West* 41, no. 1/4 (December): 205–29.

Torricelli, Fabrizio. 2018. *Tilopā: A Buddhist Yogin of the Tenth Century*. Dharamasala: Library of Tibetan Works and Archives.

Tshe ring rgyal po, Gu ge. 2006. *Mnga' ris chos 'byung gangs ljongs mdzes rgyan zhes bya ba bzhugs so*. Lhasa: Bod ljongs mi dmangs dpe skrun khang.

Tucci, Giuseppe. (1956) 1986. *Minor Buddhist Texts*. Rome: Istituto Italiano per il Medio ed Estremo Oriente. Reprint, Delhi: Motilal Banarsidass.

van der Kuijp, Leonard. 2010. "Za hor and its Contribution to Tibetan Medicine, Part One: Some Names, Places, and Texts." *Bod Rig Pa'i Dus Deb, Journal of Tibetology* 6: 21–50.

——. 2013. "On the Edge of Myth and History: Za hor, Its Place in the History of Early Indian Buddhist Tantra, and Dalai Lama V and the Genealogy of Its Royal Family." In *Studies on Buddhist Myths: Texts, Pictures, Traditions and History*, edited by Bangwei Wang, Jinhua Chen, and Ming Chen, Shanghai: Zhongxi Book Company, 114–64.

——. 2015. "A Fifteenth Century Biography of Lha bla ma Ye shes 'od (947–1019/24): Its Prolegomenon and Prophecies." In *Tibet in Dialogue with Its Neighbours: History, Culture and Art of Central and Western Tibet, 8th to 15th Century*, edited by Erika Forte et al., 341–75. Wiener Studien zur Tibetologie und Buddhismuskunde 88. Beijing: China Tibetan Research Center.

Vitali, Roberto. 2004. "Glimpses of the History of the rGya Clan with Reference to Nyang stod, Lho mon and Nearby Lands (7th–13th Century)." In *The Spider and the Piglet*, edited by Karma Ura and Sonam Kinga, 6–20. Proceedings of the First International Seminar on Bhutan Studies. Thimphu: The Centre for Bhutan Studies.

Vogel, Alicia H. 1997. "Atisha and the Kadam School: The Reformation of Buddhist Practice in Tibet." MA diss., University of Wisconsin–Madison.

Wangchuk, Dorji. 2007. *The Resolve to Become a Buddha: A Study of the Bodhicitta Concept in Indo-Tibetan Buddhism*. Tokyo: International Institute for Buddhist Studies of the International College for Postgraduate Buddhist Studies.

——. 2009. "A Relativity Theory of the Purity and Validity of Perception in Indo-Tibetan Buddhism." In *Yogic Perception, Meditation, and Altered States of Consciousness*, edited by Eli Franco and Dagmar Eigner, 215–37. Wien: Verlag der Österreichischen Akademie der Wissenschaften.

Wangdu, Pasang. 2007. "*Ke ru lha khang*: Cultural Preservation and Interdisciplinary Research in Central Tibet." In *Text, Image and Song in Transdisciplinary Dialogue*, edited by Deborah Klimburg-Salter, Kurt Tropper, and Christian Jahoda, 45–49.

Wedemeyer, Christian. 2012. "Locating Tantric Antinominianism—An Essay Toward An Intellectual History of the 'Practices/Practice Observance' (*caryā/caryāvrata*)." *Journal of the International Association of Buddhist Studies*, vol. 34, nos. 1–2: 349–419.

Williams, Paul. 1998. *Altruism and Reality: Studies in the Philosophy of the Bodhicaryāvatāra*. Richmond: Curzon Press.

Willson, Martin. 1986. *In Praise of Tārā: Songs to the Saviouress: Source Texts from India and Tibet on Buddhism's Great Goddess*. London: Wisdom Publications.

Index

LIVES OF THE MASTERS

"Since the time of Buddha Shakyamuni himself, Buddhists have been accustomed to recollect the lives of great teachers and practitioners as a source of inspiration from which we may still learn. The Lives of the Masters series continues this noble tradition, recounting the stories, wisdom, and experience of many accomplished Buddhists over the last 2,500 years. I am sure readers will find the accounts in this series inspirational and encouraging."

—His Holiness the Dalai Lama

"The lives of the most important Buddhist masters in history written by the very best of scholars in elegant and accessible prose—who could ask for more?"

—José Cabezón, *Professor of Tibetan Buddhist Studies, University of California Santa Barbara*

Books in the Series

Atiśa Dīpaṃkara: Illuminator of the Awakened Mind
Gendun Chopel: Tibet's Modern Visionary
Tsongkhapa: A Buddha in the Land of Snows

Please visit www.shambhala.com for more information on forthcoming titles.